DEATH BEFORE BIRTH

DEATH BEFORE BIRTH

Canada and the Abortion Question

Edited by E. J. Kremer
and E. A. Synan

GRIFFIN HOUSE *TORONTO 1974*

©E. J. Kremer and E. A. Synan, 1974

ISBN 0 88760 070 0

Published by Griffin Press Limited
461 King Street West, Toronto M5V 1K7
Canada

All rights reserved. No part of this book may be reproduced, transmitted in any form or by any means, electronic, mechanical, photocopying, recording, or otherwise, or stored in a retrieval system without the written permission in advance of the publisher.

Cover design: Brant Cowie
Printed in Canada

Acknowledgement

This volume has been published with the help of a grant from De Rancé, Incorporated, of Milwaukee, Wisconsin, U.S.A.

Contents

Introduction   James M. Cameron   *1*

SECTION ONE: ABORTION IN CANADA

ABORTION IN CANADA, 1960—1966   Alphonse de Valk   *14*
  1. The Canadian Press   14
  2. The Professions   18
  3. Agitation: The Voices of the Churches   23
  4. Agitation: The Canadian Medical Association and the Canadian Bar Association   27
  5. "Reform is under way!"   31
  6. The Law on Contraception   33
  7. The Law on Divorce   35
  8. Summary   37

ABORTION IN CANADA: THE 1969 LAW AND ITS AFTERMATH
C. Gwendolyn Landolt   *44*
  1. The 1969 Law on Abortion   44
  2. Debate in the House of Commons   45
  3. The Effects of the New Law   46

PROBLEMS IN "SELECTIVE" ABORTION   Hubert C. Soltan   *49*

SECTION TWO: THE HUMANITY OF THE UNBORN

INTRA-UTERINE LIFE AND DEVELOPMENT   E. Dawne Jubb   55
　1. The New Human Life and the Maternal Organism   55
　2. Variations in the Pace of Growth and Development   56
　3. Some Milestones of Intra-uterine Life   57
　4. Terminating a Developing Human Life   58

THE MERCHANTS OF CALUMNY   Donald De Marco   61

"ON BEING HUMAN"   Robert E. Tully   76
　1. The Definist Approach to What a Human Being is   77
　2. The Emergentist Approach to What a Human Being is   82

SECTION THREE: THE ABORTION DEBATE

ABORTION AND THE RIGHT TO LIFE   Lloyd Gerson   90
　1. The Range of Rights   90
　2. The Right to Life   93
　3. The Right to Life of the Unborn   95

ABORTION AND PLURALISM   Elmar J. Kremer   99
　1. Two Arguments from Pluralism   99
　2. Evidence bearing on the Humanity of the Unborn   102
　3. Pluralism on Human Development and the Right to Life   106
　4. Pluralism on the Right to Life of Infants   111
　5. Are Anti-Abortion Laws Enforceable?   113

ABORTION AND THE UNWANTED CHILD   Ian Gentles   117
　1. The Extension of Protection for the Immature   117
　2. The Unwanted Child Argument for Abortion: Deformed Children   118
　3. A Swedish Study of Unwantedness   119
　4. Parental Attitudes, Pre-Natal and Post-Natal   121
　5. Overpopulation and Technology   122
　6. Alternatives to Abortion   124

A FEMINIST FOR LIFE   Jessica Pegis   127

SEEDS, A DISCUSSION OF EUTHANASIA AND ABORTION   Denyse Handler   132

PROBABILISM AND POSSIBLE ABORTIFACIENTS   John Gallagher, c.s.b.   137
  1. The Balance of Probabilities   138
  2. Probabilism   139
  3. Doubt in the Mind of the Person Choosing   140
  4. Difference of Opinion Among Experts   141

SECTION FOUR: ABORTION AND THE LAW

LAW AND THE SINS OF THE MOTHERS   Edward A. Synan   146
  1. English Common Law
  2. Roman Law   147
  3. The Contexts of the Cases   149

QUERIES ABOUT "ABORTION TO SAVE THE MOTHER'S LIFE"   P.J. Micallef   154
  1. The Medical Viewpoint and the Law's Interpretation   155
  2. The Moralist's Position   159

ROE v. WADE: A CANADIAN PERSPECTIVE   Philip Slayton   167
  1. The Majority Judgment in Roe v. Wade   167
  2. The "Right to Privacy"   169
  3. The Three-Trimester Approach to Abortion   172

A PSYCHIATRIST'S EXPERIENCE WITH LEGAL ABORTION IN CANADA   Eloise Jones   177
  1. Origins of the 1969 Change in Canadian Abortion Law   177
  2. A Psychiatrist's Experience with Women Seeking Abortion   178
  3. Abortion and the Future of Society   183

INDEX OF PROPER NAMES   187

Introduction

By James M. Cameron

James M. Cameron is the first "University Professor", St. Michael's College, University of Toronto.

Reading what is today written on the topic of abortion, both in the able essays that constitute this book and in other published writing, is a curious experience, at least for me. The terms in which the debate is set out and the spirit in which it is pursued suggest that the problem is tractable, that with a small amount of common sense and some good will agreement in principle can be reached. Plainly this isn't happening. There isn't even an ideological line-up[1] to explain the passionate disagreements that our society endures in this battle over morality and public policy. All this perhaps suggests that the disagreements are much deeper than they may seem if we look at them within the context of formal debate.

When I say that the disagreements over abortion go much deeper than they seem to do if we look at them in the context of formal debate, I mean that a view of abortion may seem to have force as part of a more general outlook on questions of social morality; and that such a general outlook is not necessarily a logically ordered whole. One wouldn't in fact in our society find it strange, though perhaps it *is* strange, that a man should be a firm opponent of capital punishment for murder and a firm defender of abortion on demand. Again, it strikes me as bizarre that people living in a sub-culture in which abortion on demand is approved should be exercised about Animal Liberation. Here we seem to be in Laputa. It strikes me as quaint that President Nixon, in the course of waging war in Indo-China, should express his opposition to abortion. Most of all, it is surely very strange that arguments used by Protestant Christians who approve of abortion are of a utilitarian kind; that is, it is argued that abortion is in itself an evil but that it may be done in some circumstances when the over-all consequences are held to be beneficial. I myself was brought up in the Scottish Presbyterian tradition and I learned very early that it was strenuously believed by those within this tradition that one of the peculiar marks of Roman Catholic immorality was the doctrine that bad means may be employed to bring about a good end. And it was the glory of Protestantism to have rejected this wicked doctrine. I am quite confident that my grandparents thought there were things that were simply forbidden; that one might not perform an act of idolatry even to save the city, that lying was always forbidden, that "it is a sin to steal a pin/As much as any other thing". I think they would have been opposed to the killing of human life in the womb in the way they would have been opposed to adultery, theft, covetousness and failure to keep the Sabbath holy. In short, I am inclined to think that the controversy over abortion is not a controversy over *one* moral problem between people who are otherwise in general agreement; it is a point at which there is argument between people who belong to different sub-cultures. Argument is all the same worth while, first because logic is no respecter of sub-cultures, secondly, because we all in fact belong to one general culture and no one sub-culture is totally opaque to another.

In what follows I confine my speculations to the historical culture within which I and all the other contributors live: what may loosely be called "European" culture. This is of course an immense composite thing and there may be wide divergences over how to characterize it; but there can be no doubt that it is historically continuous with classical antiquity, with the Middle Ages, with the Enlightenment, and I include within these periods all that is well-known about their work in philosophy, natural science, theology and the systematic study of morality. It seems to me not contentious that this culture is present and on the whole dominant in Europe and the Americas and in some of the former colonial areas of the European powers. It is plain, too, that there are cultures, Buddhist and Hindu, for example, that are in certain important ways though not in all very different from European culture. To maintain any superiority of European culture as a whole over other cultures would no doubt be foolish; but it ought to be said that the Human Rights of the UN Declaration of 1959, a Declaration which specifically endorses the rights of the unborn, probably make sense as products of the European cultural tradition rather than of other traditions, though I would not wish to suggest that in other traditions such rights are not cherished. But the predominance of European culture in such political and moral matters is just a fact. Perhaps I ought also to make it clear that in this connection I am not talking about European practice. This has often violated the norms embedded in the culture.

Now, it seems plain that in the history of a culture there may occur large shifts in moral theory and practice, and that sometimes theory follows practice, sometimes theory anticipates practice. The great shift represented by the growth of religious toleration is a case where practice preceded theory, at least on the whole. But the shift in the attitude to chattel slavery occurred well in advance of the legal abolition of that institution. But whatever may hold of sequences that fall under the description of historical causation, there seems to be in some sense a "fit" between the moral change and the circumstances of society. That *cuius regio eius religio* was not a necessary formula for maintaining social peace was learned, not speculatively, but following the demonstrated existence of social concord in religiously mixed societies. The emancipation of chattel slaves was successful in societies where, under the conditions of a market economy, this institution no longer offered any general advantages to the free population. I want to ask, therefore, if there is something like a "fit" between the very common contemporary approval of abortion among humanists, and among many Protestant Christians, many Jews, and not a few Catholics, and other circumstances in our society that would seem to give strength to the approval and practice of abortion. (I ought to make it clear that when I speak of "approval of abortion" I don't have in mind the approval of abortion on demand. Some people will accept this happily but most would, I think, feel uncomfortable about it.)

Perhaps the most important feature (from the standpoint of our present discussion) of our culture today is that it is a contraceptive culture. By this I don't just mean that a great many people use contraceptive methods of various kinds; but that the power of women to prevent conception tends to transform the institution of marriage, making the procreation of children something that is optional, not in the normal case a necessary consequence of the marriage relation. From this there comes the idea that since conception can be prevented at will there is no need to confine heterosexual acts to those who are married. And from this there comes the idea that whatever gives pleasure is all right, inside or outside marriage; so that perverse acts are all right; they are the private concern of individuals, and it doesn't matter if those engaging in sexual activity are of the same sex, or even, perhaps, as in the case of bestiality, of the same species.

There is no straight logical implication between approving of fornication and homosexual relations and approving of abortion. The arguments for the two sets of practices are different. Indeed, as anyone with experience in counselling adolescents will testify, it isn't all that uncommon to find young people who engage in non-contraceptive intercourse, thinking contraception to be unnatural—not in the old "natural law" sense but in a romantic sense—but who do not scruple to ask for an abortion. Such attitudes may be self-contradictory but they are not plainly so. But one thing does follow from the separation of sexual pleasure from procreation: when, despite all precautions, conception does take place its being outside the intentions of the pair in question means that it is thought of as accidental, an unsolicited misfortune, just in the way one might be eating wholesome food and without realizing it swallow some injurious object that had been concealed in the food. In this way of thinking sexual activity is not an activity apt for the purpose of procreation; it is apt for the purpose of pleasure and may turn out to be procreative *per accidens*. It is rather like breathing in a crowded 'bus. One may catch a cold through inhaling a virus; but this is accidental, an unintended consequence of doing what one has to do, namely, breathe. Sexual activity without the intention of procreating is as much a part of ordinary human life as breathing.

Mrs. Judith Jarvis Thomson, in an influential article, writes that if parents "have taken all reasonable precautions against having a child, they do not simply by their biological relationship to the child who comes into existence have a special responsibility for it".[2] Notice that this argument doesn't resemble the utilitarian style of argument often favoured by supporters of abortion in some circumstances. Nothing is said here about whether or not carrying the child to term is judged likely to have bad consequences of some kind for the mother or the family. The right to abort rests upon the pregnancy's not having been intended. My guess is that in the future this kind of argument will more and more be used to justify liberal abortion policies.[3] We shall hear less and less of the special circumstances—physical or psychological ill-health, bad family circumstances, and the rest—that have been a feature of the initial stages in the campaign for liberalized abortion laws. Mrs. Thomson's argument would supply some kind of rationale for the judgment of the United States Supreme Court in *Roe v. Wade*.[4] The reliance of the Court on the right of personal privacy protected by the Constitution as amended is surely incredible. But if we take it as a major presupposition of our society that the enjoyment of non-procreative sexual activity is a general right, then Mrs. Thomson's position seems to make a kind of harsh sense, even though it may at bottom be sophistical.

There is certainly something wrong with Mrs. Thomson's argument. She distinguishes the case of those who "accidentally" conceive despite the taking of all reasonable precautions from that of those who conceive without bothering or wanting to take contraceptive action. In the latter case the biological connection is thought to provide at least *prima facie* ground for supposing that a responsibility is assumed. Here again there seems to be some kind of parallel between procreation and infection. If I know myself to be infectious as a consequence of my having some noxious disease and I don't do anything to stop its being passed on to another person, then I am responsible if someone else becomes infected. But if I don't know myself to be infectious then it looks as though I am responsible only in the weak "causal" sense of "responsible". But perhaps the parallel is more apt and goes deeper than we have so far determined. Let us suppose that the disease in question is syphilis, a disease that can normally be caught only through some kind of sexual activity. And let us suppose that the case is that of a syphilitic man (or woman) who infects his (or her) sexual partner. Two stories are possible. First, the person is syphilitic and knows it. Here the responsibility in the strongest possible sense for the partner's contracting the disease seems indisputable. There is no need for the person to go through some additional performance, verbal or other, to show that the responsibility has been assumed. Second, the person has no knowledge that he (she) is syphilitic; but he (she) has engaged in promiscuous sexual activity and, knowing like the rest of us that such activity carries with it a high risk of infection with venereal diseases, has taken all the precautions known to science against contracting a disease. Nevertheless, unknown to himself (herself) he (she) has syphilis and infects his (her) partner. The parallel with Mrs. Thomson's cases already quoted seems close. But we should surely hesitate to confine responsibility in our latter case to the causal sense of responsibility. For this there are two reasons. Syphilis is a disease of some gravity; and it is a matter of common knowledge that syphilis may be contracted by those who fornicate promiscuously and that the symptoms of syphilis are often hidden.

If the parallels with Mrs. Thomson's cases hold, as I believe they do, then how are we to account for Mrs. Thomson's failure to see that out of a biological relationship a full responsibility does arise? My conjecture is as follows. I think she is saying that in the case of a conception which occurs despite the taking of all contraceptive precautions the conception is not intended, and this is of course true in one obvious sense of "intended". But it is also true that a sexual act was intended and it is a matter of common knowledge that such sexual acts are apt to bring about conception, even in circumstances where there is an attempt to avoid this consequence. Sexual activity in adult human beings is always intentional. Since, unlike the fabled primitives of Malinowski who had not hit upon the connection between copulation and conception, we know copulation between fertile persons is of such a nature that it is apt to bring about conception, conception can't be thought to lie outside the intentions of the parties concerned in such a way that the conception can be repudiated. Only in a society in which sexual activity is thought to be apt for pleasure but not, except on chosen occasions, apt for procreation could an argument of the kind Mrs. Thomson advances seem plausible. There seems to be a "fit" here between the nature of a contraceptive society and the demand for a liberalized abortion law or, with some, for a removal of abortion altogether from the jurisdiction of the courts. Here is the great shift in our culture.

It seems plain from the general drift of the essays in this book that it is coming to be seen that the question of abortion does not primarily (*pace* the utilitarian arguments of the United Church's spokesmen) raise questions in ethics; the questions rather lie in that field of philosophy, whatever we call it, that is relevant to deciding whether or not life in the womb, from conception to delivery, can be said to be human. Only when this question is decided can serious moral questions about the killing of life within the womb be raised.

The answer to this question is a matter of what it is reasonable to judge. We now have knowledge about the nature of human life from conception to birth that people didn't have a few years ago. A reasonable judgment now cannot be the same as it was in the ancient world or the Middle Ages or even the nineteenth century. For example, intricate questions were at one time raised about when the foetus became "ensouled". Quickening was thought to be possibly a sign of this. Now we know that the entire physical development of the child and the adult is contained in the genetic code present in the zygote. In an Aristotelian sense of *psyche,* the soul is present as an organizing or formal principle from the beginning. But such technical language is unnecessary. We have simply to note that there is no clear line to be drawn at any point in the development from zygote to newly-born infant. From this it seems to follow that deliberate abortion is a kind of homicide. I suspect that some supporters of the practice of therapeutic abortion would not disagree with this. But if it *is* a kind of homicide, then the question we have to ask is in what circumstances, if any, a particular act of homicide is justified, and this may make it necessary, as is evident from many of the contributions, to discuss the circumstances, again if any, which justify homicide.

Once we grant that feticide is homicide it seems likely that arguments for and against the propriety of killing the foetus will be of the kinds we are already familiar with in moral and political theory. The situation may be viewed either as one in which there is *prima facie* a conflict of rights, or as one in which the action is assimilated into that class of actions which are justified as cases of self-defence.

Let us look first at abortion described as an act of self-defence. It seems that an attacker who seeks to take away the life of another has in so doing forfeited his own right to life; to kill an aggressor is not to violate a human right. What circumstances entitle us to count someone as an aggressor? I am inclined to think that the limiting case would be that of someone guilty of manslaughter. It is characteristic of one who is found guilty of manslaughter that he has not that degree of guilty intention which goes with murder but that he is in some degree blameworthy in respect of the circumstances that led to the death of the victim. He might therefore be said in a slightly figurative way to be an "aggressor", though it would be important to distinguish this case from that of an attack by a murderer. Now, consider a case beyond the limit, the case of a tapeworm, or a flash of lightning. Of course, we can speak of the savage onslaught of the storm or the insidious attack of the tapeworm, and we can speak of lightning conductors and medicines as means of self-defence. But if we defy the malice of the heavens or the cunning of the tapeworm we are operating quite outside the field of human rights. Our attribution of malice to the heavens or cunning to the tapeworm is a figure of speech. No moral question arises as to whether or not it is all right to put up a lightning-conductor or kill a tapeworm by swallowing a pill. Now a foetus is no more capable of framing an intention and thus maliciously attacking than is the storm or the tapeworm. But whereas to speak of the innocence of the storm or the tapeworm is to use, perhaps for the purpose of irony or satire, a trope,[5] in the case of the foetus its innocence is absolutely literal, as it is in the case of a baby. Its being unable to attack constitutes its innocence; its being properly called innocent rests upon its being human. There are parents who batter their young children under the impression that when they cry or wet the bed they "only do it to annoy/Because they know it teases"; but we recognize that such parents are either mad or criminal. The justification of abortion on the ground of self-defence seems to be a non-starter.

The other way of justifying abortion for those who agree that it is a case of homicide is by noting that there may be a conflict of rights between the mother and the foetus. This view underlies the old law concerning abortion which until recently prevailed in Canada and throughout the United States, the law which forbade abortion except where it was necessary to save the life of the mother. So far as direct abortion is concerned, this situation has been changed by medical advances into one of mainly theoretical importance.[6] Indeed, I am not sure that any of the other situations in which abortion is now considered a justifiable procedure are clearly to be understood as situations within which there is a conflict of rights. Under the old legislation the foetus was plainly a subject of rights, so that abortion was straightforwardly a criminal procedure except in one peculiar case. But now other justifications in addition to the saving of the life of the mother are adduced: the safeguarding of the health of the mother (both physical and mental), the preservation of the standard of life of the family, the effect upon other children in the family, and so on. And it is also held, though other issues are perhaps involved here, that a child may be aborted if it is merely probable or possible that it will suffer from some physical or mental defect or even if in some sense it may be "unwanted".

Not all these situations are concerned with questions of rights and in many of them there is a strong disposition for those who advocate abortion to deny that the foetus can properly be called human. If this could be shown to be so, then the question would not be one that concerned a conflict over rights, for the foetus is not to this way of thinking a possible subject of rights, the United Nations Declaration notwithstanding. Now, if it could be shown that the foetus is not a subject of rights, the topic of abortion could cease to occupy legislators and those concerned with general social policy. Of course, it might still be the case that abortion was socially important because it led to widespread neurosis in females who had had abortions or to other undesirable psycho-physical consequences. But it could no longer be thought to be *prima facie* a criminal act.

The great variety of justifications of abortion that rely upon arguments of a utilitarian type — that the consequences of aborting the foetus will be better than the consequences of letting it go to term — seem to suffer from the general defects of all arguments of this type. There is no doubt about the fascination this kind of argument has for people in our society. For example, the use of atomic bombs against Hiroshima and Nagasaki and some of the military operations by the United States in Indo-China were defended by arguments about consequences. But what ground have we, from our knowledge of history or from any other kind of knowledge, for thinking that the future will sustain our expectations? We are not God. And what holds of secular expectations in general also holds of particular expectations. Any child may have a good life, despite all handicaps, and any child of excellent physique and high intelligence may have a bad life and turn out to be an enemy of the human race. It seems to me of the utmost importance that at the very least supporters of abortion in a variety of circumstances should admit that it is the comfort and convenience of families and parents that are in question. Talk about the wretchedness of the boys and girls who would come into existence if they were not aborted at the foetal stage is humbug. We don't know of any human being whether or not he will be a blessing or a curse to himself and to others. The thought that we may take away the gift of life from any man, no matter how criminal he may be, is mind-shaking; that we should take away the gift of life on speculative and hypothetical grounds from those who are at the earliest stages of their lives strikes me as beyond reasonable understanding. Even those who won't allow that killing a foetus is violating a human right must admit that to kill a foetus is to stop at the outset a development which would otherwise issue in a man or woman capable of walking the earth and of sharing in the flow of thought, feeling and activity that is human life.

It has often been suggested that one of the main considerations in the minds of those who oppose a liberalizing of the abortion laws is that abortion may provide a dangerous precedent for the killing of young children or of adults who are in one way or another troublesome to society. I think this consideration is an important one and I am not at all clear that it would be prudent to accept any assurances from the supporters of abortion that fears in this matter are unwarranted. Once we begin to develop criteria for deciding what *value* we are to put on this or that human life we seem irresistibly carried towards a vast programme. Professor Kremer cites the statement of the United Church's Joint Committee on Abortion to the effect that "the foetus is considered to have intrinsic worth but not equality of value with actualized persons".[7] Teachers sometimes have difficulty in elucidating the term *hubris* by means of examples. I suggest this statement of the United Church's Committee on the matter of the comparative value of different human lives provides us with a rich example.

The history of the movement for the reform of the abortion laws in Canada, the United States and Great Britain is not encouraging from the standpoint of those who fear that once certain precedents are established great changes cannot be prevented. All this has been stated and analysed in the brilliant essay "Abortion in Canada, 1960-1966". We note that the campaign for the extension of grounds for abortion takes the view that opposition to changes in the abortion laws rests upon a sectarian morality or a communal fad, like vegetarianism or abstinence from the flesh of the pig. Vegetarians don't in general agitate for the legal prohibition of the killing of the brutes for food, though they no doubt hope that in time people will come round to their way of thinking; nor do Jews regard the eating of pork by non-Jews as sinful. The parallel is at best a feeble one. Again, in a very short space of time the movement for reform changes from a small spring to a raging torrent. Churches, professional bodies, the press, are carried along by a great flood of opinion. Of course, there are many different schools of thought among the reformers from conservatives (therapeutic abortion only after a stringent process of inquiry and in the early stages of pregnancy) to the revolutionaries of Women's Liberation (abortion free of cost and solely on the demand of the pregnant woman). A great many assertions about matters of fact are made during the progress of the movement. It is asserted as a matter of fact that there are x illegal abortions in Canada every year. Others say it is $x+y$ or $x-y$. In any case, it is suggested that the way to get rid of backstreet abortions is to make abortion legal under not too onerous conditions. Statistics, for what they are worth, from countries with much experience of legal abortion, bearing on the continuing practice of illegal abortion are minimized or ignored. There is a strenuous effort to run together the questions of contraception and abortion, so that abortion is presented as a kind of auxiliary service to the general work of family planning clinics. Inevitably, much use is made of forecasts of over-population in the world of the future, forecasts which, whatever their value, have less application to Canada than to any other advanced country. Altogether, people tend to receive the impression that there is a mass of statistical evidence, logically powerful argument, compassionate considerations only the hardhearted or the cruel could ignore, such that the question is really from the standpoint of civilization and morality decided. Surely whatever is agreed upon by the mass of the medical and legal professions and the vocal sections of the Protestant churches can't very well be wrong. What is absent from this tumultuous movement is any patient discussion of the possibility that questions of human rights are involved. This, despite the explicit reference to the unborn in the United Nations Declaration of Human Rights, and despite the oath of Hippocrates which for many centuries has been held to summarize the ethos of medical practice. The oath includes the following:

> The regimen I shall adopt shall be for the benefit of my patients according to my ability and judgment, and not for their hurt or for any wrong. I will give no deadly drug to any, though it be asked of me, nor will I counsel such, and especially I will not aid a woman to procure abortion.

I do not suggest that either the Declaration or the Hippocratic oath is a decisive consideration. Only such authority belongs to documents of this kind as argument and good sense can approve. But their prestige and, in the latter case, the venerable tradition surely mean that argument against abortion is not a Roman Catholic oddity. It was until very recently the attitude of most Protestants [8] and Jews and it is not clear that changes in the attitudes of these bodies rest upon any very distinguishable or compelling chain of argument.

I have suggested that there is a "fit" between the new view of abortion and the rationale of a contraceptive society. I want to make it plain that I do not think that the two topics hang together in such a way that disapproval of abortion entails disapproval of all forms of contraception. Just as the ethos that flourishes in a contraceptive society doesn't entail that abortion is morally permissible, so a belief that abortion is morally impermissible doesn't entail anything one way or the other about the legitimacy of contraception. My personal view is that contraception within the context of a fruitful marriage and contraception in other circumstances raise distinct moral issues; but these are questions I do not intend to pursue at this time.

Father Edward Synan, in his learned contribution to this volume, has shown that the right to life of the unborn was respected under the Common Law and the Roman Law, and this during periods when both traditions sanctioned much brutality. Even in periods when a man might be disembowelled alive or a woman burned, one who was with child might "plead her belly". It is strange that, in a period when in social life our practices have become so much gentler, in this matter men's hearts have become harder. It is with the foetus as it is with the peasant masses of Asia, as it was with the millions in the Soviet concentration camps under Stalin, and with the Jews, gypsies and other selected groups in the transports towards the gas chambers under Hitler: all these are not or were not *present* to us, as our families and neighbours are. It would be—would have been—uncomfortable to admit their presence, and so there is an elaborate process of rationalization according to which the foetus is not human, offenders against Soviet orthodoxy are un-persons, Jews and gypsies are sub-human. Such failures of vision can also be termed failures of the imagination and of sympathy. It will be said that sympathy is also owing to the woman burdened with much child-bearing, for example, or to the young victim of rape. It is obvious that there can be and often is a failure of such sympathy and opponents of abortion ought to make a special examination of conscience in this matter. But it does not seem a good remedy for this failure to eliminate from the world by death those who are present in a hidden way: the unborn.

In likening abortion to the killing of men and women in the Russian and German concentration camps and gas chambers I seem to be moving the question of abortion outside the field of moral discussion altogether. One does not engage in moral discussion with a Yagoda or an Eichmann. Indeed, I think there *are* some among those who press for changes in the abortion laws or who wish to take the whole question of abortion outside the jurisdiction of the courts with whom discussion is not useful. I do not know what can be said to those who claim that a woman has an absolute right to an abortion in circumstances to be determined by her alone. This seems to be the view of some spokesmen of Women's Liberation. I hope they will read Miss Pegis' moving contribution; but Miss Pegis is asking for a conversion rather than an acknowledgement that a dialectical victory has been won. But it strikes me there are many who defend a liberalized abortion law with some diffidence. They are reluctant to give no value to foetal life, in part because it is just a matter of experience that women with child are dedicated to a serious task. Also, it is hard for any one today to avoid that modification of the imagination brought about by Freud, who pushes the history of consciousness and the earliest acts of our inward drama back to our life in the womb. The ending, through crushing, or suction, or poisoning, of this mysterious life growing in the obscurity of the womb seems an affront to our natural piety. Those who with some reluctance are prepared to countenance an abortion in the hard case do so because they think other values than that of the life in the womb may be in jeopardy. Health, family stability, the chance for women to develop their talents, all these are rightly valued; and it is thought that in the exceptional case abortion is justified. Two things have to be said. First, it seems at least the problem of means and ends deserves to be looked at with some care. If it is intolerable that one innocent man should suffer for even the most compelling reasons of state—the Dreyfus affair posed just this question in our fathers' time—then the taking of innocent human life by abortion looks a fearful act. Secondly, there is no evidence to show that a carefully designed abortion law expressly concerned with the hard case will hold under existing pressures. The example of Great Britain is not reassuring for those who wish to hold the line for a conservative abortion policy. Those who agitated to bring about the legislation now in force in Britain denied repeatedly that they were asking for abortion on demand. But in many cases the safeguarding procedures have dwindled to the merest formalities; and those hospitals that have insisted on operating these procedures with some strictness are much criticized and under severe pressure. It looks as though in practice the conservative line can't be held. This ought especially to trouble those Christians who favour a conservative abortion policy. It is always comfortable to think that in any matter there must be a *via media*. Perhaps in this matter of abortion there just isn't.

Footnotes

[1] "...the Catholic view...is or was maintained by Jews, by Indians of both hemispheres, by a variety of tribes...and even by some contemporary atheistical biochemists who are political liberals." Roger Wertheimer, "Understanding the Abortion Argument", *Philosophy and Public Affairs,* vol. I, No. 1, 1971. It should also be noted that Catholic opinion is not absolutely unanimous. See the citations from Bishop Francis Simons and Father Charles E. Curran in Micallef pp. 159-61 below.

[2] "A Defence of Abortion", *Philosophy and Public Affairs,* vol. I, No. 1, 1971, p.65.

³Its strength is that it as least evades the sophistry of "a woman has a right to control over her own body".
⁴See Philip Slayton, "*Roe v. Wade:* A Canadian Perspective", p. 167 ff. below.
⁵Cp. the Presbyterian cat who was hanged for Sabbath-breaking in the old song.
⁶See P.J. Micallef, "Abortion to Save the Mother's Life," pp. 154-66 below.
⁷Cited in Elmar J. Kremer, "Abortion and Pluralism", pp. 108-9 below.
⁸Cf. the 1960 declaration of the General Council of the United Church. "Christian conscience cannot approve abortion, either as a means of limiting and spacing one's family, or as a relief to the unmarried mother, because it involves the destruction of human life." This is qualified by approval of therapeutic abortion under strictly defined circumstances; but the declaration of principle is firm enough and is strikingly different from what will be said by United Church spokesmen ten years later. On all this see de Valk, pp. 14-43 below.

Section One: Abortion in Canada

Abortion in Canada, 1960-1966

By Alphonse de Valk

Alphonse de Valk is Assistant Professor of History, St. Thomas More College, University of Saskatchewan.

1. THE CANADIAN PRESS

Abortions were first openly advocated in Canada in the late fifties. In August, 1959, *Chatelaine,* the Canadian women's magazine, published what was probably the first article in a popular Canadian periodical to call for legalized abortions.[1] Though the article's headline ended in a question mark the author left no doubt that Canada's abortion law should be amended. She called the law "the world's harshest", and claimed that it forced "desperate women to seek help from a vicious back-room racket that often deals in death". As support for future change she pointed to the discussions in Britain and the proposal of the American Law Institute. While events had not yet advanced that quickly in Canada, she could point to a recent symposium on the meaning of "therapeutic abortion" by the *University of Toronto Medical Journal* in which several doctors had expressed their preference for a different law.

In favouring a revision of the Criminal Code clause on abortion, *Chatelaine* was to remain alone among popular magazines for half a dozen years. Canada's national magazine, *Maclean's,* published by the same Toronto company as *Chatelaine,* did not broach the subject until 1967, although, like practically every other public organ in the country, *Maclean's* had earlier attacked the birth control clause of the Criminal Code.[2] However, *Chatelaine* did receive support from two other important publications, the United Church *Observer* and the Toronto *Globe and Mail.*

In its 19th General Council of 1960 the United Church had already approved the legality of therapeutic abortions for physical or mental reasons. At that time this Church still disapproved of abortion either as a means of family planning or as relief to the unmarried mother.[3] But from then on the thinking of many ministers and official bodies in this Canadian Church was to go through a rapid evolution.[4]

A United Church minister of Vancouver, the Reverend Ray Goodall, published an article in favour of permitting abortion in the March, 1963 *Chatelaine*. He charged that the Canadian abortion law was not only wrong but cruel and "grossly immoral". "There is no human life in an embryo; it is simply living tissue", he stated, and "human life begins with birth and therefore abortion can never be the destruction of human life".[5] The same author had earlier made a strong plea for world-wide scientific birth control in a 1961 issue of the United Church *Observer*, claiming, among other things, that "abstinence and continence are fine for saints and celibates; the majority of men and women are neither".[6]

In a May, 1963 issue of the *Observer,* the Rev. Goodall repeated his *Chatelaine* plea in a somewhat more subdued tone.[7] It was the counterpart to a lead article by the Rev. Gerald Paul who in the March issue of the same magazine argued that abortion was wrong.[8] That article in turn, was a reply to an earlier *Globe and Mail* editorial calling for a change in the law. Four years later the same Rev. Paul published in *Chatelaine* a laudation on the exciting and liberating new morality: "New Moralists insist that charity... not chastity, is the chief virtue; the New Morality insists that persons are more important than principles. The New Morality is not anti-Christ; rather, it is the church catching up to Christianity".[9] As one illustration among many of how quickly a man changes his mind, the minister, campus chaplain by then, mentioned that once he, too, had taken a strong stand against abortion.[10]

While *Chatelaine* espoused legalized abortion openly among its women readers, and the *Observer* raised both pros and cons in a more balanced context among members of the United Church, the Toronto *Globe and Mail* had become the most formidable protagonist of the legalization of abortion among the general public. It supported the movement from the beginning and, indeed, has been primarily responsible for systematically drawing the attention of the wider public to the issues.

Among the first reports on opinions in Canada, a Canadian Press story published in the *Globe and Mail* at the end of August, 1961, set off a chain reaction of lasting consequence. A top official of the British Columbia division of the Canadian Medical Association, Dr. E. C. McCoy, had called for modification of the law to allow legal abortions for broad physical or mental reasons. The report stated that members of

Parliament for the Vancouver area, NDPers as well as Conservatives, favoured a thorough investigation of the matter by the federal government. Another doctor, P.L. McGeer, professor at the University of British Columbia, was also quoted as forecasting that abortion would eventually become a scientific question rather than the moral one it was now. Furthermore, the report gave the opinion of Professor Michael Wheeler at the UBC School of Social Work that induced abortion was "no more suitable a subject for the Criminal Code than suicide, contraception or voluntary sterilization". "But", said the professor, "the chances of getting agreement on this in Canada are about as good as for those for the re-unification of Germany."[11]

The very next day the *Globe and Mail* made a first attempt to prove Mr. Wheeler's forecast wrong. In an editorial entitled "The Abortion Issue", the *Globe and Mail* recapitulated the information of the previous day, adding that in the opinion of Professor Douglas Cannell, head of the obstetrics department at the University of Toronto, "the general feeling was that the laws do need revision". Referring to illegal abortions and to the fact that many women were obviously following a moral code of their own, the editorial somewhat cautiously queried whether "such women should be permitted to make their own moral decision". This is a question, it said,

> which is beginning to be asked seriously not only in Canada, but in the United States, Britain, and a number of European countries. The churches have a right to present their view of the moral issue to their adherents; but is this perhaps where their right should stop and that of the individual begin? A law which is rejected by the public is seldom a sound law... [12]

Having drawn attention to the issue of abortion for the first time, the paper then invited seven representatives of the professions and the churches to express their views in a series of articles. In October, 1961, under the title "Murder or Mercy", the *Globe* presented the views of Norman Borins, Q.C.; the Rt. Rev. F.H. Wilkinson, Anglican Bishop of Toronto; Gordon George, Superior of the Jesuit province of Upper Canada; Dr. B. Schlesinger, lecturer in the School of Social Work, University of Toronto; Dr. Abraham Feinberg, rabbi emeritus of Holy Blossom Temple, Toronto; Dr. L. Harkins, obstetrician-gynecologist for the Toronto Academy of Medicine; and G.P. Gilmour, former president of McMaster University.[13]

Mr. Borins favoured an extension of the law permitting abortion, first, to save the life of the mother, secondly, to prevent serious physical or mental injuries, and finally, in the case of sexual assault. "The effect of the law in its present state", he said, "is not to eliminate abortion but to compel secrecy and abortions by unqualified abortionists". The Anglican bishop found it difficult to regard an unborn life and a mature personality as of equal merit. He supported Dr. Fletcher's opinion expressed in the book, *Morals in Medicine,* that "to refuse to interrupt or prevent a pregnancy from rape would be an obvious injustice". Father Gordon George rejected abortion absolutely on the grounds that an evil means may never be used, not even to procure some presumed good.

Dr. Schlesinger attempted to show that reasonable people had accepted abortion throughout history and that the opposition to it was only the result of the Church's attempt to make the sexual act as difficult as possible. Quoting from Rattray Taylor's book, *Sex in History,* he traced the whole opposition to abortion to a mistranslation of Exodus 21, 22 by the church father Tertullian.[14] Professor Schlesinger recommended amending the law to allow abortions for medical, eugenic and humanitarian reasons as well as for mental health. Rabbi Feinberg accepted much the same reasons but with much graver caution and concern for moral values. He reiterated the principle that one life may not be sacrificed to save the life of someone else, but explained that the Talmudic approval of abortion to rescue the mother did not contradict this principle because the embryo was not considered to be really alive and possessed of a soul until extrusion and the completion of the birth-process.

Dr. Harkins explained that some therapeutic abortions were actually being carried out in hospitals for both medical and mental reasons. He welcomed clarification of the law in that respect and forecast that most doctors would be reluctant to request widening of grounds for abortion. Finally, Dr. Gilmour rejected the "No, even though..." attitude of "certain authoritarian" churches in favour of the "Yes, but..." answer. He approved abortion whenever beneficial, while expressing hesitation and reserve because of the complexity of the problem. Thus, of the seven participants only the representative of the Catholic Church opposed abortion outright.

Except for a half dozen letters to the editors immediately following the series "Murder or Mercy", the *Globe and Mail* did not bring up abortion again until 1963. The Toronto paper, and presumably most Canadian papers, did give extensive coverage to the thalidomide tragedy and to such events as the VandePut trial in Belgium in November, 1962, and the earlier case of Mrs. Finkbine of Arizona.[15] While the thalidomide crisis was short-lived it was, nevertheless, of great and lasting importance. First, it suddenly revealed that many people were quite prepared to allow and accept abortion. Secondly, it became clear that they were prepared to do so on the mere *possibility* of a baby being born seriously deformed.

The next occasion for comment came in December, 1962, when Judge Ken Langdon of Oakville publicly recommended that abortion be made legal for unmarried girls under 16 and for victims of rape and, also, that voluntary sterilization be made available for parents of large families. On January 2, 1963, the *Globe and Mail* congratulated the judge for his forthrightness. Without direct mention but with clear reference to the August 1961 news report and to its own series of articles in October of that year, the editorial continued:

> Pressure for reform of the laws governing abortion has been growing in recent years at many levels of Canadian society. Highly placed members of the legal, medical and university professions have urged the extension of legal abortion. The National Council of Women presented a brief to the Royal Commission on Health Services which disclosed that illegal abortion is the commonest cause of maternal mortality in Canada. Leading clergymen of major Protestant communions and of the Jewish faith have endorsed extension of legal abortion. Members of Parliament representing all four political parties have also gone on record as favoring extension.

The *Globe and Mail* further declared that a law which no longer conformed to the practices of society could bring all law into contempt and that Canada's law had attained this status "because it was fashioned to meet a particular moral code which is no longer embraced by the majority of Canadians". It concluded by recommending that abortion be legalized as proposed by Mr. Borins and Judge Langdon.[16]

2. THE PROFESSIONS

The *Globe and Mail* editorial of January, 1963 may be taken as the beginning of the second, more public and organized phase of the movement for the legalization of abortion in Canada. Although any such division remains arbitrary, the January editorial is useful as a dividing line, because it does mark the beginning of a period of activity by a greater variety of organizations and publicity media. As noted above, both *Chatelaine* and the United Church *Observer* were to run articles strongly in favour of abortion, the former in March, the latter in May, 1963. More important, perhaps, the year 1963 also marked the beginning of stirrings among the professional bodies, including the Canadian Medical Association and the Canadian Bar Association.

It must not be supposed that the more public phase of the movement for widening the abortion law was managed or controlled by a central organization. It started rather with spontaneous actions of unrelated semi-public bodies, often as a consequence of developments in what many people considered related areas, such as birth control, contraceptives, divorce and homosexuality. Perhaps the most that may be assumed is that those who took the initiative in proposing changes shared similar views on the place of morality in society.

Canadian Bar Association

An important moment of the second phase came at the time of the annual meeting of the Canadian Bar Association at Banff in September, 1963. As in other countries, it was the legal profession which first introduced the question in a systematic form in Canada, under the umbrella of its own large, respected and influential organization.

A resolution for the amendment of the Criminal Code to legalize abortion was proposed at the meeting of the Association's Section on Criminal Justice. It was sponsored by the British Columbia Sub-section of the same name under chairmanship of A. Stewart McMorran. The proposed resolution suggested a Termination Board and offered three grounds for legal abortions: a) danger to the mother's life or health; b) unwanted pregnancy due to rape or a similar unlawful act; c) danger of a mentally or physically defective child.[17] It did not include, therefore, the socio-economic grounds recommended in Britain. There was considerable opposition to the whole idea from the start, but especially to the introduction of the third and last category, that of abortion in case of danger of a defective child. According to the chairman this had been added because of the horror expressed for deformations such as found in the thalidomide babies.[18]

The British Columbia Sub-section had also submitted a brief of the B.C. Catholic Lawyers' Guild opposing the motion on the grounds that the "direct taking of an innocent life . . . is an act clearly forbidden by the laws of God and of our country". This was strongly opposed by Mr. George L. Murray of Vancouver who claimed that, in his opinion, "mixing our religious views with our views as lawyers is a terrible mistake". According to him, "it was once said that Christianity is not a part of the law of Canada". [19] Whether Mr. Murray believed himself to be summing up the state of affairs as it was or as he would like it to have been, was not clear; in any case Mr. John Scollin of Winnipeg declared it was nonsense to say that the law had no relation to the Judeo-Christian spirit. Whereupon Mr. Arthur Dawe of Okanagan Mission, B.C., describing himself as a non-Christian, objected to Christians speaking for all the people of the country. For good measure he added that "only an inhuman person could oppose this progressive step".[20] It was soon clear to everyone that the matter was highly controversial and would require further study.[21] It was decided that the provincial Sub-sections on Criminal Justice would require time for such study and consequently the proposed resolution was held over till the following year.[22]

The postponement incurred the ire of the Toronto *Globe and Mail* which declared the step "regrettable" and a less than courageous "stalling for time". The editorial attacked as "pointless" the position of the spokesman for the B.C. Catholic Lawyers' Guild, Mr. Bruce Emerson, when he said that the abortion issue should not be taken up, because "apart from legal implications, it has religious, social, moral and sociological implications, and in my opinion, the least of these is the legal one". The law of Canada "already permits abortion when it is performed to save the life of the mother", declared the *Globe and Mail,* going on to say that the resolution was "a mild one" in view of the necessity to "prevent needless deaths" resulting from illegal abortions. The *Globe and Mail* saw the key point of the issue as follows:

> ... what he (Mr. Emerson) is really saying is that the law should not permit some individuals to abide by their own standards of morality, even when society as a whole is not affected.

The *Globe and Mail* concluded:

> This raises the whole difficult problem of how far the law should be based on a code of morals, or ethics, which is in turn based on religious belief not shared by many people subject to the law.[23]

At the 1964 annual meeting in Montreal, the 1963 abortion resolution of the CBA was deferred for a year once more. The chairman of the Criminal Justice section could report no more than that the provincial Sub-sections had done "insufficient work". [24] In fact, when the Bar Association met at Toronto in September, 1965, that is, two years after the original introduction of the resolution, the chairman of the Criminal Justice Section had to admit again that no written reports had been received from other provincial Sub-sections.[25] This time, however, on his assurances that abortions had definitely been discussed by the Subsections even though no written reports had been sent in, the resolution was brought forward for consideration after the Section itself had voted approval first.

On September 3, the Canadian Press could report that "legalizing of abortions was urged Thursday by the criminal justice section of the Canadian Bar Association". But CP also reported that it appeared doubtful whether the proposal would get the backing of the full association this time.[26] And indeed, once again the resolution did not come to a vote. There was too little time left and there were too few people still at the Conference to pass a resolution on such a controversial issue. Instead, it was decided that all members of the Association be sent a copy of the resolution and that the matter be definitely placed on the agenda for the annual meeting in 1966. It was further suggested that contact be made with the medical profession to ascertain the views of the doctors.[27]

Canadian Medical Association

Like the legal profession, the Canadian Medical Association, too, had begun to discuss the question of therapeutic abortion in 1963. In spite of the fact that British Columbia doctors had first raised the issue in 1961 and had sparked the interest of the *Globe and Mail* at that time, it was Ontario which took the lead in the medical association. On the initiative of the Executive of the Section on Obstetrics and Gynecology, the Ontario Medical Association authorized a special committee for the study of sterilization and therapeutic abortion in its Council meeting of May, 1963. The terms of reference required a review of therapeutic abortion (and sterilization) from the standpoint of:

1. The medical indications for procedures of therapeutic abortion and sterilization.
2. Proper hospital machinery for the assessment of such cases.
3. Legal aspects involved in the carrying out of these procedures.[28]

The Board realized that a study of abortion should be conducted "under the premise that the medical aspects, legal requirements, and religious implications are three distinct areas which must be taken into account". However, it obviously felt competent to study only the medical and technical side of the problem.

Some light on the thinking of the Board at this time is provided by the aims of the study which, in addition to a report on "the modern aspect of this problem" are stated as "Recommendations either for changes in the

(Ontario) Public Hospitals Act or for new legislation".[29] The Board apparently did not envisage the possibility that the law might remain unchanged. Another indication of the trend of thought was the fact that therapeutic abortion was to be studied together with sterilization as if there were no qualitative difference between the two subjects.

As for the choice of personnel, the Board was advised "that a senior and highly respected member of the Section (on Obstetrics and Gynaecology) had volunteered to chair the committee". This proved to be Dr. D.M. Low.[30] He was invited to head the section and was subsequently joined by Dr. D. E. Cannell, representing the Maternal Welfare Committee, and Dr. K. G. Gray, both of whom had already indicated that they desired a revision of the law. [31] Together with Dr. M. G. Tompkins of Halifax, these men were to remain the key medical men on the abortion question. Dr. Low and Dr. Cannell presented the Ontario report to the CMA; Dr. Low and Dr. Tompkins, chairman of the CMA Maternal Welfare Committee, were the CMA representatives who met with the representatives of the Canadian Bar Association; and all four men, together with Dr. Aitken, the assistant-secretary of the CMA, presented the CMA case at the hearings of the Commons committee considering legislation to legalize abortion in the Fall of 1967. At that time Gerald Waring, in his 'Report from Ottawa', wrote as follows in the medical journal:

> Dr. Aitken acted as spokesmen for the CMA delegation, which also included Dr. Gregg Tompkins of Halifax and Dr. Douglas Cannell and Dr. Donald Low of Toronto, three distinguished practitioners and teachers of obstetrics and gynecology, and Dr. Kenneth Gray of the Clarke Institute of Psychiatry.
>
> Dr. Lewis Brand (PC, Saskatoon) referred to them as "distinguished lawbreakers" and Robert Stanbury (L, York-Scarborough) as "the biggest gathering of criminal abortionists ever held in Canada"—a bantering reaction to Dr. Cannell's admission that "I and my colleagues have been breaking the law now for a long time", both in performing therapeutic abortions and in advising patients on methods of contraception.[32]

In short, all four men had long since been convinced of the need for change in the abortion law and were now committed to help bring it about. Dr. Low, moreover, was also to play an important part in shaping the official views of the United Church, in virtue of being its chief medical advisor on the question of abortion.[33]

The Sterilization and Therapeutic Abortion Committee reported to the Council of the Ontario Medical Association in May, 1965, two years from the date of its inception. It recommended that operations terminating a pregnancy be lawful if performed "to preserve the life or physical or the mental health" of the mother, and if they were done in a properly qualified place and manner, after consultation of an abortion committee.[34] The Committee wanted it understood that it had not considered it their function "to encourage 'wide' liberalization" of abortion procedures but "rather to make them legal and to provide ... better precautionary standards for the protection of both the public and the profession".[35]

Although the committee had suggested further consultations with other medical sections, the Council decided to approve the recommendations without delay. Within a week the *Globe and Mail* could print an editorial congratulating the OMA for having joined the "growing chorus of responsible voices" calling for abortion reforms. Repeating its statement of September, 1963, that the existing law permitted abortions even though only to save the life of the mother, the paper called it "a hard and cruel law" which "is so vague, so completely dependent on interpretation, that few lawyers, let alone doctors, profess to know what it means". Declaring once again that the problem had its roots in religious controversy, it concluded with the demand that "this law ... be amended to save the health as well as the lives of mothers and to enable doctors to perform their duties according to their conscience and their calling."[36] The *Ontario Medical Review* reprinted the 1965 editorial in its regular feature "Clipper's Corner", just as two years earlier it had reprinted the September, 1963 editorial.[37]

After adoption by the Ontario Council, the recommendations were presented to the parent body, the Canadian Medical Association, and its appropriate sub-section, the Committee on Maternal Welfare. The latter met in November, 1965, having in the meantime received the proposed resolution of the Criminal Justice Section of the Canadian Bar Association. After studying the lawyers' resolution the committee formulated a proposal which was basically the Ontario model with slight modifications in wording.[38]

3. AGITATION: THE VOICES OF THE CHURCHES

The second and preparatory phase of the movement for legal abortions may be said to have drawn to a close at the end of 1965; from the beginning of 1966 the movement was marked by a rapid growth of interest on the part of the general public. During the third phase those who favoured legalization became more impatient; those who opposed it began to take more serious notice of it. Also, important professional and national organizations went on record in favour of a revision of the law. And while in Britain abortion moved into its last legislative phase under international attention, in Canada abortion entered its first legislative phase by being referred to a Standing Committee of the House of Commons.

Yet, while these events were significant steps in the political and legislative evolution of the abortion issue, both public and parliament were, for the time being, more occupied with two other issues: birth control and divorce. Like abortion, both issues touched upon marital morality and, like abortion, both required changes in the Criminal Code. Thus their treatment in parliament provided not only an indication of what might happen to the abortion issue, but, in fact, prepared the way for similar treatment.

In Great Britain the abortion debate had assumed sharp religious overtones early in 1966 after the Board for Social Responsibility of the Church of England issued an abortion report on December 31, 1965.[39] By the standards of committed abortion reformers, the Anglican Committee ranked almost as reactionary. It rejected abortion on demand, or terminating life for the prevention of possible deformed babies, or abortion for rape. Yet when it came to proposing legislation, it recommended such vague wording as to make the grounds very broad indeed, justifying abortion not only when the mother's life was threatened, but also when her health or the well-being of her family were endangered. It suggested making "serious injury to the mother's physical or mental well-being" an indication for legal abortion, authorizing doctors to "take into account the patient's total environment, actual or reasonably foreseeable".[40]

The Roman Catholic primate, John Cardinal Heenan, replied to this statement in his diocesan journal. "Until recently," he wrote, "the accepted view of Christians and, so far as I know, of all believers, has been that direct killing of the child-to-be is immoral." He went on to say that

> It is only because of what is called the liberalizing of the law against abortion that the Catholic attitude has begun to appear eccentric—as if abstaining from killing the foetus in the womb were a Catholic foible like abstaining from meat on Friday...[41]

The Cardinal charged that the Committee deliberately rejected the Christian tradition of viewing the killing of the foetus as a form of homicide by declaring this tradition to be too simple a principle to fit the complexities of the case. "If it is justifiable," he wrote,

> to kill the foetus which may be born deformed because, for example, the pregnant mother has contracted German measles, it is hard to see why children who manage to be born deaf, blind or otherwise handicapped should not be ... put to death.[42]

Hardly were Cardinal Heenan's words in print before the bill came up again in the House of Lords and the Anglican Bishop of Exeter, the Right Rev. Robert Cecil Mortimer, walked out of the debate in protest against attacks upon the unborn child.

While Canadian Catholic weeklies passed on to their readers the words of the British Cardinal Heenan, the national monthly of the Anglican Church in Canada, the *Canadian Churchman,* reviewed favourably the report of its British Sister Church.[43] Indeed, this report eventually provided the basis for the policy formulation of the Canadian Anglican Church in its submission to the House of Commons in the fall of 1967. The Anglican brief recommended the report to the Commons Committee.[44]

In Canada, too, the issue began to be explained more and more in terms of religion and Church membership, following the direction indicated by the *Globe and Mail.* Often, appearances seemed to confirm that only Roman Catholics opposed the legalization of abortion. Dr. D. M. Low, speaking at the annual meeting of the United Church of Canada's Board of Evangelism and Social Service held in February of that year, reported that out of 177 active treatment hospitals in Ontario only the 40 Roman Catholic-administered hospitals totally disapproved of abortion. Furthermore, out of 187 obstetricians and gynecologists surveyed in Ontario, 169 approved widening the grounds of therapeutic abortions. The remainder were, presumably, once again Roman Catholics.[45]

The notion that only Catholics opposed abortion found further credence when the largest Protestant Church, the United Church of Canada, appeared ready to accept wider grounds for legal abortions. At the above-mentioned February meeting of the Board of Evangelism, the secretary of the Board, Rev. R. J. Hord, blamed the law for consigning thousands of women annually to "illegal back-room abortionists".[46] A resolution was passed in favour of legal abortions, not just when a mother's life was endangered, but also when her mental or physical health was threatened. While in 1960 the General Council had started its statement on abortion with the clause that the "Christian conscience cannot approve abortion", in February, 1966, the Board of Evangelism made no mention of this. Instead, it declared that the sections on abortion in the Criminal Code were "conflicting, leaving the impression that abortion is wrong and even murderous in all circumstances". It also denounced "the air of secrecy and guilt surrounding abortions". The Board's decision was duly publicized before it was sent on to the General Council.[47]

When the General Council met for its 22nd annual meeting six months later, in September, 1966, a resolution based on the proposal of the Board of Evangelism was readily adopted. It justified abortion "when the life of the foetus threatens the life or health of the mother".[48] None of the four hundred clerical and lay delegates stood to oppose it. Rev. A. R. Huband of Toronto was quoted as saying that "Every child has a right to be well born, and in some cases this means the right not to be born at all."[49] Favouring birth control and favouring abortion, he said, involved "a reverence for a quality of life rather than for life itself".[50]

National Organizations

While some Churches gradually changed their position, other organizations, too, took a stand. Some were small, like the Planned Parenthood Group in Edmonton, which in April voted in favour of widening the abortion laws.[51] Others were of medium size, such as the 45,000 member Central Ontario Women's Institute which called abortion laws archaic and futile.[52] One group, the National Council of Women of Canada, was very large. A federation of approximately 1800 organizations with 800,000 members, this body was the first national organization to go on record in favour of legal abortions. It adopted a resolution as early as June, 1964, during its annual meeting in Hamilton. Subsequently, the resolution was presented to the government twice, on January 21, 1965, and again on January 31, 1966. Although it urged the government to establish a Royal Commission to provide "an objective and non-partisan basis for amending the law", it also called the existing law "confused, conflicting, outdated, and in certain instances, cruel and unjust", thus leaving no doubt about its own attitude. The reason given for this resolution was the need "to bring these laws into conformity with the realities of Canadian life".[53] Among the various national bodies only one organization defied the trend. At its 46th national convention in Hamilton in September, 1966, the Catholic Women's League, representing

160,000 women mainly in English-speaking Canada, urged the government to reject broader abortion laws.[54]

4. AGITATION: THE CANADIAN MEDICAL ASSOCIATION AND THE CANADIAN BAR ASSOCIATION

During 1966, the Canadian Medical Association and the Canadian Bar Association also completed the internal process of consultation. Before presenting their proposal to the general meeting of the Canadian Medical Association, the Committee on Maternal Welfare, which was in charge of the abortion resolution, desired to seek further consultation with the CBA. As a result of the initiative of the Committee on Medical Aspects of Traffic Accidents, the CMA had already adopted a motion at its annual meeting in June of 1965 to investigate the possibility for a Medical-Legal Liaison Committee in conjunction with the CBA.[55] The initiative was put to good use and the Chairman of the Maternal Welfare Committee, Dr. M. G. Tompkins, together with Dr. Low, discussed the abortion resolutions with representatives of the CBA in Ottawa on two Saturdays in April 1966.[56] In these meetings the doctors strongly disagreed with the lawyers' proposed Termination Board and they questioned the CBA's third ground for legal abortions, the possibility of a defective child.[57]

Unable to agree, the medical men went ahead with their own recommendation. In a May issue, the Canadian Medical Association's journal could report that the Executive Committee meeting on April 29 and 30th had received reports from 24 Standing Committees for submission to the annual meeting in Edmonton, including a recommendation of the Maternal Welfare Committee that "sterilization and therapeutic abortion should be made lawful when performed under certain circumstances".[58] Two months later newspapers reported that the CMA in its annual meeting at Edmonton had officially approved the legalization of abortion. A motion to add to the medical resolution the indications for legal abortions proposed by the CBA had been defeated and the approved resolution was still essentially the same as the one proposed a year earlier by the Ontario Medical Association.[59]

Again the *Globe and Mail* had cause to cheer. Under the title "A Long Overdue Reform", it called the CMA's decision "a landmark". "More important perhaps than the recommendation itself," the paper wrote, "was the rationale behind it. Dr. M. G. Tompkins, chairman of the association's committee on maternal welfare, put it rather well when he said that an amendment to the Criminal Code to permit therapeutic abortions would only 'legalize what has been done and is being done'." The *Globe and Mail* interpreted this statement to mean that in the opinion of the CMA, legalization would nullify the need for illegal back-street abortions which the paper estimated "at between 20,000 and 120,000 annually".[60] Dr. Tompkins, however, was probably referring to the small number of therapeutic abortions already being carried out in hospitals. One year later, at the hearings of the Abortion Committee of the House of Commons, he and his colleagues refused to commit themselves to the view that legal abortions would necessarily reduce the illegal ones. Their answers ranged from "I don't know", to "It is possible, but not very likely".[61]

In spite of the disagreement with the medical men the Canadian Bar Association, too, proceeded with its own, slightly revised, resolution. By this time its proposal included a lengthy second part dealing with provincial Termination Boards which were supposed to judge the necessity of an abortion in cases of criminal assault. A copy of this resolution was sent to all members of the association in June, 1966, in preparation for discussion and a vote at the Bar Association's annual meeting in Winnipeg in the following August.[62]

The CBA debate at the end of that month was lively and at times emotional. It lasted three hours and illustrated two things. First of all, it showed that the climate of opinion among the population had shifted so much that approval of the resolution was a foregone conclusion. Secondly and more significantly, it indicated the almost totally diverse roads by which proponents and opponents of the resolution had arrived at their respective positions.

The arguments for and against never met on common ground. The division between pros and cons was not one between those who found different answers to the same question; rather it was a division between people who had answers to different questions. Insisting that their own questions were the more important and legitimate ones, overriding consideration of any others, they found themselves in opposing positions. Those who favoured the resolution were interested only in asking: What is to be done about illegal abortions here and now? On the other hand, those who opposed the resolution wanted first an answer to the questions: Is abortion moral or immoral? Is it good or bad for society? Proponents of wider grounds for abortion had no patience with these questions, while opponents of abortion revision were maddened by the suggestion that something could be presented as a solution when no one had examined its principles or consequences. In this sense, then, the division was basically one between pragmatists and idealists, between those who stressed the importance of practical solutions and "getting on" with it without bothering much about "religious or philosophical niceties", and those who believed these same "niceties" to be essential in upholding ideals and, therefore, fundamental for a sane society.[63]

By design rather than by accident, those who wanted an answer first to the more general question proved to be mostly "conservative" or "fundamentalist" in religion. Accustomed to consider matters in the light of basic (religious) principles, they refused, therefore, to discuss *illegal* abortions separate from the question of abortion as such. Nevertheless, their opponents could make them look like men who not only dragged their heels and who were unwilling to come to grips with "reality", and who also ignored the virtues of compassion and charity.

The resolution was introduced by the Chairman of the Criminal Justice section, Stewart McMorran of Vancouver, who explained the details of its two parts, but did not state the reasons for this bill other than that "there is nothing being forced on anyone" and that England which was pretty good at things done in the realm of law, had just passed an abortion law in the House of Lords.[64] The seconder of the original motion in 1963, Anthony C. Bazos of Toronto, stated the issue more clearly and more directly. According to him, the sole purpose of the resolution was to protect the pregnant female seeking an abortion. "You are not being asked, any of you people," he said to his colleagues, "to say that you are legalizing abortions... you're aiming to protect the pregnant female."[65]

Mr. Bazos' view was supported by Donald Diplock, one of the three Bar representatives who had met with the medical men in Ottawa. Mr. Diplock explained that a major concern of their meetings had been the question of how to stop illegal abortions. "It would suffice," he said, "to eliminate illegal abortions if the medical profession were allowed to operate, say, within the first sixteen weeks of pregnancy"; after that period, he suggested, it should be done for the purpose of saving the mother's life. Although he himself recognized the question as basically one of *moral* attitude, not of medical or social facts, he said that he failed to understand these moral objections because, when a spontaneous abortion occurs "no one thinks that a human being has died, only that a potential child has failed to be born".[66]

Except for the passing reference to it by Mr. Diplock, not one of those who favoured legalizing abortion or widening the grounds for abortion seemed interested in discussing the issue of human life. Undoubtedly this reflected the widespread unwillingness of the public in general at this time to examine this aspect. Some people believed or assumed without further reflection that human life was not involved at all, thinking, perhaps, like the American Professor of Psychiatry, Thomas Szasz, that an abortion should be available in the same way as an operation for the beautification of the nose.[67] At the Winnipeg convention the issue of human life was mentioned, however, and no one was allowed to go home without hearing something about it as well as about other philosophical and practical objections to the CBA resolution. These were presented by Alex Sarchuk, Crown prosecutor in Winnipeg.

Mr. Sarchuk, quoting extensively from religious and medical sources, argued that life was bestowed by God, not by man; that one could not justify destruction of innocent human life; that everyone agreed that the child is human just before birth; that since it is impossible to demonstrate the precise time when the unborn becomes human, it leaves the moment of conception as the only rational choice; that except for emergencies to save the mother's life, churches such as the United Church and the Anglican Church had opposed abortion as recently as 1960 and 1958; that there was much dispute whether or not therapeutic abortions were good medicine; that medical indications for therapeutic abortions were minimal; that some psychiatrists held that there were no real psychiatric grounds for termination of pregnancy either; and that in the early months of pregnancy doctors could not state whether a child would be born defective. "I submit," he concluded, "that if abortion is made readily available, responsibility will not be encouraged, legal and illegal abortions will increase, and the indications for abortion will become more liberal as women demand readier access to this solution."[68]

Following the speech of Mr. Sarchuk, Saul Froomkin, speaking for the Manitoba Criminal Justice Sub-section, quickly announced that, notwithstanding Mr. Sarchuk's remarks, the majority of the Manitoba Sub-section favoured the resolution. When other lawyers, too, spoke against the resolution, they made just as little impact as Mr. Sarchuk. Among them was Sydney Paikin, speaking for himself and for his Hamilton partner, John White. Mr. Paikin argued that there was no doubt that therapeutic abortions were legal the only time they counted, namely, when necessary to save the mother's life. In rejecting a widening of grounds he again stressed the rights of the unborn child, quoting the presumably impeccable authority of the United Nations' 1959 Declaration on Human Rights. This Declaration stated that:

> The child by reason of its physical and mental immaturity needs special safeguards and care, including appropriate legal protection *before* as well as after birth.

It was all to no avail. The majority of lawyers were not to be budged. The general mood was summed up by Mr. David Bowman of Winnipeg.

Classifying the objections as religious and moral, he dismissed them therefore, as purely private opinions of no real concern to the rest of society. "Lord knows we have heard, on so many questions over the years, this kind of argument!" he exclaimed under applause. "And surely we, who do not have these moral objections, have the right to say to the moral objectors, 'Let us, let us, too, have our rights'."[69] Without explaining whose rights or what rights he meant and not satisfied with merely brushing arguments and opponents aside, he presented his own views on morality: "And surely, further, Mr. Chairman, there can be nothing more immoral, nothing more irreligious than turning medical practitioners and decent people into criminals in the way which our present legislation does."[70] After having thus implied that people become criminals because of some law and not because they perform acts harmful to society, presumably no one was surprised when Mr. Bowman concluded by ridiculing "all the exaggerated fears of what will happen if this thing is adopted". He placed these fears in the same classification as the fears of British Lords a hundred and thirty years ago when these august gentlemen supposedly expected a national revolution after pickpocketing had been removed from the list of capital crimes.

The vote crowned with success the three-year campaign led by the B.C. Bar, and the CBA endorsement of legalized abortions was hailed by a number of persons across Canada. Stephen Lewis of the Ontario NDP, whose bill for liberalized abortion laws had died on the order paper at the Ontario Legislature in the spring, said that all Canada should applaud the stand. His father, David Lewis, federal NDP member for Scarborough West declared: "There is a desperate need in Canada for such a change in the laws." Dr. R. F. Stackhouse, professor of religion at Wycliffe College in Toronto, columnist for the *Toronto Telegram* and member of the Anglican delegation to the House of Commons hearings in December, 1967, recommended all possible support for the association's stand.[71]

5. "REFORM IS UNDER WAY!"

Progress for the revision of abortion laws at the beginning of 1967 can best be summed up by the confident words of Mr. Ian Wahn, Liberal MP for Toronto-St. Paul, in January: "Reform is under way!" Commenting on these words, Mr. Gerald Waring, in his regular column in the *Canadian Medical Association Journal,* reported that "in a few days it will be a full year since this reform-minded lawyer-MP introduced a bill in the Commons to relieve medical practitioners of the risk of criminal liability... This session the abortion bill is scheduled to get a commission hearing."[72] If he had written two weeks later, he could have said not only that the government in Ottawa had decided to give the abortion question an airing in a House of Commons' Committee— a decision made in the spring of 1966—but also that the Prime Minister, Mr. Pearson, had now hinted that abortion reform might actually be included in a proposed revision of the Criminal Code.

The Prime Minister and his cabinet were no doubt influenced by the authority of the CMA and the CBA resolutions, as well as the pressure from other organizations. A hint of possible legislative action came at a reception of a delegation of the National Council of Women of Canada on Monday, January 30th. Calling Canadian abortion laws "unjust", the President Mrs. H. H. Steen of Vancouver submitted the Association's brief for a third year in a row and asked again for a royal commission to investigate the matter. Mr. Pearson replied that he was not sure a royal commission was needed or even desirable and that the question might be considered later in the current session of Parliament.[73]

There can be little doubt that the government would not have seriously contemplated new abortion legislation at this time, if it had not been for the fact that other issues involving marriage, morality, and law, had preceded the abortion issue and were receiving a sympathetic hearing from the general public. One of these issues was the legalization of contraceptives; another was the widening of grounds for divorce. To many people it seemed natural that the removal of contraceptives from the Code would be followed by the legalization of sterilization and abortion. That was the way the *Globe and Mail* saw it. "Abortion and birth control are closely related subjects", an editorial following the Prime Minister's announcement stated, "and it would not be unreasonable, if one of them is to be dealt with, to expect that consideration of the other will come soon."[74] Edmonton's *Western Catholic Reporter* protested the editorial. "We submit", the weekly warned, "that it is unreasonable to talk of contraception and abortion in the same breath... The government of Canada will make a great mistake if it ever forgets the difference between contraception and abortion."[75] The fact of the matter was that a great many people were doing just that, including Ian Wahn in his already mentioned bill.

Mr. Wahn's bill consisted of two parts, part one on abortion; part two on contraception. Together with three other private bills which dealt with contraception only, it was referred by the House of Commons to its standing Committee on Health and Welfare on February 21, 1966. In his statement of purpose at the Committee's first hearing, it became clear that Mr. Wahn did not distinguish between the two issues.[76] In explaining that the Committee would deal first with the contraception issue only, the chairman, Dr. Harry Harley (L, Halton) pointed out that the two issues differed in principle, "one being the prevention of conception and the other being the destruction of conception". However, the chairman assured Mr. Wahn that the Committee considered abortion part of the mandate given to it by the Commons and that the issue would not be shelved but considered later.[77] Thus, consideration of abortion was ensured a full year before the hearings on this subject actually started.

In the same spring session of 1966, after it had referred the four bills on contraception to the Committee on Health and Welfare, the Commons also sent the Committee on Justice and Legal Affairs seven private bills on divorce. In the past, private bills on both these subjects had either been "talked out" or let die on the order paper without any debate. The move to refer them to committee indicated a new approach to these issues and was no doubt the result of growing pressure on the government to deal with them. As the Minister of Justice, Lucien Cardin, declared in the House: "These two subjects are no longer taboo, Previous governments have been hesitant in dealing with them—I think properly so— but we cannot close our eyes to them. We have had a number of briefs from interested organizations which were very well argued and they are being studied."[78] The key question was, of course, how parliament and the government intended to treat these very touchy and controversial issues.

6. THE LAW ON CONTRACEPTION

All four private bills on contraception proposed to change Section 150 of the Criminal Code which prohibited selling, distributing or advertising "any means, instructions, medicine, drug or article intended or represented as a method of preventing conception or causing abortion or miscarriage". Robert Stanbury (L, York-Scarborough) and Ronald Basford (L, Vancouver Centre) desired that the provisions of the Code on contraception should not apply to authorized agents such as doctors, nurses, family planning agents, etc.; Robert Prittie (NDP, Burnaby Richmond) and Ian Wahn wanted to eliminate contraception from the Criminal Code altogether.

In questioning the position of MP's Prittie and Wahn, Robert Stanbury came at once to the key question when he noted that their position "perhaps suggests that no element of this field is worthy of treatment in criminal law". He himself thought that there were aspects of public health and safety, and public morality "which still have a place in criminal law in this matter of birth control".[79] His view was similar to the view of the Canadian Bar Association which in its brief later in the year also wanted sales of contraceptives legalized but still thought restrictions on advertising desirable. On the other hand, the Canadian Medical Association sided with Messrs. Prittie and Wahn and favoured the direct elimination of all references to contraceptives from the Code.[80]

Possible explosive religious overtones of the contraception issue were defused fairly early in the hearings—insofar as they needed defusing at all—when Jean Paul Matte (L, Champlain) read a letter from two priest professors into the Committee's record, explaining that in their view Catholics would not do morally wrong if they favoured proposed changes in the Criminal Code.[81] Accepting a suggestion made two years earlier by the *Globe and Mail*, the principal author declared that in his opinion existing Canadian law held illegal even the Church's marriage preparation course, insofar as these mentioned (Church-approved) birth control methods. The two theologians then referred to the explanatory notes of Mr. Wahn's bill.[82] They simply agreed with him, stating that the "function of law is not exactly that of morality and that human law is not meant to forbid or punish all evil actions". A spokesman for the Voice of Women pointed out to the Committee that in the book, *Brief to the Bishops,* Toronto Catholic lawyer John O'Driscoll had taken a position "exactly as set out here" by Father Vezina.[83]

Authoritative confirmation of these views came when the Catholic Bishops of Canada responded to an invitation of the Committee and submitted a brief in October 1966. The Bishops declared that they would not oppose any changes in the legislation on contraceptives if "safeguards against irresponsible sales and advertising ... were provided" and if personal freedom was protected.[84] They gave as their reason that, in their opinion, legislation on contraceptives was an example where it does "not serve the common good to translate moral laws into civil laws". In order to turn a wrongful act into a statutory crime punishable by law at least four conditions should be fulfilled, the bishops said:

1. It should first of all be clear that the wrongful act notably injures the common good;
2. The law forbidding the wrongful act should be capable of enforcement, because it is not in the interest of the common good to pass a law which cannot be enforced;
3. The law should be equitable in its incidence—i.e., its burden should not fall on one group in society alone;
4. It should not give rise to evils greater than those it was designed to suppress.[85]

The Bishops considered the existing law inadequate and deficient under all four conditions "independently of the morality or immorality of various methods of birth prevention". They added, however, that they wanted "to make it abundantly clear that the modification of Civil Law in no way implies the modification of God's moral law". They also warned that the application of these principles would be quite different in regard to that part of the Code which had to do with abortion.[86]

The Committee of Health and Welfare sent its final report to the Commons on December 5, 1966. It recommended that birth control be removed from the Criminal Code, declaring that the dissemination of family planning information should be free from any fear of illegality. Family planning, the committee stated, is a personal affair and "the state should not interfere with action or laws in any way to influence such a personal decision". While the Committee expressed gratitude for the views of the Churches and others, it did not respond with much vigour to their fears of blatant advertising and uncontrolled sales to minors. The parliamentary body merely suggested that "necessary regulations on the distribution and advertising of contraceptives" be placed under the Food and Drugs Act.[87] This suggestion was accepted by the government later on and while undoubtedly it had some effect on the quality of contraceptives, it was to prove entirely ineffective in restricting their distribution.

7. THE LAW ON DIVORCE

The Special Joint Committee of the Commons and Senate on Divorce, announced on March 15, 1966, began its hearings in the fall of 1966. Nine private bills were referred to it, eight from the House of Commons and one sponsored by the 88-year-old Senator Roebuck.[88] Here, as in the matter of contraception, the climate of opinion favoured liberalization. All nine bills proposed to add to the hitherto sole ground for divorce, adultery, others such as desertion, cruelty and incurable insanity. Some bills even suggested drunkenness, drug addiction, frequent criminal convictions, or non-support.[89]

Like birth control, divorce again was an international issue. For example, in April 1966, New York State changed its divorce law for the first time since its enactment 179 years earlier. The new law included homosexuality, sodomy, cruel and inhuman treatment, abandonment for two years, imprisonment for three consecutive years, and living apart for two years following either a separation agreement or a formal court decree of separation. New York Catholics had opposed an even more liberal bill, charging that it was not meant to "reform" but simply intended to make divorces easier, thus undermining the family structure by introducing divorce by consent.[90]

In Canada the United Church was among the first religious bodies to submit a brief to the Divorce Committee, presenting a serious study which included a hundred-page brief by the Pastoral Institute of the United Church in Calgary on the concept of "marriage breakdown". The church suggested a "totally new" divorce law, making "marriage breakdown" rather than "marital offences" the basis for granting divorces. As an intrinsic part of its proposal it also requested new marital court procedures to deal with distressed marriages and help with the preservation of marriage and family life.[91]

Like the United Church brief which was supported by the Anglicans, other submissions also suggested that marriage ought to be protected by positive measures. Among the strongest expression of these views was the brief of the Roman Catholic Bishops submitted in April, 1967. While leaving the "details about grounds for divorce that would be acceptable or not" to the "well-informed conscience" of legislators, they stated that "we cannot overemphasize that an indiscriminate broadening of the grounds for divorce is not the solution to the problem of unhappy marriages". Instead they suggested an extensive rethinking of the entire body of legislation dealing with marriage and the family as a part of a revision of the divorce law, including important changes in the procedures of divorce courts.[92]

The joint Committee of the Senate and House of Commons concluded its hearings in the late spring of 1967. It submitted its report and draft bill to the government in the middle of June. Although empowered to report on both the divorce law itself and on "the social and legal problems relating thereto", the report and the bill it proposed dealt with the law only, under the title "Divorce (Extension of Grounds) Act". In fact, the Committee had ignored the bulk of the testimony. It simply declared the other matters to have been outside the scope of its investigations.[93] The suggested divorce courts, judges and trained investigators, the report said, might cause delays and "far from making divorces simpler and cheaper, might well have the opposite effect".[94]

Observers of the parliamentary scene detected two other reasons why the proposal for positive government action had been rejected. First of all, the fear that it might cost money and secondly, a refusal to accept marriage reconciliation as a proper government task. At least that was the way the Churches saw it as expressed in their joint statement of protest which was formulated after the publication of the Committee's recommendations. Signed by representatives of the Anglican, Catholic, Lutheran, Mennonite, Presbyterian and United Church communities, the statement expressed the deep disappointment of the Churches. Their own study of the 1,600 pages of proceedings, they stated, clearly indicated three areas in which there had been general agreement among those who had submitted briefs. These principles were that the federal government should take a creative lead in programs fostering successful marriages; secondly, that the social requirements for successful marriages would not be attained by a single legislative act; and thirdly, that federal divorce law should not merely play the purely negative role of facilitating the burial of some dead marriages.[95] The joint statement was submitted to Justice Minister Trudeau on November 8, 1967, filed away, and not heard from again.

By the end of 1967, then, the attitude of both parliament and government was clear. On the one hand they were willing, even anxious, to remove matters such as contraception and divorce from the supervision of the law; on the other hand, they proved unwilling to assume responsibility for positive action. That this attitude was fully approved in some quarters, was made clear by an editorial in the *Winnipeg Free Press* following the third and final reading of the new Divorce Bill in the House of Commons.[96] The editorial noted that "fortunately" nothing came of the efforts of some members to introduce the "marriage-breakdown" concept as the sole evidence for divorce. The danger of that proposal was, the paper pointed out, that the state would have to set up "a moral and social inquisitorial system".

> It is evident from some of the things that Justice Minister Trudeau had said that he wishes our courts to remain legal, and not become moral, institutions. Whether some of the advocates of marriage-breakdown as the sole ground are or are not aware of it, the principle of marriage-breakdown would hand over to the courts whole areas of our lives that are not the business of the courts. The present adversary principle leaves the courts with a theoretically simple decision to make: Is there a legal case for the ending of a given marriage? The marriage-breakdown principle, as the sole ground, would involve the courts in something quite different and something utterly abhorrent to our traditions.

8. SUMMARY

By the close of 1966 strong voices had been raised in Canada in favour of the revision of the Criminal Code. These voices probably represented a considerable section of public opinion, especially in English-speaking Canada.

Canadian public opinion had been influenced by three developments: the introduction of a bill for the legalization of abortion in Britain, a country which had traditionally influenced Canada in matters of legal theory and legal precedents; the discussions of abortions in the popular mass media of the United States; and the occurrence of the "thalidomide crisis", which revealed that the horror of cruelly deformed babies was such that many people almost instinctively preferred abortion. Public opinion had been shaped from within the country by the Toronto *Globe and Mail*, supported by *Chatelaine* and the United Church *Observer*.

By the end of 1966, a number of national organizations had indicated support for the amendment of the abortion clauses in the Criminal Code. These groups included the principal representative bodies of the legal and medical professions as well as the largest Protestant church, the United Church of Canada. Their motives and solutions differed in detail, but their overall thrust was identical: they agreed on the need to prevent the evil effects of illegal abortions and on permitting abortions for the sake of the mother's "health". They disagreed about what the word "health" should mean, and what other "grounds" or "indications" should be permitted.

Articulate opposition to abortion law revision, meanwhile, had been almost non-existent. Aside from the unsuccessful efforts of a handful of individuals, no efforts had been made to stop or even analyze the sudden trend in favour of extending the grounds for abortions. Inarticulate opposition, however, was widespread but rested mainly on traditional religious and moral authority. While by the end of 1966 the largest church in the country, the Roman Catholic Church, together with its affiliated organizations and press, had indicated opposition to revision of the law, as yet, this church had done little to explain its stand either to its own members or to the country at large. Moreover, its position as well as that of traditional religious authority in Canada in general had been weakened by two factors. First, the largest Protestant church, the United Church of Canada, together with the Anglican Church in Great Britain, denied that there were insuperable theological objections to abortion. Secondly, the Canadian Catholic Church itself had accepted revision of the Criminal Code in two other areas of marital morality which it had hitherto opposed: birth control and divorce. On the grounds that civil law must serve the common good, it had reluctantly withdrawn its opposition to revision of the law after acknowledging that this common good appeared more harmed than served by the existing legislation. Many people now thought that the common good would also be served by "legalizing" abortions.

The abortion controversy had also given renewed emphasis to another development promoted in Canada principally by the *Globe and Mail:* separation of law and morality. The *Globe,* chief advocate of abortion law revision among the general public, had observed in 1963 that abortion "raised the whole difficult problem" of the relationship between law and morality. By the close of 1966 the paper had repeatedly asserted that abortion was a question of private morality and that law, therefore, should not be concerned with it. As an explanation as to why the law had made abortion its concern in the past, the paper had offered religious beliefs, which it now declared to be both outmoded and representative only of a minority.

From the beginning of 1967 on, the struggle between pro- and anti-revisionists was to increase in intensity. In the spring of 1967 the *Globe and Mail* felt it necessary to challenge the renewed refusal of the Catholic hierarchy to accept abortion. At the same time the paper was to attack the Pearson government for refusing to commit itself to revision of the law, hoping to force the government's hand by revealing that some abortions were being done in hospitals for reasons other than saving the life of the mother.

Footnotes

[1] Joan Finnigan, "Should Canada Change its Abortion Law?", *Chatelaine*, August, 1959, pp. 17, 103ff.

[2] There were two descriptive articles in the French language edition of *Maclean's* before this date: "Le Drame de l'avortement," March, 1963, and Constantineau, G., "Une séance chez l'avorteur numéro 1 de Montréal", November, 1966. The birth control clause was attacked in "Hypocrisy in the Criminal Code: 'preventing conception' is an offense", Editorial, *Maclean's*, March 21, 1964, p. 4.

[3] "Christian conscience cannot approve abortion, either as a means of limiting or spacing one's family, or as relief to the unmarried mother, because it involves the destruction of human life. However, if in the judgment of reputable medical authorities the continuation of pregnancy seriously endangers the physical or mental health of the mother, therapeutic abortion may be necessary."

[4] By 1971 the Council had come to accept abortion as a private matter between a woman and her doctor, morally justifiable not only in medical but also in certain social and economic circumstances, and to be freely available on request.

[5] Rev. Ray Goodall, "Is Abortion ever right?" *Chatelaine*, March 1963, pp. 40 and 48. *Chatelaine* did not mention abortion again until 1966: Earl Damude, "The Medical Discovery that could legalize Abortion", Sept. 1966, pp. 35ff. Also see editorial August 1967. *Chatelaine* opposed the 1969 legislation and has favoured its repeal and abortion on demand since.

[6] R.M. Goodall, "Our crowded world needs Scientific Birth Control", U.C. *Observer*, Feb. 15, 1961.

[7] Ray Goodall, "A Case for Induced Abortion", U.C. *Observer*, May, 1963, pp. 15-16.

[8] "Abortion is Wrong", United Church *Observer*, March 15, 1963, pp. 16-17.

[9] Rev. Gerald W. Paul, "The New Morality", *Chatelaine*, June, 1967, pp. 29, 95-96.

[10] *Op. cit.*, p. 96. As another illustration he hinted at his changed feelings about euthanasia.

[11] "Relaxation of Federal Abortion Law is asked by B.C. Doctor", *Globe and Mail*, August 31, 1961, p. 1.
[12] *Globe and Mail*, Sept. 1, 1961, p. 6.
[13] *Globe and Mail*, Oct. 2-10, p. 7.
[14] Rev. Ray Goodall repeated the same story in his *Observer* article of May, 1963 (see above). In reality, approval of abortion has been the exception and opposition to it has been constant throughout history with the earliest references going back to the Sumerian Empire and the Code of Hammurabi, 2000 and 1800 B.C. respectively. Christianity also opposed abortion from its beginning. For a detailed account, see P.V. Harrington, "Abortion — Part VIII", *Linacre Quarterly*, Feb. 1968, pp. 43-60, summarizing the doctoral dissertation, *The Crime of Abortion in Canon Law*, by R.J. Huser, 1942, Catholic University of America.
[15] The VandePut trial is discussed in Chapter One of A. de Valk, *Morality and Law in Canadian Politics, The Abortion Controversy*. The Finkbine case occurred in August, 1962. Mrs. Finkbine, a Phoenix housewife and local television performer, believed her baby might be deformed. Upon being denied an abortion in Arizona, the then 30-year old mother of four flew to Sweden for an abortion. The foetus was reported deformed. Her case was mentioned again, for instance, by Joan Hollobon in an April 1967 *Globe and Mail* article reporting on a few abortions being done in Canadian hospitals for the same reasons. *Globe and Mail*, April 11, 1967, p. 1.
[16] "Two Problems to be Faced", Editorial, *Globe and Mail*, Jan. 2, 1963.
[17] *Proceedings* of the Canadian Bar Association, Forty-Seventh Annual Meeting, 1965, p. 90. The Proceedings of 1963 and 1964 do not give the text but apparently the 1965 resolution was little different from the original 1963 proposal.
[18] *Op. cit.*, pp. 92-93.
[19] Ralph Hyman, "Canadian Bar Stalls B.C. Bid to Have Abortion Laws Relaxed", *Globe and Mail*, Sept. 3, 1963, p. 3. Quote from Catholic Guild's *Brief on Proposed Changes of the Law on Abortions*, September 1963, p. 2.
[20] *Ibid*.
[21] *Proceedings*, CBA, 1965, pp. 92 & 93.
[22] *Proceedings*, CBA, 1963, p. 177.
[23] "The Moral Issue", *Globe and Mail*, September 7, 1963.
[24] *Proceedings*, CBA, 1964, p. 194.
[25] *Proceedings*, CBA, 1965, p. 98.
[26] "Legalizing abortions urged", Saskatoon *Star-Phoenix*, Sept. 3, 1965, p. 2.
[27] *Proceedings*, CBA, 1968, pp. 92 & 93.
[28] Number 96 in "Transactions of Council", May 10 and 11, 1963, O.M.R. *(Ontario Medical Review)*, July, 1963, p. 418.
[29] *Op. cit.*, Numbers 95 and 97.
[30] *Ibid*.
[31] "Transactions of Council, May 25 and 26, 1964", *O.M.R.*, August, 1964, p. 606.
[32] *C.M.A.J.*, Vol. 97, November 11, 1967, p. 1233. See also Standing Committee on Health and Welfare, *Minutes of Proceedings and Evidence* (re abortion), No. 4, Oct. 31, 1967, p. 104. (Hereafter referred to as *Proceedings — Abortion*)
[33] *Proceedings — Abortion*, 1968, No. 18, Feb. 6, 1968, p. 599.
[34] "Transactions of Council", May 10, 11, 1965, *O.M.R.*, July 1965, pp. 505-6.
[35] *Report* of the Special Committee on Therapeutic Abortions and Sterilizations, p. 1.
[36] "Free the Doctor", *Globe and Mail*, May 18, 1965.

[37] *O.M.R.*, June, 1965, p. 461.
[38] For text, see "Transactions", Report of the Committee on Maternal Welfare, *C.M.A.J.* (Canadian Medical Association Journal), Vol. 95, Sept. 3, 1966, p. 487.
[39] *Abortion: An Ethical Discussion*, Westminster, Church House, 1965.
[40] Letitia Fairfield, "Abortion and the Law", An Anglican Committee's Views. *The Tablet* (London), Jan. 15, 1966, p. 69.
[41] *Westminister Cathedral Chronicles*, February issue, as quoted in *Western Catholic Reporter*, Edmonton, Feb. 24, 1966, p. 3.
[42] *Ibid.* See also *Prairie Messenger*, Saskatchewan's Catholic weekly, Feb. 16, 1966, p. 2.
[43] "Some abortions may be justified", *Canadian Churchman*, March 1966, pp. 12 and 19.
[44] *Proceedings—Abortion*, 1967, December 15, Appendix "BB", p. 474.
[45] "Pressure to ease Abortion laws...", *Western Catholic Reporter*, Feb. 24, 1966, p. 3.
[46] *Ibid.*
[47] "Churchmen urge wider ground for legal abortion", *Globe and Mail*, February 16, 1966, p. 3.
[48] *Proceedings—Abortion*, 1968, Feb. 6, Appendix "LL", p. 627.
[49] "United Church backs therapeutic abortions", *Globe and Mail*, Sept, 13, 1966.
[50] *Ibid.*
[51] *Western Catholic Reporter*, April 21, 1966, p. 1.
[52] Canadian Press report, "High abortion rate...", Saskatoon *Star Phoenix*, November 6, 1965.
[53] For text of 1964 resolution, see *Proceedings— Abortion*, 1967, Dec. 8, p. 396. The press stressed the Royal Commission more than the abortion aspect. The *Globe and Mail* report of June 1964 refers only to the Royal Commission. Its January 1965 report mentions only birth control.
[54] *Globe and Mail*, Sept. 1, 1966; *Prairie Messenger*, Sept. 7, 1966, pp. 1 and 16.
[55] "Association News" in *C.M.A.J.*, Vol. 94, Jan. 15, 1966, p. 149.
[56] April 2nd and April 23rd, 1966, "Administrative Reports 1965-6", *Canadian Bar Journal*, Oct. 1966, p. 381.
[57] *C.M.A.J.*, Vol. 95, p. 487.
[58] "Association News", *C.M.A.J.*, Vol. 95, May 21, 1966, p. 1137.
[59] *C.M.A.J.*, Vol. 95, Sept. 3, 1966, p. 487.
[60] *Globe and Mail*, June 18, 1966. The editorial was reprinted in the *Ontario Medical Review*, (*O.M.R.*, July, 1966, p. 545.)
[61] See *Proceedings—Abortion*, 1967, No. 4, pp. 98ff.
[62] "Adminstrative Reports, 1965-6", *C.B.J.*, Oct. 1966, p. 381. Records of the debate appear in *Proceedings* of the Canadian Bar Association, Vol. 49, 1966, pp. 74-120.
[63] This division is not to be taken as applying under all circumstances. The 1963 debate of the CBA clearly indicates that some of those who favoured removal of abortion from the Criminal Code did so precisely on philosophical grounds, insisting that Christianity cease to be the dominant morality. See above, pp. 28-29.
[64] *Proceedings*, Canadian Bar Association, Vol. 49, 1966, pp. 81 and 83. The reference was to Lord Silkin's bill.
[65] *Op. cit.*, p. 109.

[66] *Op. cit.*, p. 114. During the 1968 hearings of the House of Commons Committee on Abortion it was pointed out that in Catholic hospitals a foetus is traditionally baptized and buried in a cemetery whenever possible. *Proceedings — Abortion*, 1968, No. 19, Feb. 8, p. 642.
[67] Thomas Szasz, "The Ethics of Abortion", *Humanist*, Sept/Oct. 1966, p. 148.
[68] *Proceedings*, CBA, 1966, p. 91.
[69] *Proceedings*, CBA, 1966, p. 102. See also *Globe and Mail*, August 31, 1966, p. 1.
[70] *Proceedings*, CBA, 1966, p. 102.
[71] News report, *Toronto Telegram*, August 31, 1966. Report was reprinted in *O.M.R.*, Sept. 1966, p. 702.
[72] "Report from Ottawa", *C.M.A.J.*, Vol. 96, Jan. 21, 1967.
[73] *Globe and Mail*, Jan. 31, 1967, p. 8.
[74] Editorial, "A distant hope flickers", *Globe and Mail*, Feb. 4, 1967.
[75] Editorial, *Western Catholic Reporter*, Feb. 9, 1967.
[76] Dr. Brand (PC, Saskatoon) remarked: "I think he is using the words 'birth control' to include therapeutic abortions". Standing Committee on Health and Welfare, *Minutes of Proceedings and Evidence*, (hereafter referred to as *Proceedings, Birth Control*). No. 2. March 3, 1966, p. 35.
[77] *Op. Cit.*, p. 34.
[78] "Commons committees study divorce, birth control bills", *Prairie Messenger*, March 9, 1966, p. 16.
[79] Bernard Daly, "MP's may draft 'most forward' family planning law", *Prairie Messenger*, March 16, 1966, p. 8. See also *Proceedings, Birth Control*, 1966, p. 42.
[80] Bernard Daly, "Briefs heard on contraception", *Prairie Messenger*, March 30, 1966, p. 3. The CBA resolution went back to Sept. 7, 1963, and the CMA resolution also to 1963. *Proceedings, Birth Control*, 1966, pp. 55 and 58.
[81] The priests were Rev. Louis P. Vezina, O.M.I., superior of the Oblate Fathers' centre for ecclesiastical studies in Ottawa and Director of the Institute of Pastoral Studies, St. Paul's University; and Jean Guy Lemarier, O.M.I., moral theologian. See "Vote favoring changes in Code on birth control not immoral", *Prairie Messenger*, March 30, 1966, p. 1. Also *Proceedings, Birth Control*, March 22, 1966, p. 84.
[82] Mr. Wahn's explanation of his Bill C-40 reads as follows: "The purpose of this bill is to exclude criminal liability, in circumstances where there is no serious danger to the public interest, in respect of acts of birth control which more properly should be left to the individual conscience and to ecclesiastical and moral laws and not made the subject of criminal legislation".
[83] *Ibid.* It may be noted that the spring hearings of the Health and Welfare Committee on Birth Control were very poorly reported in the daily newspapers. The country was pre-occupied with the Gerda Munsinger affair and the capital punishment debate in the house. The meeting of March 22nd was not reported at all in five papers examined (Halifax *Herald*, Montreal *Gazette*, Ottawa *Journal*, Toronto *Globe and Mail*, Winnipeg *Free Press*). The book in question was Harris, Paul T., edit., *Brief to the Bishops: Canadian Catholic Laymen Speak Their Minds*, Toronto, Longmans, 1965.

[84] See: *Contraception, Divorce, Abortion: Three statements by the Canadian Catholic Conference*, Ottawa, 1968, pp. 64. See also *Prairie Messenger*, Oct. 19, 1966, p. 1; *Western Catholic Reporter*, Oct. 13, 1966, pp. 1, 5, 15; *Proceedings, Birth Control*, Oct. 11, 1966, pp. 466ff. "RC bishops won't fight legislation making contraceptive sales legal", *Globe and Mail*, Oct. 12, 1966, p. 12.
[85] *Contraception, Divorce, Abortion*, p. 17. See also Editorial, "Recipe for workable laws", *Globe and Mail*, October 14, 1966.
[86] *Op. cit.*, p. 18.
[87] Third Report to the House, *Proceedings, Birth Control*, 1966, pp. 590-1. Also "Commons hears report on contraceptives", *Prairie Messenger*, Dec. 14, 1966, p. 2. "Birth Control Report Tabled in Commons", *Globe and Mail*, December 6, 1966.
[88] *Proceedings of the Special Joint Committee of the Senate and House of Commons on Divorce*, Oct. 18, 1966, no. 1, p. 3. Hereafter referred to as *Proceedings—Divorce*.
[89] Cf. B. Daly, "Bills on Divorce Under Study", *Prairie Messenger*, March 23, 1966, p. 3.
[90] *Western Catholic Reporter*, May 5, 1966, p. 2. Britain was to introduce a Matrimonial Causes bill early in 1967.
[91] "United Church submits brief on divorce", *Prairie Messenger*, Dec. 7, 1966, p. 8. *Proceedings—Divorce*, 1966, p. 374. Even though the United Church believed that marriage should be a life-long union, the brief said, the Church had presented its submission on divorce because it wanted to acknowledge that Christian partners do fail in marriage. As explanation for making a presentation to a parliamentary committee, the brief gave compassion for all members of society, not just its own members, as reason. *Proceedings—Divorce*, 1966, p. 376.
[92] "Bishops express views on divorce", *Prairie Messenger*, April 12, 1967; Text: April 19, p. 8. "Catholic Bishops end opposition to reform of divorce legislation", *Globe and Mail*, April 7, 1967, p. 11.
[93] See B. Daly, "New Divorce Proposals: Reconciliation Measures Weak", *Western Catholic Reporter*, July 6, 1967, p. 1.
[94] *Ibid.*
[95] "Joint Church Statement on Divorce", Nov. 1967, reprinted in *Contraception, Divorce and Abortion, op. cit.*, pp. 50-54. Text also in *Prairie Messenger*, Nov. 22, pp. 3, 15, "Revive dead marriage, don't bury it". See also "Measures to prevent broken marriages not included, churches complain", *Globe and Mail*, Nov. 9, 1969, p. W2.
[96] "Grounds for Divorce", *Winnipeg Free Press*, December 20, 1967.

Abortion in Canada: The 1969 Law and its Aftermath

By C. Gwendolyn Landolt

C. Gwendolyn Landolt, a lawyer and mother, is President of the Right to Life Association of Toronto and Area.

1. THE 1969 LAW ON ABORTION

The present Canadian law on abortion was passed by the House of Commons on May 14, 1969, as part of a wide-ranging Omnibus Bill, which introduced more than a hundred changes into the Criminal Code. The previous law simply ruled against induced abortion, and allowed for the destruction of the unborn child only when it was necessary to preserve the life of the mother. The present law retains the general regulation against induced abortion but permits exceptions under certain circumstances. The following subsections of Section 251 of the Criminal Code give the main thrust of the new law:

(1) Every one who, with intent to procure the miscarriage of a female person, whether or not she is pregnant, uses any means for the purpose of carrying out his intention is guilty of an indictable offense and is liable to imprisonment for life.

(2) Every female person who, being pregnant, with intent to procure her own miscarriage, uses means or permits any means to be used for the purpose of carrying out her intention is guilty of an indictable offence and is liable to imprisonment for two years.

(4) Subsections (1) and (2) do not apply to

a) a qualified medical practitioner, other than a member of a therapeutic abortion committee for any hospital, who in good faith uses in an accredited or approved hospital any means for the purpose of carrying out his intention to procure the miscarriage of a female person, or

b) a female person who, being pregnant, permits a qualified medical practitioner to use in an accredited or approved hospital any means described in paragraph (a) for the pur-

pose of carrying out her intention to procure her own miscarriage,
if, before the use of those means, the therapeutic abortion committee for that accredited or approved hospital, by a majority of the members of the committee and at a meeting of the committee at which the case of such female person has been reviewed,
- c) has by certificate in writing stated that in its opinion the continuation of the pregnancy of such female person would or would be likely to endanger her life or health, and
- d) has caused a copy of such certificate to be given to the qualified medical practitioner.

(6) For the purposes of subsections (4) and (5) and this subsection
- f) "therapeutic abortion committee" for any hospital means a committee comprised of not less than three members each of whom is a qualified medical practitioner, appointed by the board of that hospital for the purpose of considering and determining questions relating to terminations of pregnancy within that hospital.

2. DEBATE IN THE HOUSE OF COMMONS

The proposed Omnibus Bill was first made public on December 21, 1967. There was a good deal of debate as to whether the Members of Parliament should be allowed to vote on the abortion amendments apart from the rest of the bill, and whether they should be permitted to vote "according to conscience" rather than be pressed to vote along party lines. In the end there was a separate vote on the abortion provisions, in the form of a vote on a motion to delete all references to abortion from the Omnibus Bill. Only two members of the majority Liberal Party voted to delete the abortion provisions from the bill.

It would appear that many legislators were unaware of the ramifications of the new law. The spokesmen for the Liberal government, which sponsored the bill, was Justice Minister John Turner. The Liberals held 155 of the 264 seats in the House of Commons, and only a handful of Liberals questioned Mr. Turner's interpretation of the proposed law. "The proposed law," Mr. Turner said, "does not authorize the taking of foetal life; it does not promote abortion. It simply removes certain categories of abortion from the present place they have on the list of indictable offenses." Earlier the same day he had said, "The fact is that the present state of the law is not clear and one of the overriding purposes of the legislation is to clarify it."[1] Several months later he said, "Also, I should like to draw to the attention of the house the fact that the substance of these amendments does no more than recognize what has actually been happening already in a number of hospitals with respect to therapeutic abortions."[2]

A different interpretation of the new law was made by members of the New Democratic Party, who generally approved of unrestricted legal abortion (with the exception of John Burton, who represented Regina East). The proposition that the new law was a step in that direction was voiced by John Gilbert (NDP, Broadview): "In the minds of some honourable members the addition of the word 'health' only brings the law up to date as interpreted by the courts. This may be so but to me it creates a different atmosphere and different attitudes. We are beginning to regard the problem of abortion as a human or social problem rather than as a criminal act."[3]

Mr. Turner rejected a proposed amendment adding a "conscience clause" to protect doctors and hospitals from pressure to do abortions, saying, "Section 237 as amended imposes no duty on the board of a hospital to set up a therpeutic abortion committee; it imposes no duty on any medical practitioner to perform an abortion; it imposes no duty even on a medical practitioner to initiate an application on behalf of a patient."[4]

When the question was asked whether abortions were to be paid for out of "medicare hospitalization", Mr. Turner replied, "Oh, no."

Everyone seemed to agree that the new legislation did not permit abortion for eugenic reasons. Thus, Mr. Turner stated flatly, "The bill has rejected the eugenic, sociological or criminal offense reasons."[5] Mrs. Grace MacInnis (NDP, Vancouver-Kingsway) deplored the fact that the new law would not allow eugenic abortions, saying that it is "the height of irresponsibility for people to bring into today's world children who are deformed."[6]

3. THE EFFECTS OF THE NEW LAW

How do the above statements compare with the actual results of the law five years later? Contrary to Mr. Turner's statement that the new law would merely provide a clear legal basis for the sort of practice previously occurring in some Canadian hospitals, the new law has in fact led to abortion on demand in some hospitals. This situation has resulted from the vagueness of the law, which allowed each therapeutic abortion committee to interpret "threat to the health" of the mother in any way it chose. In the words of Dr. W. H. Allemang, Senior Staff Obstetrician and Gynaecologist at Toronto General Hospital, it came to be assumed that any "unwanted pregnancy constituted such a threat", the result being "free abortion on demand".[7] Similarly Dr. Ayao Noguchi, Chief of Staff at Northwestern Hospital, Toronto, has said that the new law is open to so many "conjectures" that he is inclined to approve all requests for abortion submitted to his therapeutic abortion committee, allowing for the facilities available.[8] Dr. Allemang points out that, by 1972, the number of induced abortions at Toronto General equalled the number of live births, and for 1973 the number of induced abortions (2631) exceeded the number of live births (2326). Similarly, at McMaster University Hospital in 1973, the number of induced abortions (527) exceeded the number of live births (304).

The abortion rates for the entire country, as reported by Statistics Canada, are as follows:

	Number of Induced Abortions	Induced Abortions as % of Live Births
1970	11,152	3.0
1971	30,949	8.3
1972	38,853	11.2

The understanding that abortions would not be performed for purely eugenic reasons under the new law, has also turned out to be mistaken.[9] Such abortions are put through under the pretext that continuing the pregnancy would be likely to "threaten the health" of the mother. And, despite Mr. Turner's response to the question about "medicare hospitalization", legal abortions are now covered by public health insurance in every province.

Only one of Mr. Turner's points has stood up at all: no hospital or doctor has so far been forced by any level of government to participate in abortion. However, it would appear that Mr. Turner did not anticipate the sort of pressure which would be brought to bear. On October 5, 1970, Mr. Loffmark, provincial Minister of Health in British Columbia, said that he might "order all B.C. hospitals to grant legal abortions". Such an action, he said, would be based "on the grounds that hospitals supported by public funds will have to face up to their public responsibilities".[10] The Ontario Minister of Health, Mr. Lawrence, made similar remarks, withdrew them after they caused protests, and then said he was confident that all Ontario hospitals would be doing abortions in a few years.[11] At its 1972 Annual General Meeting, the Family Planning Federation of Canada unanimously passed a resolution urging "all Canadian provincial and territorial governments to require all hospitals receiving public funds to make . . . therapeutic abortion as requested by patients in consultation with their doctors available as part of their service".[12] Finally, a general report on health services in British Columbia, prepared for the province by Dr. Richard Foulkes and released on January 17, 1974, recommends that all publicly funded hospitals be required to perform abortions.[13]

It is clear from the above that the 1969 law on abortion has had results quite unlike those intended by the majority of the legislators when it was passed. The time has come for Parliament to admit that a mistake was made and to take steps to give more effective protection to the lives of unborn children in Canada.

Some will say that the unborn should have no protection and that abortion should be considered a private matter. However, abortion raises a fundamental question of justice and is not a private matter.

The law has consistently given more and more legal recognition to the rights of the unborn child, who has been given legal rights in tort, property and equity cases, as well as under the criminal law. It is only during the past decade that some have attempted to undermine these rights by demands for easy abortion.

To deny protection to the unborn is to accept a concept totally alien to our system of justice — that one person has the right to decide privately to take the life of another human being without being answerable for this action. The principle that every human life is to enjoy equal protection of the law has been like a golden thread giving unity and strength to the fabric of the English system of law. If we now break that thread, we do so at our own peril.

Footnotes

[1] *Hansard,* January 23, 1969, p. 4722.
[2] *Ibid.,* April 28, 1969, p. 8058.
[3] *Ibid.,* February 25, 1969, p. 5925.
[4] *Ibid.,* April 28, p. 8058. Section 237 became Section 251 in the revised code.
[5] *Ibid.,* May 6, 1969, p. 8397.
[6] *Ibid.,* January 27, 1969, p.4846.
[7] W.H. Allemang, "Therapeutic Abortions — Some Considerations of the Current Problem", a paper presented to the National Canadian Conference on Abortion held at St. Michael's College, Toronto, May 23-25, 1972.
[8] *Toronto Star,* April 14, 1972.
[9] See the essay by Dr. Hubert C. Soltan in this volume.
[10] *Globe and Mail,* December 18, 1970.
[11] *Globe and Mail,* February 1, 1972.
[12] *Family Planning & Population,* a Quarterly Newsletter published by the Family Planning Federation of Canada, Spring, 1973, Vol. 1, No. 1.
[13] Reported in A. de Valk, "Abortion Coercion Feared in Canada", *Western Catholic Reporter,* February 10, 1974.

Problems in "Selective" Abortion

By Hubert C. Soltan

Hubert C. Soltan is Associate Professor of Anatomy and Paediatrics, University of Western Ontario.

A growing number of well educated and "ecologically aware" young couples in Canada are turning their attention increasingly to the "quality" of their future children. Technological advances and attitudinal changes are making this possible, since the former preoccupation of this social group with "quantity" and spacing of children has been lessened by the variety, effectiveness, availability and acceptability of contraceptives. Today many young married couples expect their physician to advise them, not only on how to achieve or avoid pregnancy but also how to have the type of children they want — or at least to prevent the birth of the type of child they do not want. These desires are stimulated and sometimes aggressively pursued because of society's changed attitude and legislation which permits and encourages the abortion of "unwanted" foetuses, for whatever reason they are unwanted.

During the last five years the classical approach to investigation and counselling of couples who are at appreciable risk to conceive a child with one or other of several hundred genetically determined diseases has been significantly augmented. This widening scope of genetic counselling has been made possible by the development and medical acceptability of techniques which result in a direct study of cells or fluids produced by the foetus and obtained by the technique of trans-abdominal amniocentesis during the early part of the second trimester of pregnancy (13 to 18 weeks). The purpose of this procedure and subsequent laboratory testing is to determine, as accurately as possible, the genetic or chromosomal constitution of the foetus and so to draw conclusions about its expected clinical state after the birth. The number of genetic conditions where this is becoming a practical possibility is growing year by year. This new development is heralded by some as opening a whole new era in preventive medicine as applied to genetic disease.

If the information obtained by amniocentesis determines that the foetus is abnormal, the parents who have already pre-decided on an abortion in such an eventuality request their physician to proceed with this course of action. The foetus now becomes "unwanted" because it has been shown to be genetically abnormal and clinically affected. The importance of obtaining this information well before the end of the second trimester of pregnancy is obvious since the decision to abort or not to abort must await this information. On the other hand, if the foetus is shown not to have the chromosomal or gene defect for which it was at appreciable risk, it becomes "wanted" and pregnancy hopefully proceeds to its joyfully awaited outcome.

This approach to abortion and the "unwanted" foetus is a novel one, made possible by rapidly developing technology. It presents physicians, genetic counsellors and society at large with several difficult medical and ethical dilemmas which need more discussion than they are presently receiving. This area of abortion is usually referred to as "selective abortion" following pre-natal or ante-natal or intra-uterine diagnosis.

The various reasons proposed for selective abortion are illustrated in Table 1. The complete type of selective abortion, alluded to earlier in this essay, is depicted first in Table 1. It covers the situation where intra-uterine diagnosis can tell precisely whether or not the child will be affected with the disease in question. The fourth category of Table 1 is the classical (non-selective) situation which has concerned genetic counsellors for many years. This is where intra-uterine diagnosis is not yet possible and where the probability for the foetus to be affected follows patterns of single gene inheritance according to Mendelian Laws (e.g., 25%, 50%). Although both these categories present ethical problems for couples and physicians who, for moral reasons, do not accept abortion on any genetic grounds, it is the middle two categories which present ethical and legal difficulties to the greatest numbers of couples and physicians. This is so because, in each instance, there is a high probability of aborting a normal, healthy foetus. In the "Community Genetics" type the probability of the foetus being normal is close to 100% yet abortion could be performed when parents, physician and hospital abortion committee are agreed that the rights and interests of the genetic pool of a future generation take precedence over the right to life of a foetus (and subsequent child and adult) who has the potentiality of producing offspring with hereditary disease with an appreciably increased probability when compared to that of the general population. This type of concern may seem to be a marginal indication for abortion on genetic grounds, but a number of such cases have occurred on this continent. In jurisdictions where abortion is available on demand, if not in law at least in practice, the demands of a "socially aware" young couple committed to preventing the pollution of the gene pool of future generations may place the attending obstetrician in a difficult medical and ethical dilemma.

The number of abortions selectively performed for genetic reasons, particularly in the first three categories of Table 1, is very small in Canada today; probably less than 100 out of the almost 31,000 legal abortions performed in Canada in 1971. However about fifteen hospital or university laboratories across Canada are carrying out intra-uterine genetic diagnoses from samples of amniotic fluid and foetal cells obtained by amniocentesis for this purpose (as compared to 121 such laboratories listed in September, 1971 for the entire world). The wider application of this technique, coupled to the rapidly growing ability to identify (in utero) an ever widening selection of genetic diseases and their carrier states, indicates that this work will increase in volume and diversity.

Intra-uterine diagnosis and selective abortion can be considered as "genetic engineering" only in the restricted sense of preventing the birth of some individuals who might make a disproportionate contribution of deleterious genes to the genetic pool of the future population. The prospect of the human genetic engineer, who is able to design or alter the genetic code of a particular gamete or early embryo in line with exact specifications, is still some years away. However, some of the technology which the genetic engineer will have to master to achieve this end is currently being developed. It arises as a by-product of the developing science of foetology and intra-uterine diagnosis but also flows from the experimentation with human fertilization and early human development in the laboratory.

Many of the genetic diseases which can currently be terminated prenatally by intra-uterine diagnosis and subsequent destruction of the affected foetus are associated with moderate to profound mental retardation, others involve chronically handicapping or progressive physical diseases. The legal killing of foetuses with these conditions has accentuated the problem which society faces with respect to children and adults with similar conditions. "Infanticide" and its more emotionally neutral synonyms are no longer unmentionable words in the vocabulary of the "new" Eugenics.

TABLE 1. CLASSIFICATION OF "GENETICALLY BASED" REASONS FOR ABORTION

Type of "Selective" Abortion	Description	Examples
Selective on Basis of Specific Genetic Condition	Foetus with specific chromosomal or genic abnormality which always results in pathological phenotypic abnormality.	1. Down's Syndrome (Mongolism). 2. Tay Sachs Disease.
Selective on Basis of "Community Genetics"	Foetus is a chromosomal or genic heterozygote without pathological phenotype.	1. Balanced $^{13}/_{14}$ chromosomal translocation. 2. Heterozygote for Tay Sachs Disease.
Partially Selective	Foetus where intra-uterine diagnosis, in the present state of knowledge, is limited to a determination of sex rather than genotype or abnormal karyotype.	Male foetus conceived by woman heterozygous for an X-linked disease, such as Duchenne Muscular Dystrophy or Hemophilia A (Factor VIII deficiency).
Non-selective	An unplanned pregnancy where both parents are heterozygous for an autosomal gene which, in homozygous recessive form, results in serious genetic disease. Where one parent is affected or at high risk to become affected with an autosomal dominant disease.	1. Both parents heterozygous for gene for Cystic Fibrosis. 2. One parent affected with, or at high risk to develop, Huntington's Chorea.

GLOSSARY OF GENETIC TERMS

ALLELE—Alternative form of the gene found at the same locus on homologous chromosomes.

AMNIOCENTESIS—Technique of obtaining a sample of amniotic fluid and any foetal cells which it might contain. The most widely-used technique in the intra-uterine diagnosis of genetic disease.

AUTOSOME—Any one of the 22 pairs of chromosomes in Man not involved in sex determination.

CHROMOSOME—The visible carriers of genetic information in the nucleus of the cell. The chromosomes are most readily studied microscopically in the dividing cell. In human cells there are 46 chromosomes normally; a set of 23 derived from the mother and 23 from the father.

DOMINANT—Attribute of trait (phenotype) which is expressed when the responsible gene is present in heterozygous state or "single dose". The phenotype in the homozygote may or may not differ from that in the heterozygote.

EMBRYO—Early developmental stages prior to the time that the embryo becomes known as a foetus.

FOETOLOGY—The study of the foetus.

GAMETE—The mature sex cell, sperm in the male and ovum in the female.

GENE—Basic inheritance unit of the genetic code.

GENETIC CODE—The base triplets of deoxyribonucleic acid (DNA) and ribonucleic acid (RNA) which carry the genetic information.

HETEROZYGOTE (carrier state)—Individual with two different alleles at a given locus. Also used to identify an individual with visible differences in two homologous chromosomes (e.g., translocation heterozygote).

HOMOLOGUES (homologous chromosomes)—Partner chromosomes having corresponding loci which pair at meiosis. One homologue is derived from the mother (ovum), the other from the father (sperm).

HOMOZYGOTE—A genotype consisting of identical genes (alleles) at a given locus (e.g., AA or aa).

LOCUS—The precise location of a gene on a chromosome.

MEIOSIS—The special type of cell division occuring in the gonads by which gametes, containing half the number of chromosomes of "body" cells, are produced.

MENDELIAN LAWS—Fundamental laws describing the simple patterns of inheritance first enunciated by Mendel in 1865.

PHENOTYPE—The observable (often clinical) characteristics of an organism (patient) due to the action and expression of a particular gene, genes or chromosomal aberration in a particular environment.

RECESSIVE—Attribute of trait (phenotype) which is expressed only when the responsible gene is present in homozygous state or "double dose". However, subtle differences may be detectable in the heterozygote.

TRANSLOCATION—The displacement of part or all of one chromosome to another, usually non-homologous, chromosome.

Section Two: The Humanity of the Unborn

Intra-uterine Life and Development

by E. Dawne Jubb, M.D.

Dawne Jubb is Associate Professor of Obstetrics and Gynaecology, University of Toronto.

Thanks to our rapidly advancing technology much of the mystery and conjecture about human reproduction and human intra-uterine growth and development has been replaced by direct observations and scientific facts. The molecular chemistry analysis of chromosomes, genes, RNA (ribonucleic acid) and DNA (deoxyribonucleic acid) has led to the establishment of reliable criteria by which human life can be identified with certainty, and the distinction made between an individual live human cell able to reproduce only itself, and a live human fertilized ovum which by a natural and continuous process will mature through the various stages of human existence to maturity and old age. Once conception has occurred, new human life is present which from this beginning to the end of its existence will be distinguishable from every other human being by virtue of chromosomal differences.

1. THE NEW HUMAN LIFE AND THE MATERNAL ORGANISM

The usual place for conception and growth of new human life is in the reproductive organs of the adult human female, but as has been shown by the development of "test tube" babies, and the artificial placenta, the mother's biological contribution from conception on is one of only nourishment and protection, and is artificially replaceable. Support systems outside of the human uterus have been developed, albeit imperfectly, in research laboratories for the first few weeks of human life and, again, more perfectly in the premature intensive care units in major medical centres for weeks from 20 to 40 of human life. That a human embryo or foetus will not live if its intra-uterine protection and nourishment are cut off does not destroy its separability but rather describes the conditions under which life will not continue.[1]

At no time is the new human life part of the maternal organism, although usually it is nourished and protected within a maternal organ (uterus) which is specifically for this purpose. Even before implantation in the wall of the uterus, the developing new life is responsible for the maintenance of the pregnant state in the maternal metabolism, and its tissues, which are antigenitically different from those of the mother, set up protective mechanisms to prevent maternal immunological responses from causing it distress.[2] The female who is pregnant is thus already a parent providing for her offspring. The very changes in her physiology which, when noted, can establish that the pregnancy is there are actually a measure of the support and protection she is already beginning (willing or unwilling, aware or unaware) to give to the new life. She no longer has the choice of being or not being a parent—she already is a mother, and if at any time in its existence, intra-uterine or extra-uterine, the new life dies or is killed, the fact of her motherhood does not cease; she becomes the mother of a dead offspring rather than of a living one. (In passing it can be noted that the contributing male is also a parent once a pregnancy has occurred, but since his contribution to the support and protection of the new life is indirect through a loving relationship with the mother and then the child, its omission is not lethal but certainly results in irreparable emotional damage to the child eventually.)

2. VARIATIONS IN THE PACE OF GROWTH AND DEVELOPMENT

From conception on, human life is a complex, dynamic, rapidly growing organism with a specific pattern of maturity and function. The pace of growth and development in the first 40 weeks (intra-uterine) is faster than that after birth, but the process is the same—as long as the specifically suitable nourishment and support systems are supplied the maturation continues in an orderly pattern and the functioning genes are programmed in at the appropriate time: e.g. heart begins beating at 24 days, reflexes begin at 42 days, air breathing begins at birth, secondary sex characteristics develop at puberty, etc. The pattern of intra-uterine development for human beings has been well studied and documented by workers in the medical specialties of Embryology, Foetology and Neonatology. Just as

Intra-uterine Life and Development • 57

in post-natal life where there are established norms of development by which a child's growth and maturation is considered precocious, normal or deficient (e.g. age of sitting unaided, age of walking, age of teeth appearing, age of secondary sex characteristics appearing), the same is true for the ante-natal states of development and a diagnosis of growth retardation can be established while the child is still in the uterus.

3. SOME MILESTONES OF INTRA-UTERINE LIFE

Some of the "milestones" of intra-uterine life which have been well documented are as follows:

17 days—Blood cell formation has started.[3,4]
20 days—Heart and primitive intestine formed.[3,5]
24 days—Heart starts to beat.[3,4,5]
33 days—Cerebral cortex is formed.[6]
5 weeks—One-third of one inch long.
—Limb buds sprout.[3,7]
6 weeks—Sex organs sprout.[3,7]
—Full skeletal system.[3,7]
7 weeks—Reflexes begin.[3,7]
8 weeks—Two inches long, well proportioned, small scale infant with familiar external features.
—All internal organs present.[7,3,5,4]
—Stomach produces digestive juices.[6,8]
—Specific electroencephalogram—conscious experience possible,[6,8]
—Kidneys begin to function by extracting uric acid from foetus blood.[6,8]
—Bone begins to replace cartilage in skeletal system.
9 weeks—Sex hormones elaborated.[16]
—Makes a fist if palm is stroked.[9,10]
10 weeks—Turns the head away, squints and frowns if forehead is touched.[9,10]
12 weeks—Thyroid gland functioning.[17]
—Capable of sucking.
14 weeks—Opens the mouth and swallows regularly.[13]
16 weeks—Eight to eleven inches in height.
—Starts to urinate.[7,6,11]
—Vocal cords are complete.[9,6,3]
—Fingernails appear.[7]
—Primitive eggs and sperms are formed.[7,6,3]
20 weeks—Twelve inches tall and 450 grams in weight.[7]

— Hair grows, eyebrows, eyelashes and scalp,[3]
— Calcification of bones,[6,7]
— Sleeps and wakes.[12,13]
— Reacts to outside noise and vibrations.[6]
24 weeks — Fourteen inches tall.
— Psychological individual differences noted.[8]
— Intra-uterine transfusion accomplished.[13]
— 10% survival rate extra-uterine with present support systems. [14,15]
28 weeks — Red, wrinkled skin, eyelids reopen. [7,6]
32 weeks — Sixteen inches tall, average 1670 grams weight.
— Testes descend into scrotum and subcutaneous fat starts depositing.
36 weeks — Skin fades and wrinkles smooth out.
— Fingernails project to fingertips.
40 weeks — Twenty inches tall, average 3150 grams.

4. TERMINATING A DEVELOPING HUMAN LIFE

Any honest review of the current medical status of human intra-uterine life demonstrates conclusively that a separate human life is present from conception and that this human life matures and grows according to an orderly and predictable pattern which begins intra-uterine and continues through the immediate post-natal period, infancy, childhood, adolescence, maturity and old age. Obviously, this life process can be terminated at any time in its continuum by direct attack upon it or by withholding or interfering with its support systems. Direct attack on human life after birth is usually referred to as "battering" of a baby and "assault" of an adult. The intra-uterine assault and battering by curette or suction apparatus, usually referred to as "therapeutic" abortion, is no less an attack on human life although it is usually performed out of the direct vision of the attacker. Interference with the support systems of the growing and maturing human life is also called by different names at different times but is always detrimental to the developing human and can be lethal. Obvious post-natal examples are "child neglect" involving food and warmth, and in adults suffocation and exposure to the elements, for example, fire or cold. Pre-natal examples include the hypertonic saline injection method of abortion which causes an intra-uterine chemical burn, usually fatal, and hysterotomy which results in exposure of the developing human to room air and temperatures, supports which are unsuitable for it.

Whenever the subject of abortion is being considered, one must remember that no matter how performed or by whom, the purpose of the procedure is to terminate the natural development of a new human life. Even at the present stage of our rapidly developing modern sciences — genetics, embryology, foetology and perinatology and all of biology — the humanity of the unborn new life from conception can be conclusively established. Any organism with the chromosomes and genes proper to a human being can be nothing less than human. Human life exists only in human beings and all human beings are persons. There is no basis, in fact, for conclusions to the contrary. To use the excuse so often quoted by lawyers and other professionals that the doctors do not agree when human life begins, is to allow oneself to opt out because one can find others who do not, or will not, give due consideration to scientific evidence when it is presented to them.

Equal protection of the right to life (regardless of the stage of development or degeneration) from arbitrary attack — as well as full recognition of the supremacy of *that* right over the lesser rights to liberty and the freedom to pursue one's own happiness—is well founded in Western tradition and Anglo-Saxon law. Accordingly, no mother was *required* by Canadian law to sacrifice her life for her child, born or unborn. It is also true that the teaching of the Roman Catholic Church has never *required* a mother to sacrifice her life for her born or unborn child, though the Church has always taught "a man can have no greater love than to lay down his life for his friend",[18] which is true of Christian charity and is above the law. Most discussion about abortion has centred about the rights of the mother, the rights of the family or the rights of society. Little, however, has been said in regards to the rights of the being most directly affected, the unborn child. Fundamental to all the rights bestowed upon the unborn is the right to life—and without this one all of the others are meaningless. The work of law is surely to protect this basic right to life for all humans.

Footnotes

[1] 282 App. Div. 542, 125 N. Y. S. 2d 696.

[2] Currie, G. A.: *The Foetus as an Allograft: The Role of Maternal "Unresponsiveness" to Paternally Derived Foetal Antigens, op. cit. supra* note 1.

[3] Patten, Bradley M., *Human Embryology*, 3d Ed., McGraw-Hill Book Company, New York, 1968, Chapter VII.

[4] Ingelman-Sundberg, Axel, & Wirsen, Cloes, *A Child is Born: The Drama of Life Before Birth*, Dell Publishing Company, New York, 1965.

[5] Rugh, Robert & Shettles, Landrum B., with Richard N. Einhorn, *From Conception to Birth: The Drama of Life's Beginnings*, Harper & Row, New York, 1971.

[6] Flannagan, G.L., *The First Nine Months of Life*, Simon & Schuster, 1962.

[7] Arey, Leslie B., *Developmental Anatomy*, 6th Ed., Philadelphia, W. & B. Saunders Company, 1954, Chapters II and VI.

[8] Gesell, Arnold, *The Embryology of Behaviour*, Harper & Bros. Publishers, 1945, Chapters IV, V, VI and X.

[9] Hooker, Davenport, *The Prenatal Origin of Behaviour*, University of Kansas Press, 1952.

[10] Hooker, Davenport, *The Origin of Overt Behaviour*, Ann Arbor, University of Michigan Press, 1944.

[11] Wood, Carl: "Weightless: Its Implications for the Human Foetus", *The Journal of Obstetrics and Gynaecology of the British Commonwealth*, 1970, Volume 77, pages 333-336.

[12] Petre-Quadens, O., *et al*, "Sleep in Pregnancy: Evidence of Fetal Sleep Characteristics", *Journal of Neurological Science*, Volume 4, pages 600-605, May and June 1967.

[13] Liley, H.M.I., *Modern Motherhood*, Random House, Rev. Ed. 1969.

[14] Monroe, *Canadian Medical Association Journal*, 1939.

[15] Hellegers, André, M.D., *National Symposium on Abortion*, May 15, 1970, Prudential Plaza, Chicago, Illinois.

[16] Abramovich, D.R.: "The Importance of Fetal Physiology and Endocinology in Obstetrics", *The Medical Journal of Australia*, Volume 2, pages 408-411, August 23, 1969.

[17] Shepard, Thomas: "Onset of Function in the Fetal Thyroid: Biochemical and Autoradiographic Studies from Organ Culture", *The Journal of Clinical Endocrinology*, Volume 27, pages 945-958, July 1967.

[18] *The Jerusalem Bible*, Gospel of John, Chapter 15, Verse 13.

The Merchants of Calumny

by **Donald De Marco**

Donald De Marco is Assistant Professor of Philosophy, St. Jerome's College, University of Waterloo.

In all of English literature, perhaps the most dramatic and devastating argument against prejudice is that given by Shylock in *The Merchant of Venice*:

> ... I am a Jew. Hath not a Jew eyes? hath not a Jew hands, organs, dimensions, senses, affections, passions? fed with the same food, hurt with the same weapons, subject to the same diseases, healed by the same means, warmed and cooled by the same winter and summer, as a Christian is? If you prick us, do we not bleed? if you tickle us, do we not laugh? if you poison us, do we not die? and if you wrong us, shall we not revenge? if we are like you in the rest, we will resemble you in that.[1]

There can be no retort to Shylock's statement. One must either recognize the facts presented and agree that Shylock is both human and deserving of equal treatment with Christians, or ignore the facts and walk away. The reason for this is that the Jew's self-defence is mounted on too fundamental a level to be undercut. He wisely avoids sophisticated reasons, academic distinctions and intellectual subtleties that could render his argument suspect, weak or unclear. His self-defence is really a self-description and in describing the elementary facts he makes his case irrefutable and undebatable.

Taking the fundamental and forthright approach of Shylock, can a convincing argument be raised in defence of the humanity of the human foetus and his right to equal protection with adults? Substituting 'human foetus' for 'Jew' and 'adult' for 'Christian', the same argument used by Shylock is set forth in defence of the human unborn against his detractors—the merchants of calumny.

1) " I am a human foetus:

In his article on "The Humanity of the Unborn Child", pediatrician Eugene Diamond writes:

> To consider the foetus not to be a separate person but merely a part of the mother has not been tenable since the sixteenth century when Arantius showed that the maternal and fetal circulations were separate—neither continuous nor contiguous.[2]

Contrary to the unscientific thinking of Justice Holmes, who once declared that the unborn child is "a part of its mother",[3] medical evidence[4] shows conclusively that the foetus is a distinct human being in its own right "with its separate principle of growth and development, with its separate nervous system and blood circulation, with its own skeleton and musculature, its brain and heart and vital organs".[5]

Genetics clearly establishes the human foetus as a member of the human race by recognizing the genesis of his 23 pairs of chromosomes per somatic cell as being derived equally from a human mother and a human father. Foetology establishes the self-hood of the human foetus by tracing the growth and development of the foetus from a single cell which neither belongs exclusively to the mother or father. Dr. H.M.I. Liley writes:

> He (the unborn baby) has his own space capsule, the amniotic sac. He has his own lifeline, the umbilical cord and he has his own root system, the placenta. These all belong to the baby himself, not to his mother. They are all developed from his original cell. [6]

The self-hood of the human foetus is further corroborated by electrocardiographic (ECG) readings of his heart beat at seven and a half weeks[7] and electroencephalographic recordings of his brain waves at 43 to 45 days (EEG).[8]

2) ... Hath not a human foetus eyes?

His eyes begin to form at nineteen days. By eight and a half weeks the eyelids become sensitive to touch. If the eyelid is stroked, the child will squint.[9] Rugh and Shettles describe the foetus after eight weeks as having "A human face with eyelids half closed as they are in someone who is about to fall asleep."[10] During the fifth month hair begins to grow on his eyebrows and a fringe of eyelashes appears.

In the sixth month his eyelids will open and close. His eyes will look up, down and sideways. The iris diaphragm will contract or dilate to admit the proper light intensity. Dr. Albert Liley of New Zealand, the world's most renowned foetologist, contends that the child may perceive light through the abdominal wall of his mother.[11]

3) ... hath not a human foetus hands, organs, dimensions, senses, affections, passions?

The hands with fingers and thumbs are recognizable by the seventh week of foetal life.[12] The lines in the hands (and feet), which will remain a distinctive feature throughout the life of the individual, are engraved at eight weeks.[13] At eight and a half weeks the palms of the hands become sensitive to touch. If the palm of the foetus is touched, the fingers will close to a small fist.[14] The child's grip at sixteen weeks is quite strong. At this time he is able to maintain his grasp on an object, such as a slender rod, while that object is being moved up and down or slightly away from him.[15]

All the organ systems are present in the human foetus by eight weeks.[16] In the ninth and tenth weeks, if the child's forehead is touched, he may turn his head away from the stimulus and pucker up his brow and frown. By the twelfth week, his organs, dimensions, senses affections and passions are present and operative.

> By the end of the first trimester (twelfth week), the fetus is a sentient moving being. We need not pause to speculate as to the nature of his psychic attributes but we may assume that the organization of psycho-somatic self is now well underway.[17]

4) ... fed with the same food,

In Shakespearian England, as scholars have pointed out, the segregated Jew did not dine in the company of the Christian. Moreover, in accordance with his Jewish tradition, his diet was markedly different from that of the Christian. The human foetus and his mother, on the other hand, are quite literally fed with the same food.

The taste buds, salivary and digestive glands develop in the foetus during the third month. At this time the baby is able to swallow and utilize amniotic fluid.[18] Although the blood of the mother and her child do not mix during foetal development, the child receives oxygen and food from his mother, through placental attachment, "much like he receives food from her after he is born".[19]

When a child *in utero* fails to receive adequate nourishment, it is possible to correct this problem by injecting supplementary nutrients directly into the amniotic fluid which he normally swallows (250 to 700 cc a day). In the words of one doctor, "We well may be able to offer the child that is starving because of a placental defect a nipple to use before birth."[20]

5) ... hurt with the same weapons,

In a recent interview, a California doctor who performed abortions was asked the following question: "Doctor, what does the aborted baby feel while it's dying?" The doctor answered, "Oh, I think that depends on your philosophy." Furthermore, he stated that the question was not an important one.[21]

To Dr. Albert W. Liley, the question of foetal pain can be answered on the basis of objective evidence and is a crucially important one. In 1963 Dr. Liley developed the first surgical technique for administering blood transfusions to the foetus within the womb.[22] According to Dr. Liley, the foetus feels pain as early as three months. In offering instructions for carrying out the surgical techniques of foetal blood transfusions, he advises his colleagues to take into serious consideration this fact of foetal pain. During the actual surgical procedure the child must be sedated and given pain-relieving medication. Dr. H.M.I. Liley, wife and research assistant to Dr. Albert Liley, and distinguished foetologist and pediatrician in her own right, remarks in her well known book *Modern Motherhood*:

> When doctors first began invading the sanctuary of the womb, they did not know that the unborn baby would react to pain in the same fashion as a child would. But they soon learned that he would. By no means a "vegetable" as he has so often been pictured, the unborn knows perfectly well when he has been hurt, and he will protest it just as violently as would a baby lying in a crib.[23]

In reference to aborting a twelve-week-old foetus by the method of dilatation and curettage (D&C, where the neck of the womb is opened to allow the removal of the foetus in pieces, by the scraping of a sharp instrument called a curette), Dr. Eugene Diamond states:

> When this procedure is done, there is little doubt that the foetus in fact, feels what is done to it.[24]

In the words of physician Gino Papola, "The curette will become mightier than the sword."[25]

The weaponry used against the unborn—curette, suction and salt, together with the methods of starvation and suffocation which follow a hysterotomy abortion, are fatal for the unborn for physiological reasons alone. Being assaulted by these weapons and methods, the adult would succumb for the same medical reasons the aborted foetus does.

6) ... subject to the same diseases,

Dr. H.M.I. Liley writes:

> No problem in foetal health or disease can any longer be considered in isolation. At the very least two people are involved, the mother and her child.[26]

The most convenient way in which the physician may diagnose the condition of the foetus is from an analysis of the amniotic fluid which surrounds the unborn child. In observing the colour, turbidity and volume of the amniotic fluid, or the enzymes and other chemicals contained therein, he is able to diagnose a long list of foetal diseases.[27] In addition, the electrocardiogram of the unborn and the analysis of his heart sounds through phonocardiography is helpful to the diagnostician.

In Ashley Montagu's book, *Life before Birth,* the author lists some of the diseases which may afflict the unborn child. The list includes pneumonia, scarlet fever, typhoid, streptococcal infections, rheumatic fever, listeriosis, syphilis, malaria, virus diseases, tuberculosis, viral hepatitis, and others. All these diseases can be transmitted from the pregnant mother to her unborn child.[28]

7) ... healed by the same means,

Dr. Liley's technique of intrauterine blood transfusion has been mentioned. Perhaps the most famous case involving a blood transfusion given to the unborn foetus occurred in 1964. Because of certain religious beliefs, a pregnant woman refused to allow her unborn to undergo a blood transfusion. The child, because of an Rh problem in his blood, vitally needed this particular operation. The case went to court. The judge ruled that the unborn's right to survival was a value which outweighed the mother's right to practise her religious beliefs in this manner.[29]

Analysis of the amniotic fluid surrounding the unborn has led to diagnoses of the adrenogenital syndrome, hemolytic anemia, adrenal insufficiency, congenital hyperanemia and glycogen storage disease. Some of these, and hopefully in the future, all of these maladies can be treated before birth.[30]

Apart from medical means, there are ways in which nature heals the injured foetus. If the child sustains a fractured limb where his mother suffered a fall, the limb will heal naturally. Even a gunshot wound (incurred at three months) would heal naturally and by the time of his birth, only a scar would remain.[31]

8) ... warmed and cooled by the same winter and summer, as an adult is?

Through temperatures both high and low as well as changes in temperature, the unborn is directly affected.[32]

When the body is colder than normal, metabolism is retarded and oxygen is circulated in the blood stream at a slower rate. This means that when the body is cooled, the brain needs less oxygen than normal. When a patient faces a lengthy operation in which he is to receive heavy amounts of anaesthesia, it is sometimes medically expedient to cool the body so as to combat the harmful effects to the brain represented by large doses of anaesthesia.

Drs. F. Wilson and C.B. Sedzmir have reported a case where a woman thirty-two weeks pregnant had been cooled in preparation for surgery. As her body temperature was being reduced, the heartbeat of her unborn child dropped from 160 to 85 beats per minute. Furthermore, when trimethaphan was injected into the woman, for the purpose of providing a relatively bloodless field for surgery, the foetus protested by kicking rather furiously. The doctors conjectured that the kicking was brought on by a state of induced anoxia (lack of oxygen) in the child caused by the drug injection. In another case, a patient's temperature was cooled to 86°F. prior to her operation. At the same time her twenty-four week unborn child's heart beat fell from 180 beats per minute to 120.[33] In both cases, after the mother's temperature returned to normal, the child's metabolic and circulatory rates returned to normal.

9) ... If you prick us, do we not bleed?

Blood cells begin to appear at about seventeen days. The heart commences development at eighteen days and although this figure is given as the normal time for such development, Marcel and Exchaquet attest to observing contractions of the heart as early as two weeks.[34]

At thirty days the heart is beating regularly sixty-five times a minute[35] and pumping blood cells through a closed circulatory system.[36] At five and a half weeks the heart is functionally complete and is essentially similar to that of an adult in general configuration.[37] By the seventh week of life, the liver manufactures red blood cells and the kidney is engaged in eliminating uric acid from the blood.[38] Straus, *et al.* have shown that the electrocardiogram of a seven and a half week foetus demonstrates the existence of a functionally complete cardiac system.[39]

The blood which the unborn sheds when aborted is his own, its type (antigens and antibodies) being determined genetically from the zygote cell at conception and not from either the mother's or father's blood type exclusively.

10) ... if you tickle us, do we not laugh?

Doctor Hellegers writes:

> If we tickle the baby's nose, he will flex his head backwards away from the stimulus.[40]

About the end of the twelfth week the vocal cords of the unborn are completed. The child, however, is unable to cry (or laugh) primarily because his voice cannot be activated in the absence of air.[41]

Dr. Liley relates an incident where an air bubble had been injected into an eight month unborn baby's amniotic sac for the purpose of locating the placenta on X-ray. The air bubble happened to cover the child's face. When this occurred, the child inhaled, allowing his vocal cords to become operative, and produced a cry which was clearly audible to all those present, including the physician and the technical assistants. The mother later reported to the doctor that the air bubble kept moving over the baby's face whenever she lay down to sleep, allowing the child to cry so loudly that both she and her husband were kept awake.[42]

11) ... if you poison us, do we not die?

Dr. Willke describes induced abortion by the method of saline poisoning in the following way:

> A large needle is inserted through the abdominal wall of the mother and into the baby's bag of water. A concentrated salt

solution is injected into his amniotic fluid. This immediately poisons the baby, causing him to convulse and die. About a day later the mother goes into labour and delivers a dead baby.[43]

There is enough scientific evidence reported to justify the claim that the unborn child is as susceptible to poisoning as the rest of the population.[44] Lead, mercury, arsenic, copper, phosporous, bromide iodide, potassium chlorate and strontium are just a few of the many inorganic poisons which can reach the child through his mother's body.[45]

Dr. P. Bernhard in 1949, Dr. J.M. O'Lane in 1963 and Dr. J. R. Zabriskie in the same year found, as a result of their extensive studies, a strong index of correlation between smoking pregnant women and abnormally high rates of spontaneous abortion and prematurity[46] (prematurity is the number one cause of death in early infancy).[47]

12) ... and if you wrong us, shall we not revenge? if we are like you in the rest, we will resemble you in that."

It is written in the Talmud that "Whoso sheds the blood of man within man, his blood shall be shed".[48]

Professor Ian Donald, Professor at Glasgow University, in reporting on 20,000 legal abortions in England in 1969 (which resulted in the deaths of fifteen mothers) states:

> We can look forward to this (legal abortion) being the dominant cause of death to young women.[49]

The Royal College of Obstetricians and Gynaecologists, in an inquiry into the effects of the first year of England's *Abortion Act (1967),* states:

> Eight maternal deaths occurred in relation to 27,331 terminations of pregnancy during the year 1968-9. This gives a mortality rate of 0.3 per thousand, which is higher than the maternal mortality rate (including abortions, criminal or otherwise) for all pregnancies in England and Wales at the comparable time. A statement issued by the Secretary of State to Parliament on 4 February 1970 reveals a similar state of affairs in respect of about 54,000 induced abortions notified from all sources during 1969; among these there were 15 maternal deaths.[50]

In a documented report presented before the Minnesota State Legislature, legal abortion mortality rates were compared with the maternal mortality rates per births. The maternal mortality rate for the state of Minnesota was established by Rosenfield et al. [51] at 14 per 100,000 live births. The deaths of women per 100,000 legal abortions in countries having a history of legal abortions showed Finland to have a rate of 66 per 100,000, Denmark 41.4, Sweden, 39.2 and Great Britain 39.2.[52]

On the basis of the mortality rates for mothers undergoing abortions in various countries where abortion was practised under legal auspices, the following conclusion was reported by the American College of Obstetrics and Gynecology:

> The inherent risks of a therapeutic abortion are serious and may be life-threatening; this fact should be fully appreciated by both the medical profession and the public. In nations where abortion may be obtained on demand, a considerable morbidity and mortality have been reported.[53]

Apart from mortality figures, non-fatal medical complications arising from induced abortions have been documented and reported, indicating the grave risks to health and fertility a woman assumes in undergoing an abortion.

Dr. Stallworthy *et al.* reported the results obtained in 1182 legal abortions in one teaching hospital in England. The report showed that nearly 17% of the patients lost more than 500 ml. of blood and 9.5% required transfusion. In addition, cervical lacerations occurred in 4.2%, and the uterus was perforated in 1.2%. Emergency laparotomy was required six times and hysterectomy was twice necessary to save life. In 27% of the patients pyrexia (high fever) of 38°C or more persisted for longer than twenty-four hours. Fourteen patients suffered peritonitis.[54]

"It is disquieting", wrote the doctors, "that postabortal infection, which is one of the common causes of death after criminal abortion, should have occurred in 27% of this series".[55]

The Stallworthy report was especially disturbing since it showed almost identical results with those reported by Sood.[56]

Dr. Droegemuller, reporting on Colorado's first year experience with legal abortion, reported that eight out of every hundred women required blood transfusions after being aborted.[57]

The incidence of major hemorrhaging following legel abortion was reported in Russia as 14.2%[58](D&C); Great Britain 21%[59] (all methods of inducing abortion), Sweden 3 to 7.8% (saline).

In Japan, the 1969 survey of the office of the Prime Minister reported the following complications resulting from induced abortion; 9% sterility after three years; 14% habitual spontaneous abortion; 4% extra-uterine pregnancies; 17% menstrual irregularities; 20% abdominal pains; 19% dizziness; 27% headache; 3% frigidity; 13% exhaustion; 3% neurosis.[61]

The Nagoya survey by the Women's Associations reported 59% were severely troubled with adverse after-effects or were in poorer health following abortions. In the Mainichi survey in 1969, 18% complained of being physically unwell after one abortion; 27% after two; 40% after three; and 51% after 4.[62]

The Swedish experience with legal abortion is well documented. Perhaps the most thorough follow-up study on women who have undergone abortions has been done by Dr. Martin Ekblad. Dr. Ekblad studied 479 women at the time of their abortion and again two to three and a half years later. He found that 10% continued to feel the operation unpleasant; 14% had mild self-reproach; 11% suffered serious self-reproach and self-regret; and 1% had gross psychiatric breakdowns.[63]

A study in Poland has shown a 14% decrease in sexual libido four to five years after abortion;[64] while the Czechs have reported decrease in libido in 33% of patients nine months after the abortion.[65]

It has been said that "You can drag a baby out of the uterus but you cannot wipe it out of the mind."[66] According to certain psychologists and psychiatrists, the feminine principle is one of receiving, keeping and nourishing.[67] Although the pregnant woman may initially deny her unborn child, once she admits she is pregnant (and she must do this to undergo an abortion) she feels an unconscious attachment to him. Because of this, many women feel that part of themselves is lost through abortion.[68]

The psychiatrist Karl Stern states that it is not infrequent that women who have had abortions break down with a serious depression or even psychosis when the time arrives when they would have given birth to their child. What is remarkable about this, notes Stern, is that the patient may very well be unaware of when that due date was, or even indifferent to the moral dimension of abortion. Her profound reaction of loss coincides with the time of birth which did not take place.[69]

A World Health Organization group of scientists have concluded that:

> There is no doubt that the termination of pregnancy may precipitate a serious psychoneurotic or even psychotic reaction in a susceptible individual.[70]

Apart from the death brought to the unborn, and the mortality or morbidity suffered by the mother as a result of abortion, there are also serious dangers to subsequent children of aborted mothers.

Fourteen years after legalizing abortion, Hungary reported a 5% increase in premature babies.[71] In addition, due to birth injury, post-natal asphyxia and atelectasis (collapsing of the lungs) which are leading cases of death in premature infants, Hungary's infancy mortality rate was 1,278.2 per 100,000 live births compared to a 549.4 per 100,000 rate for the U.S.[72] Following legalized abortion on request, the perinatal mortality rate in Hungary had doubled!

The frequency of spontaneous abortions (miscarriages) in women who have undergone legal abortions has been reported as 30 to 40% higher than in cases where women had not been aborted.[73] Furthermore, the incidence of foetal death during pregnancy is twice as great for a woman who had an abortion compared to those who hadn't.[74] Dr. Kelaris, a leading gynecologist in Greece, speaks of his country's biggest social problem being women not being able to retain pregnancies due to their having been previously aborted so often.[75]

Findings such as these have led one authority to conclude as follows:

> Induced abortion plays an important role in the development of a subsequent child ...the impact of premature birth on infant mortality and on the mental and physical development of the child is connected with the frequency of abortions.[76]

Just as Shylock, the Jew, cannot be prejudiced with impunity, neither can the human foetus be aborted without grave reprisals being suffered by his mother, her future progeny, the medical profession, and all of society. The merchants of calumny who banalize the human foetus and suppress the medical risks which abortion represents are bargaining for their own pound of flesh.

The desire to believe that the human foetus is not human and that abortion does not give rise to frequent and serious complications is very strong in some people. They would prefer that the world should bend to their beliefs rather than they themselves be enlarged by a world which is wider than will. Perhaps the essence of prejudice lies in a fear of accepting what is different. But in the case of the human foetus, this prejudice takes an ironic twist. We all contain the unborn. We are the unborn. The abortionist is the inverse of Narcissus. He hates his own repeated image. He has no memory. He has no ontogeny. The human foetus tells him how small he must be. In rejecting his own smallness, he then lashes out against the unborn. To accept one's smallness requires greatness. This is the essential paradox of man.

In accepting his smallness, his finitude, his fallibility, man honours a truth and thereby acknowledges the universe. When he insists upon nothing less than his own perfection, emancipated forever from any attachment or resemblance with the humble foetus, he acknowledges only his own vanity.

Inseparable from a fear of finitude is a terror of death. If man grows from a single cell, what fortress in this world can ever be a safeguard against his destruction? If man's life begins in the penumbra of nothingness, that shadow must remain to lurk behind his every heartbeart.

As he came forth from his mother's womb, so again shall he depart, naked as he came, having nothing from his labour that he can carry in his hand.[77]

Footnotes

[1] Shakespeare, *The Merchant of Venice*, Act III, Scene i.
[2] Eugene Diamond, "The Humanity of the Unborn", *Catholic Lawyer*, Spring, 1971, p. 174.
[3] *Dietrich v. Northhampton*, 138 Mass. 14, 52 *Am. Rep.* 242 (1884).
[4] That is to say the current findings in embryology, foetology, genetics, perinatology, and all of biology.
[5] David Granfield, *The Abortion Decision*, Doubleday, 1971, p.23.
[6] Day & Liley, *The Secret World of a Baby*, Random House, 1968.
[7] Reuben Straus *et al.*, "Direct Electroencephalographic Recording of a Twenty-Three Millimeter Human Embryo", *The American Journal of Cardiology*, Sept. 1961, pp. 443-47.
[8] J. W. Still, *Journal of the Washington Academy of Science*, 59:46, 1969.
[9] Davenport Hooker, *The Prenatal Origin of Behaviour*, Univ. of Kansas Press, 1952. G.L. Flanagan, *The First Nine Months of Life*, Simon & Schuster, 1962.
[10] Robert Rugh & Landrum Shettles with R. E. Einhorn, *From Conception to Birth: The Drama of Life's Beginnings*, Harper & Row, 1971, p.71.
[11] Albert W. Liley, "Auckland MD to Measure Light and Sound Inside Uterus", *Medical Tribune Report*, May 26, 1969.
[12] Bradley Patten, *Human Embryology*, Third Edition, Ch. 9, McGraw-Hill, 1968.
[13] Arnold Gesell, *The Embryology of Behaviour*, Chs. 4-6, 10, Harper & Row, 1945.
[14] Davenport Hooker, "Early Human Fetal Behavior with a Preliminary Note on Double Simultaneous Fetal Stimulation", *Proceedings of the Association for Research in Nervous and Mental Disease*, Williams & Wilkins, 1954.
[15] Cf. photograph in G.L. Flanagan, *op. cit.* p. 98. (Photography by the courtesy of Hooker & Humphrey.)
[16] Dr. & Mrs. J. C. Willke, *Handbook on Abortion*, Hiltz, 1971, p.21.
[17] Arnold Gesell, *op. cit.* p. 65.
[18] Carl Wood, "Weightlessness: Its Implications for the Human Fetus", *Journal of Obstetrics & Gynecology of the British Commonwealth*, Vol 77, 1970, pp. 333-6.
[19] *Amicus Curiae Brief of Some 220 Physicians, Professors and Fellows of the American College of Obstetricians and Gynecologists Before the U.S. Supreme*

Court in the Texas and Georgia Cases. Oct. term, 1971.
[20]Rafael Sevilla, "Oral Feeding of Human Fetus: A Possibility", *JAMA,* May 4, 1970, pp. 713-17.
[21]Interview between Mike Levy and Dr. Ballard, *Triumph,* March, 1972, pp. 20-23, 44.
[22]Valerie Vance Dillon, "Application for Life", *Sign,* Oct. 1968, p. 12.
[23]Dr. H.M.I. Liley, *Modern Motherhood,* Revised Edition, Random House, 1969, p. 50.
[24]E. Diamond, *op. cit.* p. 175.
[25]Gino Papola, M.D., "Abortion Today: A Doctor looks at a modern problem", *L'Osservatore Romano,* March 23, 1972, p. 10.
[26]H.M.I. Liley, *op. cit.* p. 207.
[27]E. Horger & D. Hutchinson, M.D., "Diagnostic Use of Amniotic Fluid", *Journal of Pediatrics,* Vol. 74, No. 3, Sept. 1969, pp. 503-508. W. Floyd, M.D., P. Goodman, & P. Wilson, "CT: Amniotic Fluid Filtration and Cytology", *Obstetrics & Gynecology,* Vol. 34, No. 4, Oct. 1969. Szijarto, "Modern Diagnostic Criteria of Fetal Suffering", *Fracestoro,* Vol. 61, Nov.-Dec. 1968. Parmley *et al.,* "Fetal Maturity and Amniotic Fluid Analysis", *American Journal of Obstetrics and Gynecology,* Vol. 105, No. 3, pp. 354-362.
[28]Ashley Montagu, *Life before Birth,* New American Library, 1964, Ch.X.
[29]*Raleigh Fitkin-Paul Morgan Memorial Hospital v. Anderson,* 42 N.J. 421, 201 A. 2d 537, cert denied, 377 U.S. 985 (1964).
[30]Peter Berman et al., "A Method for the Prenatal Diagnosis of Congenital Hyperuricemia", *Journal of Pediatrics,* Vol. 75, No. 3, Sept. 1969. N. O'Doherty, "The Prenatal Treatment of Adrenal Insufficiency", *The Lancet,* No. 29, 1969, 2:1194-95. A. Hodari & T. Lorna, "Experimental Surgical Procedures Upon the Fetus in Obstetric Research", *Obstetrics and Gynecology,* Vo. 34, No. 2, Aug. 1969, pp. 204-11.
[31]Dillon, *op. cit.* p. 10.
[32]Montagu, *op. cit.* pp. 187-8.
[33]*Ibid.* p. 178.
[34]M. Marcel & J. Exchaquet, "L'Electrocardiogramme du Foetus Human Avec un Cas de Double Rythme Auriculaire Verifié", *Arch. Mal Coeur,* Paris 31, 504, 1938.
[35]Flanagan, *op. cit.* p. 51.
[36]Leslie Arey, *Developmental Anatomy,* 6th edition, Saunders, 1954, Chs. II, VI.
[37]Marcel *et al., op. cit.*
[38]Gesell, *op. cit.*
[39]Straus *et al., op cit.*
[40]A. Hellegers, "Fetal Development", *Theological Studies,* 3, 7, 1970, p. 26.
[41]H. M. I. Liley, *op. cit.* B. Patten, *op. cit.*
[42]Liley, *op. cit.* p. 50. Hooker, *op. cit.* p. 75.
[43]Willke, *op. cit.* p. 28.
[44]Montagu, *op. cit.* p. 186.
[45]*Ibid.* "Tobacco Smoke and Other Poisons", p. 99.
[46]*Ibid.* p. 97.
[47] Cf. Willke, *op. cit.* p. 72. Cf. also A. J. Schaeffer, *Diseases of the Newborn,* Saunders, 1966. "... premature birth is the leading cause of infant death, and

one of the leading causes of mental and motor retardation".
[48]Quoted by Rabbi Karasich in Papola, *op. cit.* p. 10 under "Jewish Comments". This remark has been traditionally interpreted as constituting a commandment against killing the unborn child.
[49]Dr. Ian Donald, *The Scotsman*, March 9, 1970.
[50]"The Abortion Act (1967)", *British Medical Journal*, 30 May, 1970, p.533.
[51]A. B. Rosenfield *et al.*, "Recent Trends in Infant and Maternal Health in Minnesota", *Minn. Med.*, 53:807-16, 1970.
[52]Thomas Hilgers, M.D., & Robert Shearin, M.D., "Medical Complications of Induced Abortion", *Induced Abortion: A Documented Report*, Jan. 1971, p.24.
[53]Drs. Gardiner, Pisani & Mattingly, *College Statement and Minority Report on Therapeutic Abortion*, issued by the American College of Obstetrics and Gynecology, Chicago, May 1, 1969.
[54]J.A. Stallworthy, A.S. Moolgaoker, J.J. Walsh, "Legal Abortion: A Critical Assessment of its Risks", *The Lancet*, Dec. 4, 1971, pp.1245-49.
[55]*Ibid.* p.1248.
[56]S.V. Sood, *British Medical Journal*, 1971, iv, 270.
[57] W. Droegemuller *et al.*, "The First Year of Experience in Colorado With the New Abortion Law", *American Journal of Obstetrics and Gynecology*, 103:694-698, March, 1969.
[58]A.M. Lekhter, "Experience in the Study of the Sequelae to Abortions", Sovet. *Zdravookhr*, 25:27, 1966.
[59]L.O. Courtney, *Proc. Roy. Soc. Med.*, 62:834, 1969.
[60]L. P. Bengtsson *et al.*, "Legal Abortion Induced by Intrauterine Injections" (parts I & II), *Lakartidninger*, 64:5037, & 64:5046, 1967.
[61]Dr. Paul Popenoe, "Abortion in Japan", *Catholic Digest* (condensed from *Family Life*), Sept. 1971, p. 28.
[62]*Ibid.*
[63]M. Ekblad, "Induced Abortion on Psychiatric Grounds, A Follow-up Study of 479 Women", *Acta. Psychiat. Neurol. Scand. Suppl.*, 99:238, 1955.
[64]E. Midak, "Early and Late Sequelae of Abortion", *Pol. Tyg. Lek.*, 21:1063, 1966.
[65]J. Cepelak *et al.*, "Influence of Interruption of Pregnancy on the Sexual Life of the Woman", *Cesk Gynaek.*, 25:609, 1960.
[66]Quoted by Dr. Paul Marx, O.S.B., "What Sisters Should Know About Abortion", *Sisters Today*, 1972, p. 527.
[67]Helene Deutsch, *The Psychology of Women; A Psychoanalytic Interpretation*, Grune & Stratton, 1945. Karl Stern, *The Flight from Woman*, Farrar, Straus & Giroux, 1965, pp. 21-23.
[68]R. Le Roux (moderator), "Abortion", *American Journal of Nursing*, 70:1919-1925, 1970.
[69]Stern, *op. cit.* pp. 22-23.
[70]"Spontaneous Induced Abortion", report of a World Health Organization scientific group. *World Health Organization Technical Report Series*, No. 461, p. 41.
[71]A. Klinger, "Demographic Consequences of the Legalization of Induced Abortion in Eastern Europe", *Int. J. Gynec. & Obst.*, 8:680-691, Sept. 1970, p. 691.
[72]*World Health Statistics Report*, Vol. 23, No. 7, pp. 546-549.

[73] M. Kuck, "Abortion in Czechoslovakia", *Pro. Roy. Soc. Med.*, 62:831-832, 1969.
[74] World Health Statistics Report, *op. cit.*
[75] Dr. P. Marx, *op. cit.*
[76] A. Klinger, *op. cit.*
[77] *Ecclesiastes*, 5:14.

"On Being Human"

by R. E. Tully

R.E. Tully is Associate Professor of Philosophy, St. Michael's College, University of Toronto.

Being clear philosophically about whether an embryo or a foetus is a human being involves nothing less than thinking clearly about the kinds of things we call human beings. The prematurely-born infant, the athlete who has suffered a concussion and remains in coma, the elderly cancer patient kept under heavy sedation, individuals such as these are protected by law and unhesitatingly cared for because in each case a human life is at stake. But is the embryo or the foetus a human life? Does abortion pertain to what is less than or not yet a human life? Whether satisfactory answers to these questions can be given seriously depends on the clarity of the approaches taken to obtain them. And undoubtedly on the nature of the answers a good deal of our thinking about abortion logically depends.

In this essay I want to investigate two different approaches to the question of whether the embryo or the foetus is a human life. The first, which I shall call the *definist* approach, tries to describe what a human being is in terms of a set of necessary and sufficient conditions, and then attempts to apply this set to the various stages of embryonic and foetal development. I shall not be so much interested in enumerating the many different possible sets of necessary and sufficient conditions that might be listed as with the general approach to deciding the issue of humanity in this manner. The second approach, which I shall call the *emergentist*, takes the view that being a human life is not a mere collection of properties (those that would be mentioned in a definition of what a human life is) but rather is something irreducible which makes an organic compound to be a human life. Emergentism, which was a recognized philosophical position in Britain earlier in this century, has sometimes been depicted as a general metaphysical thesis about the nature of things and their properties. Fortunately, because I am concerned here with method rather than with doctrine, the merits of this general position can be ignored. It has also been sometimes branded as an anti-scientific doctrine, a charge which (as I have tried to show elsewhere) is simply not true. In any case, since leading emergentists like Alexander and Broad had really nothing to say on the question of whether being a human life was in any sense an emergent characteristic, the present discussion can remain somewhat innocent of historical controversy.

I shall say in advance that I do not think that either the definist or the emergentist approaches can conclusively settle the issue of the humanity of the embryo or foetus. (I should think rather than any claim to the contrary would be immediately suspect.) But the emergentist approach can, I think, dispense with some of the problems latent in the definist method without spawning insoluble problems of its own, and that by itself is some measure of its worth.

1. THE DEFINIST APPROACH TO WHAT A HUMAN BEING IS

The minimal conditions for being a human life are what the definist method tries to isolate. "Being rational" might be an example, on the one hand, of a condition which is not minimal, because while many of those whom we want to call human beings are to some extent and in some sense rational, there remain others, such as the new-born infant, whom we also want to count as human but who have as yet failed to give any of the conventional indications of rationality. On the other hand, "being a living organism" would appear to be an insufficient condition, since it applies equally to laboratory mice *in utero* and to the patient who has suffered irreversible brain damage and lingers on in a hospital's intensive care unit. On the definist approach, the property of being a living *human* organism will be also classified as insufficient, though it may well be a necessary condition, since a heart or kidney being maintained for transplantation is both living and human but is nevertheless not counted as a human life. Clearly, something must be present to a human living organism which makes it to be *a* human life or *a* human being. Lacking this something a human embryo will be regarded much like a heart or kidney, as a merely organic part of a human being's body which can be removed and destroyed or otherwise dealt with, given any sufficient reason.

But what then is this something which must be present to a living human organism? In searching about for a clue, the definist might want to consider what it is that, when absent, makes a human body to be from the medical point of view a dead human being. The symmetry of the comparison is initially appealing. If we know what a doctor seeks the absence of when trying to determine whether a human body has ceased to exist as a human being, we can then search for the presence of just this characteristic in order to declare that a human embryo or foetus has begun to exist as a human being. Typically, however, a doctor will base his judgment of death on a cluster of indications from the heart, lungs and brain, rather than on the basis of anything so simple as the absence of one characteristic. For example, if the patient's respiratory and circulatory functions are normal or near normal, but his brain activity has become seriously impaired, a verdict of death may well be premature. Brain activity might revive, at least partially, and the patient will remain a human being, even though from the commonsense viewpoint he has become a radically changed person. What a doctor may look for is evidence of irreversible damage, and this is not a matter of the presence or absence of some special characteristic. It is a matter of the developing incapacity of the patient to sustain his vital organic and neural functions without complex artificial support, and when such massive incapacity amounts to death may be a matter of interpretation. In a purely clinical sense, instantaneous death may well be rare.

However, when one turns to the case of the embryo or foetus, the situation appears entirely dissimilar. For in the case of an acknowledged human being what is in question is a process from life to death, from being a living human being to being a dead one, while in the case of the embryo or foetus the movement is not from death to life but from being a mere organism to being a human life (if its humanity is challenged). What was wanted was a clear indication in the uterus of the difference between human life and *a* human life, but there seems to be none here. From its first moment, the embryo is sustained by its mother, and even if the foetus could not sustain its renal, respiratory and circulatory systems outside her womb, there is evidence week by week of its moving to a position of greater stability. It is moving to be born. Nor is absence of mental activity a clear indication of non-humanity; neither is it always in the case of an acknowledged human, and in any case it will be plainly false that the embryo or foetus is forever incapacitated from undergoing a process which will lead to its full possession of normal mental activity.

Once the asymmetry between pre-natal and moribund life is seen, the definist is left to discover or suggest one or more characteristics, shared in some form by both infants and adults and rendering them human, but absent either from both embryo and foetus, or from embryo but not foetus, or from the embryo alone prior to a certain stage in its development. No small part of his job will consist in specifying any characteristic with sufficient care so that the form in which it is shared by acknowledged human beings is clearly incapable of extension to one or more of the pre-natal candidates. In previous discussions of the humanity of the foetus, two characteristics have received principal attention: mentalistic development and dependency for survival on the body of the mother. Either has been supposed to exemplify a clear difference between what was already a human life and what had not yet reached that stage. It is not of course difficult to show that there are pronounced differences between the embryo in its early week of development and the foetus which has gone beyond twenty weeks. Any handbook on embryology will furnish details. But what is wanted is a resilient argument that makes use of these details to show that an embryo which possesses only a primitive brain does not deserve to be called a human at all, rather than just a human with a primitive brain. Nor is it difficult to prove that in the present state of the medical arts both the embryo and the young foetus would find it impossible to survive outside of the mother's womb. But what is wanted is a convincing argument that such forms of life should not simply be classified as organically dependent human beings. What the definist is asked to provide is the warrant for a definition.

Suppose, for example, that mentalistic development is suggested as the crucial distinction. The definist is obliged to show that failure to have a chosen characteristic (such as the four lobes of the brain, or its cortical convolutions) makes a human organism fail to be *a* human being. Yet human organisms can fail to have the chosen characteristic in vastly different senses. The placenta which develops along with the embryo does not undergo cerebral development, nor does the anencephalic embryo; the one never as a matter of fact undergoes that sort of cellular differentiation, the other through accident or cellular malfunction is prevented from doing so. But the case of the embryo which follows a normal pattern of development is much different. It does develop the lobes of the brain at an early stage, which does in turn develop cortical convolutions at a later stage. There is only a question of time and normal circumstances. The brain of the young foetus will become progressively adapted to the use of the sensory organs developing in other parts of its body at the same time, and it is well known that the stage of development reached by the time of birth is still comparatively primitive. The infant apparently will not yet have acquired a capacity to taste, the child of two remains neurologically unsuited to read at least small print, the pre-adolescent is usually unready to cope with much abstract conceptualization. Facts such as these, when assembled, seem to expose a weakness in the definist's position. The chosen characteristic of mentalistic development seems capable of extension to several of the pre-natal candidates.

Except in a genetic sense, of course, the convolutions of the brain are not "present in" the early embryo; but the two are related by stages of development, and between adjacent stages there is a great similarity, just as there is a vast difference between vastly separated stages. The mature female is not present in the infant. But there is much that is similar between the two-year old and the early reader of three, and between the infant and fully developed foetus. It is one thing for the definist to point to the fact that the brain of an early embryo fails to resemble closely the brain of an infant, and quite another for him to suggest that this amounts to the crucial distinction of humanity from non-humanity. In their different ways both the embryo and the infant are bundles of capacities which clearly separate them in one class from the placenta, the anencephalic embryo, the ovum and the sperm. While this does not prove that the embryo is a human being, there yet appears no clear warrant for the definist to disqualify it.

If the definist is pressed for a justification, where is he to find it? The facts that are available to him are much like those just referred to, facts which do not obviously support his choice of defining characteristic. But then what will justify that choice? It will not be satisfactory to say that because embryos are very different from acknowledged humans they are therefore not human beings, for that is to ignore the probability of their development. Nor will it do to assume that no human organism that has failed to reach a certain stage of cerebral development is a human being, for that is just to beg the question. And it will be equally unsuitable for the definist to recommend or to assume that no such creature *ought* to be called a human being, since that simply ignores the need for justification. What creates these difficulties is the need to find a defining characteristic that makes (or fails to make) the living organism in the womb to be a human life. The definist seems to be cornered by the demands of his own method.

In his search for a characteristic that will work, the definist will be tempted to avoid specific properties. If he wants to use "having well-developed surface convolutions" as his candidate, the question will immediately arise: supposing that doctors can agree how to define what a well-developed surface convolution is, why should not the possession of surface convolutions relating to the immediately anterior stage allow a foetus at that stage to be counted as human as well? and what of the stage of development that comes immediately before that? And such questions would not be mere quibbling, since the development of convolutions from one stage to another can be a matter of mere days — just the time that might elapse between a hospital committee's decision to allow an abortion and the carrying out of their decision. In any case, given that the embryo's development can be regarded as a connected series of stages leading to its possession of (among other things) a mature brain, it will remain unclear what motivates the definist to select one specific stage rather than another. And so the definist will somewhat understandably drift toward generality in an effort to find a characteristic that does not have to be minutely tested for, that does not seem arbitrary, and that applies to all acknowledged humans. We noticed above that "being rational" would be an unsuitable characteristic, since it would not clearly apply to newborn infants. But "having a capacity to be rational" would be equally unsuitable, though for a different reason, because of the vagueness of the word "capacity" itself. What is to count as a capacity, and how is it to be tested for? Once again the definist faces the danger either of being too specific or of remaining both general and uninformative.

In some discussions of abortion the claim is made that the embryo or foetus could not survive outside of the mother's uterus, and so, being a part of the mother's body, it is said to be subject to her own individual rights. This is clearly an instance of the definist's method at work. Because it lacks what is taken to be an essential human characteristic, that of extra-uterine independence, the embryo or foetus is considered to be not yet a human being; and because it is considered nothing but a part of the mother's body, talk of its individual rights cannot be meaningful. But if this claim is to be plausible, the definist is obliged to offer some clarification of the chosen characteristics. What is "independence" to mean? Obviously, it cannot mean absence of dependence altogether on the part of the new-born or even young; indeed in some cultures, the infant remains exclusively dependent on its mother for survival, including its nourishment, her breasts being substituted for the placenta. It is probably more accurate to say that the journey from womb to world involves only a change in the mode of dependence. On the other hand, what if it were to become possible for doctors to remove the living organism from the womb at even the earliest stages and provide it with a completely adequate life-support? Would this confer humanity on it in the eyes of those who would refuse to regard it a human life while in the womb? It might, if prior to its removal the living organism were clearly nothing but a part of the mother's body. But often this is just what people who make use of this characteristic fail to be clear about. Something can be a part of one's body in many different ways: the brain is a part of the body, and so are red corpuscles, staph germs, tape worms, food and an imbedded cardiac pacer. An embryo is also part of a body, but even if its status as a human life is denied it has, unlike these other things, a rather unique capacity of becoming a human being. To refuse to call an embryo or foetus a human being *because* it is a part of its mother's body is naïve. Why should it be thought that the embryo or foetus cannot be both a part of the mother's body *and* a human life?

It would be a mistake to conclude from this discussion that it is impossible to arrive at a definition of what it is to be a human being, or even inadvisable to go looking for one. The difficulties we have found, however, concern a few standard attempts to clarify what is meant by being a human life, and what these attempts have in common is the proposal that the acquisition of some special physical trait or some special status (in relation to the mother) makes a human organism into a human being. It is here that we have found the definist's method faltering. The definist may want, of course, to define the human organism itself as the human being, and in one way, as we shall see, his position would closely resemble the emergentist's. But in another way even this attempt might falter if he goes on to identify the humanity of the embryo or foetus with one or more of its biological characteristics. For if this is how he chooses to explain what it is for the organism to be human, he will face a set of problems similar to those which confronted the other crucial characteristics just discussed.

2. THE EMERGENTIST APPROACH TO WHAT A HUMAN BEING IS

A striking difference between the definist and emergentist methods concerns their different starting points for analysis: what things are to be regarded as simple and what as complex. The definist, we have seen, looks upon humanity as a complex property that is resolvable into a cluster of simpler constituent properties, and he tries to answer the question of whether the embryo or foetus is human by testing for the presence of one or more of these at its different stages of development. Considering the difficulties that this approach has met with, however, the emergentist will urge that another path be followed which begins with the assumption that "being a human life" is an irreducible or simple property of some physical organisms, a property which emerges from them and belongs exclusively to them. Of course, even if "being a human life" were to be accepted as an emergent property, it would remain a separate question whether the embryo or foetus ought to be called a human being. But the starting point of the emergentist's path is what must be examined first.

Traditionally, though the tradition of emergentism is not that long, the sorts of thing that were held to be emergent were certain properties of physical objects, like "being red", and certain properties of organic compounds, like "being conscious". Among all the properties of organic and inorganic objects, those which interested the emergentists most were ones which to their way of thinking belonged only to the objects taken as wholes, but not to the parts of such objects, or at least not to the smallest parts of such objects. If a microscopic particle is part of a plastic ball, and that ball is coloured red, it would not follow, indeed it would likely be false, that the particle itself is also red. Again, supposing that a certain neuronal fibre was identified as part of a human brain, and that it was in one sense true to say that the brain was conscious or undergoing some mental experience, it would not also be true to make either assertion about the fibre itself. Emergent properties, such as these were believed to be, were contrasted with others that were thought of as characterizing even the smallest parts of the whole: "being combustible", for instance, would belong to even the microscopic particles of the plastic ball, and "having a protein component" to the neuronal fibre. So it was thought one of the family traits of emergent properties that they were found only in the presence of compounds of various sorts which had to pre-exist their occurrence—their emergence—in space and time. Samples of the colours we are all familiar with in our experience did not always exist; their appearance depended on the formation of macroscopic compounds in the universe. And because human brains did not always exist but had to evolve slowly, the kind of phenomenon that is called human consciousness had to await its time to emerge.

Another of the alleged family traits of emergent properties was their simplicity, their alleged indefinability in terms of simpler properties. Emergentists resorted to different formulations of this trait. One, for example, thought that any act of consciousness was in fact identical with those physical components of the brain on which it depended for its existence, and yet was something more than just those components acting together. His idea, apparently, was that an emergent property may depend for its existence on a complex interaction of physical properties, but that after it has come into existence there would be an impropriety in regarding it as just another physical property; it is so different from the pre-existing "material" of physical properties that it deserves to be called a new order or kind of quality. As to how it could be decided for every different sort of quality which were merely physical and which emergent, there was no satisfactory answer, nor for that matter any concerted attempt to answer. Intuition and common sense very likely played a strong part in the decision. Another emergentist tried to explain simplicity by claiming that emergent properties are those which people must have experienced in order to know what, qualitatively speaking, they are. He used the example of a "mathematical archangel" to illustrate his point: if the chemical compound of ammonia had never been discovered or encountered, he reasoned, the archangel would know many facts about the imagined compound because of already known facts about the behaviour of hydrogen and nitrogen in isolation. The mathematical archangel might even know that among those sublunary creatures gifted with a sense of smell, a strong whiff would cause irritation of the mucuous membranes of the nose. But, never having smelled it himself, the archangel would not know *how* ammonia smells; he would not know its characteristic odour.

However, if examples like the particle of the red plastic ball, the neuronal fibre and the archangel are supposed to reveal family traits of emergent properties, "being a human life" would not appear to be even a distant cousin. Assuming that there are legitimate instances of properties whose nature remains unknown until they come to be experienced, there seems to be no convincing reason why "being a human life" could not have been predicted by a mathematical archangel before the evolution of human beings. It is not a restricted observational property, one which pertains exclusively to one or another of the senses. On the other hand, the distinction between being a property of a whole and being a property of its parts might seem to allow "being a human life" to be called an emergent property. For, unlike the case of "being human", the property of being a human being is applied to what we regard as a whole, an individual — a person; it does not make sense to speak of a person's tissue or bones or blood as a human life, though these are both living and human. But when we search for the reason as to why this is the case, the issue seems to go against emergentism.

In the case of the red plastic ball we were able to see how the distinction between being a property of the whole and being a property of its parts could be made, because in fact *another* criterion could be appealed to. If we wonder whether the property of being red applies to a part of the red plastic ball, we have only to look at the part ourselves under normal conditions of lighting: if it should appear red to us under those conditions, this is a tolerably good reason for supposing that the part *is* red; and should the microscopic part of the ball fail to appear red when it is viewed under similar conditions through a microscope, then this is reason enough to consider the part not to be red. The criterion of observation is also appealed to in a modified form in the case of that other supposedly emergent property, consciousness or some particular form of conscious experience. If part of a subject's brain were removed but he still claimed to be able to have a particular type of experience, then it would likely be agreed that the experience actually characterizes less of the brain taken as an organic whole than was originally thought. The limit will have been reached when the subject reports having the experiences no longer, or when some other and more objective test indicates this to be the case. But the point remains the same, however the limit is determined, that a property can be said to be or not to be a property of certain parts when some sort of relatively objective observation can be made. And this is just what confronts the case of "being a human life" with a difficulty. There are tests for telling whether a body and its parts are human, but by what sort of test do we determine that a body possesses the property of being a human life? Observing something to be a human being is plainly different from observing it to have black hair or to be in pain, and even though sometimes, as in the case of another's pain, we do not *directly* observe that state or condition, we ourselves know what it is to be in pain and we can surmise that what the other person is experiencing is much like what we have felt. But if the property of being a human life is not directly observed, neither can the emergentist claim that like pain or other forms of conscious experience it can be *indirectly* observed. This is because any form of conscious experience is directly known by one particular person, the person who *has* the experience, while no one introspects or directly experiences his own property of being a human being.

There are, of course, numerous tests for telling whether something is a human being, ranging from our ordinary ways of observing speech and behaviour to sophisticated analyses of chromosomal structure, but to adopt any one of these approaches might strike the advocate of emergent properties as tantamount to admitting that the property of being a human being is reducible to one or another particular characteristic, which is the method of the definist. And while this would allow him to go on claiming that the property of being a human being characterizes a whole but not the parts of that whole, he could not then infer that such a property is therefore simple or irreducible. The early emergentists allowed for just such a class of non-emergent properties. A rug which is five feet square, is not composed of individual strands which are each five feet square, yet this was not considered a sufficient reason for calling "being five feet square" an emergent property. Worse still, the early emergentists never used their various forms of tests for simple properties to isolate "being a human life" as emergent. The closest they came was to call "life" itself as a property of organic compounds, an emergent. But the question of whether a human embryo or foetus is living has not been disputed, only the question of whether it is to be called a human being.

At this point, if he is determined to apply his doctrine, a protoemergentist might resort, quite literally, to invention. If he wants to avoid identifying the alleged emergent with any of the observable properties which human beings have, and if he continues to maintain that being a human life is a property of *some* sort, then he might begin to treat it as a hidden, more or less metaphysical, property. And thus the emergentist might begin to endow human beings with a new range of properties which had not so far entered the discussion. Not only would the world contain instances of reducible and irreducible physical properties as well as reducible and irreducible mental properties, there would also be found that which makes all and only human beings to be human beings, namely the property of being a human being. Clearly this proposal would accomplish very little: it would not furnish us with a clear criterion for telling when something is in fact a human being and when not—indeed, the proposal to count being a human life as an irreducible but unobservable property seems to presuppose that we already possess the means for telling in every case whether we are dealing with a human being; and in return for the conceptual burden which the proposal asks us to carry there seems to be no compensatory advantage in terms of theoretical simplicity and synthesis when compared with the definist approach. In short, this proposal would only add to our present stock of difficulties.

The impasse which the emergentist is facing appears to concern the central assumption that if being a human life is to be understood as an emergent then it must be understood as an emergent property of things (of the embryo, foetus, infant, etc.). Historically, there is some warrant for this assumption, in that much of the controversy over an emergentist view of the world has concerned the question of whether and in what sense any so-called emergent properties are irreducible to the physical properties of matter. But the early emergentists were accustomed to insisting that in addition to emergent *properties* there were also emergent *kinds* — mind and spirit being sometimes mentioned as examples. Although this aspect of their doctrine might not itself be the resolution to the difficulties we have met, it might still provide a clue that could lead to one.

The clue is that "being a human being" does not stand for a simple, irreducible property which makes a complex physical organism to be a human being, rather, the complex physical organism *itself* is an irreducible, simple kind of thing. A human being is to be undertood as one who displays a cluster of different sorts of properties relating to physical appearance, social behaviour, varieties of experiences, and use of language, each of these relating to the others in complicated ways. A human being *has* an experience of pain, for example, *describes* it to others, *ascribes* a similar experience to another human, and *consoles* another. In the life history of an individual these different sorts of properties will not always be present together. Language is lacking to the infant, conscious experiences and feelings to the patient in a coma. And yet both are easily admitted to be human beings. The properties which qualify something to be a human being are not hidden, not unobservable, and not difficult to grasp, because they are the very ones we as human beings commonly use to identify others of our kind. But no one of them is *identical* with what "being a human life" means. If anything is identically human it is the person himself, not his properties.

It ought to be realized that what the emergentist is doing when he follows out his clue is more a philosophical reminder than an empirical discovery. What he reminds us of is the fact that we possess some very fundamental categories with which we approach the world and differentiate its objects, and the objects which particularly interest him here are those which we categorize as humans. The judgment of whether an individual is a human being comes to be made in enormously different ways, and in fact the instances are rare when we can catch ourselves making just *this* judgment; more often we find ourselves responding in our words and actions to another human as though the judgment had already been made. Once made, and whether explicitly made or not, it will not later be withdrawn. Individuals who live as humans die as humans and not as something else. If a child dies not having gained the use of language, he dies an incomplete human being but a human being nonetheless. And even when a criminal has acted with gross inhumanity to his fellow humans and is under judgment of forfeiting his life, he has still not forfeited his right to be called a man. But it is also important to realize that an individual does not wait to have humanity *conferred* on him by our judgment; whatever criteria we use to make the judgment — the looks, movements, words, or even the chromosomal structure of an individual — our judgment is really a *recognition* of the presence of a human life.

The emergentist will insist that to be a human life is not identical with any of the various criteria which we employ to identify humans—for that is the way of the definist, as well as of the emergentist who treats humanity as a property. It is a misleading and ultimately self-entangling way because it fails to recognize that it is to *humans* that we ascribe language, it is *humans* which have been discovered to possess a characteristic set of chromosomes. Even if it were an established fact that humans shared an identical set of genes with the apes (as they happen to do many of their internal organs) there would be no greater difficulty than there ever was in the past in determining what to call a human being. The recognition of humanity belongs to a context of fertilization, birth, life and death. The emergentist reminds us that despite our genetic continuity with other forms of animals we remain prepared to count humans as irreducibly different.

At the same time, the emergentist is not treating "humanity" as the name of an occult, metaphysical entity, a shadowy self which accompanies us through life and makes the difference between our being humans and being mere animals. The philospher Wittgenstein once said that "where our language suggests a body and there is none: there, we should like to say, is a *spirit*". But in the case of human beings the "body" is altogether obvious; it is the complex organic compound whose character and capacities are determined at the time seed meets ovum and which from that moment will proceed to develop and fulfill its life in the variety of ways we call human. To be human is to belong to the human kind. As a living organism a human is a collection of countless parts, as a member of society he is but one part among many, but as a human being he is neither part nor divisible whole.

It therefore seems philosophically reasonable to say that the embryo will come to have conscious experiences *because* it is a human life. Nevertheless, humanity is not a causal property which is additive to the organic traits of the embryo, it is rather the sum of those traits at any stage in the life of an individual. What follows from this account is that for a foetus or an infant to undergo mental experiences does not *make* an individual to be human, nor does it constitute humanity in a specific instance. More appropriately, it is *a way of being human*. And a human being is what the embryo is and what the sperm or the ovum by itself is not. Those who would refuse to call the embryo a human life fall into the confusion of thinking that because the embryo does not yet act in the way of the majority of living human beings act it is therefore not a human at all. But given that it is human, it will so act. In the same way, the infant and the child will someday become sexually active, though they are remote from that role at birth.

Near the beginning of this essay I mentioned that neither the definist nor the emergentist positions could conclusively settle the issue of whether the embryo or the foetus is a human being. I think that it is now possible to offer a good philosophical reason for such humility. Both positions are alike in the methodological sense that both offer definitions of what a human life is: one proposes to define a human being as this or that property or set of properties, the other proposes to define a human being as an irreducibly different kind. But though it seems natural to go on to ask which is the *true* account, it is not clear that such a question makes any sense. In the analysis of philosophical arguments an assertion or a proposition which has been identified as a definition can be agreed with, challenged or rejected, shown to be warranted or unwarranted, consistent or inconsistent with what has been asserted elsewhere, criticized for its vagueness or ambiguity, or adopted as a reasonable basis for further argumentation. But when a definition serves as the starting point of a philosophical account, it is not easy to see what one is to mean by investigating it for its truth, in the sense of asking for a *proof* that it is true. For definitions are typically *laid down* as true at the outset. And in the case that we have been dealing with the two definitions are intended not to add to our stock of empirical facts but to organize the facts. Hence, asking whether either definition is true is far less preferable than asking whether either organizes the facts well. Both the definist and the emergentist proposals can be tested for the degree to which they capture in theory the concepts which we as rational individuals operate with in practice. And in this respect the emergentist account seems to lie closer to home.

This point bears on another made at the very beginning of the essay. I mentioned that a good deal of our thinking about abortion logically depends on how we answer the question, whether the embryo or foetus is a human life, and now that the answer is a little clearer I think it is to that extent clearer that abortion must be regarded as the taking of a human life. The life that is taken in any abortion is not of course a complete human life, any more than infanticide involves taking a complete human life. But if there are good reasons for allowing an abortion then these must also be good reasons for taking *any* human life, which is thus a matter for the law to decide as well as the moral conscience of the individual. Anyone therefore who would defend abortion in some circumstances ought to be prepared to defend it as killing, and not as a matter of mere medical procedure to be decided between a woman and her doctor. Those who recommend or legally sanction a "liberal" policy on abortion ought themselves to recognize the major revision in our inherited conceptual scheme which they are proposing if the unborn are no longer to be counted as humans with rights, or as humans at all. When human lives are at stake, being clear philosophically about what is being proposed has far more to it than theoretical interest.

Section Three: The Abortion Debate

Abortion and the Right to Life

by Lloyd Gerson

Lloyd Gerson is a Lecturer in Philosophy, St. Michael's College, University of Toronto.

Those who oppose abortion wish to argue that every human being has an inalienable right to life from the moment of his or her conception. The basic argument includes three points: (1) Every person has at least a *prima facie* right to protection against endangerment of that life by another. (2) This right is forfeitable, if at all, only in extreme cases such as war or punishment for great crime. (3) Each person begins his or her life at the moment of conception. Thus, the unborn child is a member of the class of those falling under the general principle expressed in (1) and (2).

Many people deny the validity of this argument, usually rejecting (1) and/or (3).[1] It is not at all clear that these people do not have the weight of common sense on their side. Are we to accord to a microscopic organism the identical right that we accord to grown, conscious persons? Is it not an excessively harsh and unreasonable theory to hold that the weight of law and morality should force us, not only to protect what is microscopically small, but to protect it with the same dedication we are bidden to bring in protecting active members of society?

1. THE RANGE OF RIGHTS

The concept of a "right" pervades law and morality and lies at the heart of the abortion controversy. In order better to understand the nature of the right with which we shall be primarily concerned—the right to life—it will perhaps be useful to begin with some considerations about rights in general.

We normally speak of "rights" in two broad senses. In the first sense we would say, for example, that a man living in Russia today does not have the right to free speech. In the second sense we would say that he has the right to free speech, yet the right is not recognized by the state. The difference between the two manners of speaking is that in the first instance the existence of the right depends to some extent upon the recognition or validation or creation by the state, while in the second instance the right is somehow in the man himself and remains so even if it is ignored or violated.

Clearly, a decision on the choice of locution will depend upon the sort of thing we conceive a right to be, the different kinds of rights which exist and a consideration of the reasons for their existence.

Some simple rights exist only if and when the state says they do. These rights refer (roughly) to activities the performance of which is permitted to people. For example, our traffic code contains provisions concerning "rights of way". In some cases we might have such rights and in others not. And the right may be revoked or its precise terms changed at any time. These "rights of way" are a reflection of the basic aim of the traffic laws and, by extension, of the legal code in general. The laws specify, among other things, situations in which we must act or refrain from acting in a certain way if the general aim of the laws is to be achieved. Notice first that in the last sentence the "must" is mitigated by the "if", that is, the imperative is contingent upon the desire of the population as a whole for the achievement of the end or purpose of the laws. Notice further that the right, in this case the "right of way", is based solely on the fact that in a given situation a person, by acting in a certain way, will be achieving the desired end—the end presumably desired by the majority of the population. Further, it is important to see that the "right of way" describes a particular situation and prescribes a particular act. It is irrelevant to the "right of way" that the driver is, say, unlicensed or impaired. One need only be driving an automobile in order to claim the right. This is not to say, of course, that the class of those who fulfill the conditions of the right may in fact be restricted in one way or another. The right, however, specifies the conditions and presupposes the reason for its existence and does not name the group which may or may not fulfill it.

Created rights are contingent in two ways. First, in a given situation we might not have the right. We might not have the "right of way" in a given situation. Second, they are usually contingent upon the existence of a legal code and general legal principles and a certain cultural environment. In a country in which there were no automobiles the "right of way" presumably would not exist. Created rights are at the bottom of a hierarchy of rights and principles of increasingly wider scope. They presuppose prior rights as the conditions of their existence and effective operation.

A different sort of example is now in order. In this country it is generally held that a man has the right to practise the religion of his choice within very broad limits. Presumably, if his religion involved, say, cannibalism he could not claim the right. This right is obviously a good deal broader and more basic than the "right of way" and so the string of antecedent conditions for its existence is much smaller than in the previous example. Yet it is a fact that some people and some governments deny that a man has a right to practise freely a religion. Granted that such a controversy exists, it is reasonable to ask for the putative source or cause of the right. The answer must surely be connected with the fact that there are certain human activities which we commonly recognize as being essential to each individual's happiness and that in order to attain this happiness these activities must be governed by each person's conscience and will. We recognize a sort of boundary around each person, any violation of which would serve to impair or destroy the unique individuality of that person. To the extent that a government or another individual violates this boundary, the person is treated as a passive object, a thing which is not human. The activities and powers which fall within the boundary I should call the "material" for essential rights, and those which fall outside the "material" for accidental rights. The rights themselves, which refer to these are, accordingly, essential and accidental. No doubt, the precise location of the border is debatable. However, anyone who agrees that there should be *some* limit upon state authority over the individual must concede that the border does exist. I shall not now attempt to determine its location, for the right with which I am concerned will be seen to be the condition of the existence of any rights at all.

I should like to distinguish the power or ability to choose a religion from the right to religious practice strictly speaking. The right does not refer to the power alone but includes the fact that others recognize the power and its (conditional or unconditional) inviolability. Perhaps such an analysis of a right into the component parts of power and recognition is not much clearer than if we were to say simply that the right exists in the man, unrecognized or not. In that case, however, we would be forced to speak of a right as being somehow a quality in a person and I am not at all sure that *that* would serve the cause of clarity. We must not, though, go so far as to conflate completely recognition and creation of a right such that if we chose not to recognize the right it would not exist. The "material" of the right, in this case the power, is no doubt present without our recognition, and it is this "material" which, in part, evokes the recognition. The essential right itself is properly considered as consisting of a "portion" of the inviolable border in addition to our collective recognition of its existence. In general, if I say that Mr. Jones has an essential right to... I am expressing the recognition that a particular activity cannot be taken out of his control without impairing or destroying the nature of the person himself. The distinction between rights that are essential and rights that are not essential is admittedly very imperfect in some cases. In other cases as we shall see, it is quite clear.

Though the right to religious freedom may be an essential right it is not obviously correct to speak of it as an absolute right. First, we should probably allow that there are certain circumstances in which the right might be temporarily suspended. For example, a soldier in the heat of the battle might be constrained to forego attendance at the church of his choice for the moment. It is important to notice that we would be moved to grant such a suspension of essential rights only when something even more basic is threatened. This brings us to the second sense in which the right of religious freedom may be said to be contingent. The right is contingent upon our recognition of a person's right to live, for without his life he cannot exercise any other right. Further, when we recognize the existence of any subordinate rights, essential or otherwise, we are led sooner or later to the recognition of their condition as being a right as well. If the *conditiones sine qua non* of religious freedom were all immune to infringement it would be incorrect to speak of them as rights. The basic condition, however, human life, is pre-eminently subject to infringement. Thus, we may speak of a "right to life".

2. THE RIGHT TO LIFE

It is a mistake to think of the right to life as nothing more than the sum of all the other rights we judge to be within the border of individual inviolability. It is prior. There are countless cases we could point to in which it is the right to life we are directly protecting and not any subordinate right. A right does not exist without the capacity to exercise it. Were a person to be incapacitated with respect to a certain essential right that would not in itself compromise his right to life. Therefore, we must separate the right to life, the condition of every other right, each of which is a subordinate right, from those derived rights. The right to life is primary.

Wherein lies the inviolability of human life? I can think of only two general sorts of answers one might give. The first is a theological answer that seeks ultimate explanation in divine authority. The other answer is expressed in the idea of social contract—the idea that, desiring the protection and recognition of my own individuality, I grant it to whomever will grant it to me. Notice that in the latter case there would still be a recognition, not a creation of the right, or at least the "material" of the right, although the recognition would be first and foremost of my own self.

The choice between these two general sorts of answers is, in my view, of the utmost importance, though for the present it may remain undecided. We may not avoid the fact, however, that if we follow the chain of the argument to its conclusion, we shall see the acceptance of one of these answers, or some version of them, as necessary for the maintenance of any ordered society. For if human lives are subordinated to any other end, then all rights are in danger of being swept away. The recognition of the right to life of every person (on the basis of either one of the above reasons), is in fact the basic condition of the existence of our fragile institutions and laws.

If we isolate the right to life we can clearly see the conditions of *its* existence:[2] simply, life itself. The right is again relative to the ability to exercise it and any living person obviously has that ability. It is perhaps a bit odd to speak about *exercising* the right to life. We might, therefore, for the sake of clarity, speak of the right to life as being a "negative" right, i.e., the right to have others refrain from endangering one's life. The separability of this right from all others is clear. A mentally retarded person does not have the right to vote, yet to deny him the right to vote is very far from denying him the right to live.

Such arguments and distinctions as I have adduced are not simply the pedantic product of the classroom. The Western world has seen a grim succession of societies which did not accept the right to life as based on the fact of human life alone, but rather considered economic or religious or political criteria as decisive. Persons excluded from the dominant group forfeited their right to life. Or, to express the point more exactly, their right to life was vulnerable to revocation in the name of whatever considerations held sway at the moment.

It was sufficient to have been a Negro in the Southern states of America in the nineteenth century to have one's life "bargained away" to "higher" considerations. A denial of the right to life renders meaningless the recognition of any subordinate right. Would it not be the most macabre absurdity to say to a man that he had the right to vote but did not have the right to live? Thus, to deny anyone the right to life entails the denial of all other rights. Can we then pick and choose between those groups who will have full rights and those who will have none? To think that we can do so for very long according to a rational and just criterion is a pitiable delusion. For having once denied the absolute primacy of human life, there is no truly stable criterion by which we could decide who is and who is not to have any rights at all. Human life will be subject to the opinions of the reigning powers. As political and religious opinion changes so too will change the groups whose lives are to be sacrificed. The right to life of no one is safe unless that right is accepted to be beyond the vagaries of partisan group beliefs. Should we be willing to acquiesce in the destruction of the rights of others as long as we think we are safely included in the "in" group, how shall we plead our own case when our masters turn their displeasure upon us?

3. THE RIGHT TO LIFE OF THE UNBORN

The existence of *de-facto* legalized abortion on demand in Canada today tragically displays the results of the failure to see clearly the meaning of the right to life. At a time when this country proudly boasts of a Human Rights Commission, the rights of one group of people are rapidly eroding.

There is no doubt that the rights of the unborn are *not* fully comparable to the rights of adults. It would be quite absurd to claim, for example, that an embryo had a right to join a labour union. That is not the issue at all. There is one right, however, in which the unborn child is on exactly the same footing as anyone else. It is a unique individual, the product of human conception, as we all are, and very much alive. If we recognize that the right to life exists for each of us precisely because, and only because, we are living human beings, then it is not possible consistently to deny this right to unborn children. If the fact of human existence is not sufficient to guarantee the right to life of the unborn, why should this fact be sufficient in anyone else? It may be the case that those who deny the right to life of unborn children allow that right to those who have been born simply because they are human. An ulterior motive is, however, very likely. There are many of these such as sentimentality, fear of reprisal, or, most likely, utility. If the last be the case, then the obvious question is utility for whom? The distinguished anthropologist Ashley Montagu has publicly declared that humanity is "an achievement rather than an endowment".[3] The "underachievers" no doubt must pay the penalty for not having quite made the grade. What, we may ask, is the "grade"? Is there any reason to doubt that once having disconnected the right to life from its proper source it will eventually be denied to yet other groups of people who do not meet the current critieria. An arbitrary criterion of human life cuts both ways. Such a criterion excludes some and includes others in equally arbitrary ways. The first trickle of euthanasia bills now pending in some U.S. legislatures indicates that the next victims will probably be old people and the mentally retarded. Indeed, what reason would there be to stop there?

Any number of objections to the claim that unborn children have the right to life have been formulated. These objections have as their common foundation the strategy of trying to show that unborn children and persons who have been born,[4] do not have "humanity" in an identical sense and so to deny the right to life to the unborn does not entail the denial of it to the rest. The right to life is upheld (so it is argued) while denying that a certain group can lay claim to that right. To defend abortion, we could either say that all humans have the right to life, but that the unborn are not human, or we could say that a certain class of humans has the right to life and a certain class does not. Either statement will entail grounding the right to life in something other than biological human life. That is, "human" will be taken to name something more than a common genetic structure.

There is no short-cut to a refutation of the arguments which variously try to select criteria for the right to life such that most or all unborn children cannot claim the right although everyone else can. Each argument must be evaluated on the particular criterion offered.

I suspect that one of the most quietly persuasive of the criteria of humanity suggested is that of consciousness. An unborn child or even a newly born child is probably not conscious. (It is not clear, though, whether this means that he or she is not in any sense aware of being alive.) Thus, before birth, or whenever consciousness begins, abortion does not deprive anyone of his or her right to life since no human being as yet exists.

As it stands, this criterion obviously will not do. For on this criterion anyone who is temporarily unconscious forfeits the right to life. A person temporarily comatose would be just as clearly excluded from humanity as the child before birth. Both are not now, but will probably soon be, conscious. It may be argued that the difference between the person who is comatose and the unborn child is that while the former has a past history of "lived existence", or consciousness, the latter does not. Against this, if a right is relative to the capacity to exercise it, no one has the capacity to "exercise" his past life; he can live only in the present, and then the future. So, the person who is comatose and the unborn child are in the same situation: unconscious in the present and capable of being conscious in the future. Presumably, one could retreat to a broader criterion, defining "conscious" as neurological activity of any sort. Neurological activity is detectable in the unborn about forty days after conception. On this criterion, therefore, any product of conception would fall outside the class of human beings before this time.

We should note, however, what the assertion of such a criterion implies. By so defining humanity we reduce its essence to a purely physiological activity which in turn leads us to question the selection of one activity rather than another. Why not, for example, reduce the essence of humanity to cardio-vascular activity which happens to begin about nineteen days after conception? If it be countered that cardio-vascular activity is possessed by many non-human animals then the criterion will do nothing more than say that humanity is defined by human activity—an instance of a circular demonstration. If the ground of the right to life is no more than a purely physiological activity it is difficult to see what meaning a "right" could have in this context. At any rate, if we did accept the inevitability of some physiological criterion, would it not make sense to take the widest possible criterion available? If, so to speak, the criterion of our criterion is not that we shall choose what is *prima facie* the widest possible one, thereby giving human life the benefit of the doubt, then our primary criterion is in danger of subordination to such extraneous considerations as political and economic utility, real or imagined. Moreover, if we took the particular criterion of neurological activity seriously, untenable consequences would follow. Should medical science advance to the stage where we could suspend brain activity during surgery in the way that we now can suspend independent heart activity, then during the operation the patient would not be human. Clearly, we are groping into the sheerest arbitrariness if we define humanity by one or another physiological activity. This is not to say, of course, that certain physiological activities are not *signs* that humanity is present.

If, however, we hold that human life begins at conception and that accordingly the right to life begins at conception, have we not fallen into the same trap of arbitrariness? I should think we had if we claimed that the ground or cause of the right to life is simply a particular genetic structure. The genetic structure, however, is a guarantee of the fact that, given the normal course of events, the unique individual product of conception will grow to possess the full array of human qualities. The genetic structure contains human potentiality. Were the unique genetic individual not allowed to develop it is undoubtedly true that the qualities it did not possess would not be destroyed. So it is true that by killing an infant we do not kill the Prime Minister that he might have become. However, we cherish the right to life of the infant as much for its unique potentiality for possessing human qualities as for what it presently possesses. Insofar as the ground of the right to life is thought to be in the actual possession of some characteristic or other the choice is arbitrary. By locating the ground in what is the unique potential of a human being (unique amongst all animals and unique in each person) we have a rational and consistent criterion, one which accords the right to life wherever a human being exists, that is, anytime from conception to death.

Surely, it takes an act of imagination to recognize that a microscopic organism is human and that is possesses any rights. When we begin to strip away the *signs* of humanity, however, and seek the source of these signs; when, for example, we realize that consciousness is only a sign of humanity, we may perhaps understand that it is the intangible potentiality made present by a unique human existence that is the foundation of the right to life. And unless we wish to make the right to life contingent upon a certain degree of the fulfilment of the potentially (what degree?) then we must affirm the right to life wherever the potentiality is to be found. Whatever human activity we might care to name as the reason for granting the right to life is to be found in potentiality in the unborn child.

It is perhaps not too bold to say that the great achievements of our culture are those institutions and customs which have collectively and severally served to develop human potential. If we choose not to respect what people can be then it is unlikely that we shall respect them for what they are and all human rights will be in jeopardy.

Footnotes

[1] (2) and (3) might be rejected, for example, by a pacifist.
[2] I use, for lack of an appropriate word, "condition" to apply both to an antecedent right and to an antecedent fact.
[3] Letter to the Editor, *New York Times*, March 9, 1967, p. 38, col. 6.
[4] The vagueness here is inevitable since I am lumping together theories which set different criteria for inclusion within the human race. One characteristic of the general pro-abortion position is that there appears to be no consensus on when human life begins.

Abortion and Pluralism

by Elmar J. Kremer

Elmar J. Kremer is Associate Professor of Philosophy, St. Michael's College, University of Toronto.

Opponents of laws against abortion[1] often cite the current disagreement about the right and wrong of abortion in defence of their position. I shall argue, on the contrary, that the existing state of disagreement favours anti-abortion legislation.

1. TWO ARGUMENTS FROM PLURALISM

One argument from pluralism was employed in an editorial in the Toronto *Globe and Mail* on March 11, 1968, against the anti-abortion law then current in Canada:

> This issue first concerns the right of any group of citizens to violate through the law the conscience of other citizens. For that is precisely what the present abortion laws do. The Criminal Code of Canada forces all Canadians—including Protestants, Jews, agnostics and others—to accept the birth of unwanted or deformed children regardless of the mother's health or the family's ability to care for children. . . .
>
> All of those offended by our laws respect the right of Roman Catholics to follow their consciences and reject abortion. But they have a right to expect Roman Catholics to let them follow theirs and accept abortion in reasonable, civilized conditions.

Aside from the appeal to religious prejudice, the editorial's main argument is that there ought not be a law which prohibits adults from obtaining abortions if they would derive significant advantages from abortion and their conscience tells them it is not wrong.

Now the fact that some adults would derive significant advantages from an act which their conscience tells them is not wrong, does not by itself prove that there ought not be legislation against the act. Indeed, most legislation would be ruled out by such an argument, including legislation against infanticide, killing the aged and not paying one's income taxes.

Furthermore, it has been claimed that the unborn child[2] is a human being with rights of his own. If this claim is correct, then the unborn child's right to have others refrain from killing him takes precedence over the right of adults to follow their conscience. In the absence of an adequate treatment of this claim about the unborn child, the fact that anti-abortion laws do not allow some people to follow their conscience is no reason for objecting to such laws.

Proponents of legalized abortion sometimes employ a second argument from pluralism in the effort to show that it is not necessary to deal with the evidence bearing on the humanity of the unborn. So long as there is disagreement in our society about the humanity of the unborn, they argue, the law ought not recognize the unborn child as a human being with rights of his own, and the question of abortion legislation ought to be decided on grounds other than the supposed right to life of the unborn child, such as the right of adults to follow their conscience. If this argument were correct, it would absolve the members of a pluralistic society of any obligation to examine the evidence for the humanity of the unborn before taking a position on abortion law.

To bring out what is wrong with the second argument from pluralism, let me compare it with a line of reasoning which might occur to an abortionist: It is not necessary for me to deal with the evidence for the humanity of this unborn child before I proceed to kill it; no doubt I ought to refrain from killing innocent human beings, but so long as there is disagreement in my society about whether an individual is a human being, I ought not base my decision about whether to kill it on its supposed humanity; rather I ought to make my decision on other grounds, such as the right of this woman who is asking for an abortion to follow her conscience, and the fact that if she cannot obtain an abortion she will be discriminated against as compared with other women who have been able to obtain abortions.

An abortionist who reasons thus overlooks the fact that his obligation to refrain from killing innocent human beings includes an obligation to make reasonably sure that an individual is not a human being before he kills it. Furthermore, his obligation to consider the evidence for the unborn child's humanity before killing it takes precedence over his obligation to allow other adults to act according to their conscience. For if he has evidence that the unborn child is a human being, then he has evidence that it has the same right to life as any other human being. Here I assume that human beings of all stages of development are equal in the sense that it is no easier to justify killing one than to justify killing another. This assumption will be defended in sections 3 and 4 below.

Returning now to abortion law, each person has the obligation to seek laws which will protect innocent human beings in his society from being killed by others, so far as it comes his way to make decisions about legislation, whether as a legislator or as a voter who elects legislators. This obligation also includes an obligation to make reasonably sure that the members of a group are not human beings before denying to them legal protection against being killed. Finally, our obligation to uphold legal protection for the life of the unborn child unless we are reasonably sure that the unborn child is not a human being, takes precedence over our obligation to allow other adults to act according to their conscience. Therefore, the fact of disagreement about the humanity of the unborn child in no way absolves us of our obligation to assess the evidence of his humanity before taking up a position on abortion law.

Sometimes the second argument from pluralism is developed with reference to groups of experts who are said to disagree about the humanity of the unborn. Thus Mr. Justice Blackmun of the United States Supreme Court, in *Roe v. Wade,* says,

> We need not resolve the difficult question of when human life begins. When those trained in the respective disciplines of medicine, philosophy and theology are unable to arrive at any consensus, the judiciary, at this point in the development of man's knowledge, is not in a position to speculate as to the answer.[3]

These references, however, do not strengthen the argument. The references to philosophy and theology are ludicrous. These professions have much to contribute to the abortion debate. But they can contribute nothing to those who, like Blackmun, wait around for a consensus. Indeed, philosophers have not even been able to agree on whether there exists an external, physical world. The case with medicine is different. This profession includes most abortionists, and is furthermore noted for its unwillingness to criticize its own members in public. On the other hand, medicine is traditionally dedicated to saving and healing human lives. One would expect the medical profession, therefore, to be torn by disagreement about whether abortion is the killing of a human being with rights of his own.

Several professions ought to be consulted in dealing with the question of the rights of the unborn. However, the question does not fall within the special competence of any learned profession. Rather it is a question which every thoughtful person ought to resolve for himself. The necessary first step toward such a resolution is to consider the evidence bearing on the humanity of the unborn child.

2. EVIDENCE BEARING ON THE HUMANITY OF THE UNBORN

Those who argue that the child conceived but not yet born is a human being emphasize the claim that the unborn child has *a human life*. Evidence for this claim can be marshalled in at least two ways, depending on how we interpret the phrase "a human life". If by a life we mean a history, a series of episodes—as in the titles of biographies, e.g. *The Life of Johnson*—then the specifically human life of an individual can be traced back continuously through childhood, infancy and prenatal existence to conception, and no further. At each stage from conception onward, the organism gives rise to the next stage by a process of self-nutrition and development. This process is the source of the continuity of bodily characteristics which is essential to the continued existence of *the same human being*. Nothing like this is found in the unfertilized ovum or the spermatazoon. Prior to conception, the ovum and the spermatazoon are, of course, alive, just as a blood cell, or an organ separated from its donor's body and being prepared for transplant, is alive. But they are not growing and developing through self-nutrition in the normal pattern of human life. Because each human being originates from the sex cells of his or her parents, we should say that life comes from life, not from non-life. But in the process of generation, life from life, there must be some point at which a new individual life begins. That point is conception.

"A human life" may also be taken to refer to a characteristic pattern of causal abilities. Here it is important to bear in mind that the abilities characteristic of human life do not spring into existence and disappear all at once, but rather unfold in a complex pattern during the person's lifetime. At a given stage, some abilities may be coming into play, others declining. The infant and the woman past menopause lack the capacity for sexual reproduction; the unborn child at five weeks gestation and the old man lack the power of taste. In this respect being a human being is quite unlike belonging to a relatively static natural kind, e.g., being a diamond.

To say that an individual has a human life at a given time is not to imply that it possesses every human ability at that time, but only that it possesses some human abilities and is at some stage in the characteristic human pattern of abilities coming into play and declining. Now when a human ovum is fertilized there comes into existence an organism capable of nourishing and developing itself by the production of further cells with a specifically human genetic structure. Therefore this organism has at least one specifically human ability. Further, because of that ability, it will, given time and normal circumstances, exhibit the full pattern of human abilities. Therefore the fertilized ovum is in the first stage of the pattern, and has a human life of its own. The earliest stages of the pattern involve the most rapid development. In the words of a standard reference work on developmental anatomy, "Almost all of the internal organs are well laid down at two months; henceforth, until the end of gestation, the chief changes undergone are those of growth and further specialization of the tissues."[4]

Both the above approaches lead to the conclusion that the unborn child is a human being in the sense of an individual living its own human life. From this we can conclude in turn that the unborn child is a person, in a fundamental sense explicated by Boethius's famous definition of *person* as *an individual substance of a rational nature*.[5] Saying that an individual has a rational nature does not imply that it is here and now able to reason, but only that it is of such a kind that it is natural for it to be or become capable of reasoning. Every human being is a person in this fundamental sense, and, so far as we know, no other animal is. Recall the experiments in which chimpanzee infants were reared together with human infants in a human environment.[6] The human infants developed the ability to communicate rationally with others while the chimpanzee infants did not, because human infants are persons while chimpanzees are not. Not that every human being inevitably becomes capable of rational activity. Such development may be forestalled not only by premature death, but also by abnormal conditions. But if a human being fails to develop this ability, a special explanation is called for. Not so with the chimpanzee or any other animal species.

So runs the basic argument for the humanity of the unborn child. I do not see how it can be denied that it makes it reasonable to think that the unborn child is a human being from conception onward.

Despite the evidence outlined above, it has been argued that the embryo or foetus simply is not a human being until it has passed some milestone after conception. The chief arguments of this type can be divided into three classes: attempts to show that the unborn child is not a human being until it has undergone some degree of maturation, attempts to show that the unborn child is a human being only after it is viable outside the womb, and attempts to show that the child is a human being only after it has been born.

Two main considerations have been advanced in defence of the view that the unborn child must undergo some degree of maturation before it is a human being. First, it is pointed out that the unborn child is *smaller* at the earlier stages than it is after some degree of maturation.[7] It may seem that the difference in size between the unborn child just before and just after a chosen stage of development is irrelevant to whether it is a human being, because the difference is very slight. However this objection can be defeated. Someone defending, e.g., a ten-week cut-off date may grant that if all unborn children of a given stage of gestation meet a presumed standard of size for being a human being, then most unborn children of a stage a few hours or days earlier also meet that standard. However, in defence of a ten-week cut-off time it may be said that prior to, say, twelve weeks of gestation, the typical unborn child is simply too small. The ten-week limit is then defended as being well on the safe side of the minimum size of a human being. As Edmund Burke said, despite the fact that no one can draw a stroke between night and day, the difference between the two is tolerably clear.

Nevertheless the appeal to size is a weak argument, especially in view of the evidence that every unborn child from conception on is living its own human life. There may be a limit of size below which an individual cannot have a human life of its own and thus cannot be a human being, just as there is a limit of size (namely, the size of a molecule of H_2O) below which something cannot be a quantity of water. However, the size of an individual, taken apart from its having or not having a human life of its own, does not determine whether it is a human being. Being a human being is not a matter of being so and so big. One who defends a cut-off line between conception and birth by appeal to size may be compared to the Indian prince in Hume's *First Inquiry* who on first hearing refused to believe the effects of frost. Such a difficulty is best cured by familiarity with the facts, in the present case the facts about the continuous development of human life from conception to adulthood.

Various cut-off dates between conception and birth have also been defended on the grounds that the organic structure of the individual is less developed at earlier stages. Thus Joseph F. Donceel has argued that the embryo is not a human person "during the first few weeks of pregnancy" on the basis of the view that "the human soul was infused into the body only when the latter began to show a human shape or outline and possessed the basic human organs. Before this time, the embryo is alive, but in the way in which a plant or an animal is alive".[8] Donceel uses the terminology of "hylomorphism", which is not germane to our discussion. Setting aside this terminology, it should be conceded that a human life is a physical, organic life which can be initiated only in an organism of a specifically human type. But this point does not rule out the presence of a human life prior to sufficient development to allow the ordinary, rough-grained distinctions among human organs. It is simply incorrect to say that there is no specifically human organic structure or vital activity present in the early stages of embryonic development. Even the zygote is an organism with functioning parts and vital activities specific to man, because of which it will exhibit the full range of characteristic human parts and activities given only time, nutrition and normal circumstances. At no time is the human embryo actually alive only in the way in which a plant or a brute animal is alive.

In fact there is no good reason to require that the unborn child pass any given stage or organic development in order to qualify as a human being. An organism at any stage of development between conception and the stage at which it begins to reason and to communicate rationally, can still be called a human being only in view of the development it will undergo, given time, nutrition and normal circumstances. Since the unborn child is from conception a living human organism, taking in nourishment and developing rapidly in the characteristically human pattern, it is just as reasonable to call it a human being at any one stage as it is at any other.

Donceel also thinks that the occurrence of identical twinning is an obstacle to those who say that conception initiates an individual human life:

> Identical twins derive from one ovum fertilized by one spermatozoon. This ovum splits into two at an early stage of pregnancy and gives rise to two human beings. In this case the defenders of immediate animation must admit that one person may be divided into two persons. This is a metaphysical impossibility.[9]

If this argument worked, it would show that the *conceptus* does not become a human being until a few days after fertilization. However the assertion, "In this case the defenders of immediate animation must admit that one person may be divided into two persons" is a *non-sequitur*. There are at least two alternatives consistent with the initiation of an individual human life at fertilization and with what we know about identical twinning: first, that at twinning a part of one person's body becomes another person, the original person continuing to exist (this is what would happen if human beings came to be cloned[10]); second, that at twinning the original person goes out of existence, the parts of its body becoming the twins.

Concerning the view that the unborn child is a human being only after it is capable of surviving outside the mother's womb, and the view that it is a human being only after birth, we can be more brief. Neither view is based on facts about the kind of life present in the unborn child. In each case it is urged that the unborn child is a human being only after it has achieved one or another kind of independence of the mother. However, from the fact that A is a distinct organism from B, it does not follow that A is independent of B. The fact that organism A depends, no matter how intimately, on organism B, is no reason to deny that A and B are really two organisms.

Further, each of these two views has special drawbacks of its own. The viability-outside-the-mother's-womb approach implies that whether an individual is a human being depends on the sort of medical equipment available and its employment for the individual's benefit. One might try to get around this difficulty by saying that the unborn child is a human being when it is viable outside the mother's womb given the full employment of ideally perfect medical technology. But then it would follow that the unborn child is a human being from conception onward. The view that the unborn child becomes a human being only at birth, on the other hand, assumes that the humanity of an individual is a matter of its location.

In summary, the arguments which have been presented to show that the unborn child is not a human being from conception onward fall far short of establishing that conclusion. The total evidence bearing on the humanity of the unborn child weighs heavily in favour of legal protection for his or her life.

3. PLURALISM ON HUMAN DEVELOPMENT AND THE RIGHT TO LIFE

I have so far operated on the assumption that human beings of all stages of development are equal in the sense that it is no easier to justify killing a human being at one stage than at another. It is now time to discuss that assumption. Some who deny that the unborn ought to be protected by law against being killed by others, do not, like those so far considered, deny that the unborn child is a human being. Rather they concede the humanity of the unborn child from conception, but argue that a human being does not have the right to life until it has passed some milestone after conception.

Clearly the mere fact of such disagreement does not justify the withdrawal of legal protection from the unborn. Otherwise, supposing that a number of people in our society were to claim, however arbitrarily, that the senile or the newborn or the members of any other minority do not have the right to life, we would be justified without further ado in withdrawing legal protection from that group. Therefore I shall examine directly the arguments which have been offered against the right to life of pre-natal humans who have not passed some milestone after conception.

The arguments of section 2 against the humanity of the unborn child dealt with size, development of organic structure, viability outside the womb and birth. Each can be recast as an argument that the unborn child has no right to life until it has passed the given milestone, even though it is conceded to be a human being from conception on.

Of the four arguments which then face us, the first can be dismissed quickly. The appeal to size is no more compelling here than it was in the earlier context. The fact the the unborn child, conceded to have a human life of its own from conception onward, has not attained a given size, does not seem to have any bearing on its right to life.

The arguments for viability outside the womb and actual birth as criteria for the right to life are based on the idea that the child has the right to life only after he has become independent of his mother. Of the two sorts of independence, I shall here consider only viability outside the womb. If viability outside the womb is not a prerequisite of the right to life, *a fortiori* actual birth is not a prerequisite. According to the argument we are considering, it is conceded that the mother and the unborn child are two distinct human beings from conception onward. Nevertheless, it is contended, until the child has become independent of the mother by becoming viable outside her womb, it does not have the right to life.

Against this argument it can be pointed out that the child continues to be dependent on adults after it is born. It may be said that the case is different before viability outside the womb because then the child depends uniquely on the mother, whereas after viability other adults can provide the necessary support. Nevertheless, unique dependence on one adult does not necessarily end at viability or even at birth, and does not preclude a child's having the right to life. For example, a young child living alone with his mother in an isolated place would depend uniquely on her and yet would have the right to have others, including his mother, refrain from killing him. Indeed it can be argued that complete dependence of one human being on another, far from removing the obligation of the stronger to refrain from killing the weaker, in fact, adds or increases the obligation of the stronger to protect the weaker.

There remains the appeal to the development of organic structure. The most plausible argument of this type is that the unborn child must have a functioning brain in order to have the right to life. For the onset of the "higher" mental processes of thinking and reasoning, as well as the occurrence of feelings and sensations, depends on the brain. But it is the fact that every human being is an individual of a rational nature, and hence a person in the fundamental sense explicated by Boethius, which creates the initial presumption that any human being has the right to life. It is not necessary that an individual have a brain in order to be a person in this fundamental sense. But the development of an individual as a person requires that he develop a functioning brain.

One weakness of this argument is the vagueness of the phrase "a functioning brain". The brain is sufficiently developed to co-ordinate the muscular movements of the unborn child prior to the eighth week after conception. However the brain is not sufficiently developed to allow the onset of conceptual activity for some time after birth. If the development of the brain at any pre-natal stage is sufficient to allow the right to life, it would seem that its development at any earlier stage would also be sufficient, including the determination of the brain in the structure of the one-cell zygote. The various stages are but so many steps toward full development. On the other hand, if the full development of the brain needed for the onset of reasoning is required, then the infant will lack the right to life for some time after its birth.

There is a fifth argument against the right to life of pre-natal human beings who have not passed some milestone after conception. According to this fifth argument, a pre-natal human being has the right to life only after it has attained to a certain degree of *value* to which it attains only after it has passed the given milestone. A modified version of this argument attributes some sort of right to life to human beings at every stage of their development but attributes a *greater* right to life to those who more nearly approximate the standard stage of development, on the grounds that they have a *greater value*. Once passed the milestone which defines the standard stage of development, all human beings are attributed by this argument *full* value and the *full* right to life.

Recent statements of the United Church of Canada indicate that it has adopted a modified version of the fifth argument. Thus the United Church's Joint Committee on Abortion has said,

> The foetus is considered to have intrinsic worth but not equality

of value with actualized persons.... As the foetus approaches term, increasingly grave reasons are morally required for abortion. Only in the most extreme emergencies would we consider that a possibly viable foetus could be aborted and a living infant, even very premature, has all the rights society bestows on any living citizen.

The position is complicated, however, by the ambiguous phrase "potentially a human being". The same committee quotes with approval from an early statement,

> Since an embryo develops from very simple beginnings to the complex life of a child, we think of it as gaining value as the days and months of pregnancy continue.... We regard the foetus, especially during the first seven months as potentially a human being though not yet one.[11]

The phrase "potentially a human being" is ambiguous. It may mean "what is not a human being but can become or is in process of becoming a human being". On this interpretation the United Church's position seems to be that the foetus is a human being only after the seventh month. From the seventh month to birth it would seem to have some right to life based on its value as a human being, but, not having attained *full* value (that, apparently, comes only with birth), it would not have the *same* right to life as those already born. Prior to the seventh month reasons of unspecified gravity would be required to justify killing it, because of its status as a "potential human being".

"Potentially a human being" is also sometimes used to mean "an immature human being". On this interpretation the United Church's position seems to be that the unborn child is a human being from conception onward, but may be killed for lesser reasons at earlier stages because it is less valuable, full value, once again, being attained only at birth. For simplicity's sake I shall consider only the second interpretation. Whether it is the correct interpretation of the United Church's position can be left to others to decide.

That there are differences of value among human beings cannot be disputed. But it is not at all clear that these differences qualify the right to life. Further, if we are going to say that a human being's right to life depends on his or her value, why should we single out one of the many types of value? Maturity is a sort of excellence, and therefore a more mature human being is, in one way, more valuable that a less mature human being. But why should the excellence of maturity be thought more relevant to the right to life than other sorts of excellence, e.g., intelligence or moral innocence? Last year a doctor with major responsibility for a hospital clinic at which many abortions are performed, said to me that when he considered the sort of women who came to his clinic for abortions, he sometimes thought it would be better, if it were medically and legally possible, to kill the mother and save the child. Taken literally, his suggestion would be outrageous, but no more so than the suggestion that the unborn child may be killed for the benefit of the mother, on the grounds that the unborn child, being less mature than the mother, is less valuable.

I have so far argued that the existing pluralism about the humanity and the right to life of the unborn child provides no reason for withdrawing the protection of the law. I have also argued that the total existing evidence about the humanity and right to life of the unborn child weighs heavily in favour of legal protection for his or her life.

These arguments will draw from some quarters the retort: It's fine for someone as sure of his position as you seem to be, to propose laws against abortion. But what about those who are equally sure that you are wrong and those who are unsure of their position?

There are some who assert that it is *beyond doubt* that the unborn child is not a human being or does not have the right to life prior to passing some milestone after conception, but their number is small. To maintain their position they must claim either that there just isn't any significant evidence of the humanity and right to life of the unborn, or that what evidence there is is definitely and unquestionably outweighed by evidence on the other side. Neither claims seem to me at all credible.

It is quite a different matter to remain somewhat uncertain as to the finally correct solution while granting that there is significant evidence in favour of the humanity and right to life of the unborn. Someone in this position ought to consider the question of the burden of proof.

There are at least two ways in which the burden of proof might be distributed in the debate about the legal protection of the unborn: (a) The burden of proof might fall primarily on those who would defend the unborn. That is, one ought to favour legal protection of the unborn only if it is for him beyond all reasonable doubt that the unborn child is a human being with the right to life. (b) The burden of proof might fall primarily on those who would withdraw the legal protection of the unborn. That is, if one has significant evidence that the unborn child is a human being with the right to life, he ought to support legal protection of the unborn until and unless it is demonstrated to him that the unborn child is not a human being with the right to life.

Clearly (b) is the correct assignment. Even the likelihood that a given legal arrangement will permit many innocent persons to be killed by others implies that we ought to reject that legal arrangement.

4. PLURALISM ON THE RIGHT TO LIFE OF INFANTS

Our discussion of the implications of pluralism for abortion law would be incomplete if we overlooked the growing disagreement in our society about the right to life of infants. It is becoming a commonplace for genetecists to urge that the right to life of the newborn not be recognized by law for some time after birth so as to allow for the elimination of any "defective" babies who happen to get born. As Dr. Hubert Soltan says in his contribution to this volume, "'Infanticide' and its more emotionally neutral synonyms are no longer unmentionable words in the vocabulary of the 'new' Eugenics."[12] Among philosophers, too, it appears that essays in defence of infanticide may become something of a fad. It is likely that the legislators who appealed to pluralism to justify withdrawal of legal protection from the unborn will soon have to ask themselves whether pluralism also justifies withdrawing legal protection from the newborn.

Those who argue against the right to life of the infant are committed to the view that an actually living human being must meet some further condition before he or she has the basic right to life. Typically the attempt is made to specify his further condition in terms of "consciousness" or "self-consciousness". Michael Tooley, for example, asserts that an individual has the right to life only if

> it is the case, or was at some time in the past, that the individual is capable of envisaging a future for itself and of having desires about that future, is capable of possessing the concept of a continuing subject of experiences and other mental states, is itself such an entity, and possesses self-consciousness, or at least the capacity for self-consciousness.[13]

Similarly, S.I. Benn says that in order to have any rights at all, *a fortiori* in order to have the right to life, it is necessary that one have the capacity to "be aware of oneself as the subject of enterprises and projects that could be forwarded by choosing to exercise one's rights", a condition which he also describes as a "level of self-consciousness".[14]

Both Tooley and Benn argue as follows against the right to life of the infant: There is no morally (or legally) relevant difference between an unborn child and an infant; therefore, if the infant has the right to life so also does the unborn, and the "liberal" position on abortion must be abandoned; but the liberal position is correct; therefore, the infant does not have the right to life.[15] It would be interesting to know how many people are sufficiently dedicated to a permissive position on abortion to accept infanticide on the grounds that it is implied by that permissive position.

Neither Tooley nor Benn estimates the age at which a human being would finally have the right to life. Tooley ventures that it is not important to estimate this age: "There is no serious need to know the exact point at which a human infant acquires a right to life. For in the vast majority of cases in which infanticide is desirable, its desirability will be apparent within a short time after birth."[16] Why he thinks adults would not find it desirable to do away with infants some time after birth, or how his restriction on the right to life would be expressed in law, he does not say. It is worth noting, too, that the arguments of Tooley and Benn would permanently deny the right to life to human beings presumed too mentally defective ever to be capable of employing concepts.

Both Tooley and Benn adopt the view, held by a number of seventeenth century philosophers, including Descartes and Locke, that the identity of a subject of human thinking is not the identity of a human organism. Since a person is an individual for whom it is natural to be a subject of thinking at some stage of its existence, this view implies that *being the same person as x* is not strictly equivalent to *being the same human organism as x*.

Now the identity of a human person is treated in law as equivalent to the identity of a human organism, and it is difficult to imagine how it could be otherwise. Imagine, for example, an individual disclaiming legal responsibility for a past act carried out by his body on the grounds that he had since undergone a change of personality, or, conversely, claiming legal title to the property of a deceased millionaire on the grounds that he was the millionaire "reincarnate". Such claims would be legally rejected because the law operates on the assumption that y is the same human person as x if and only if y is the same human organism as x.

No doubt Tooley and Benn would want this legal equivalence restricted to the identity of a human organism after it has matured to the point where its behaviour (including speech) reflects the employment of concepts. But neither gives a cogent reason for thus restricting the identity of a person. Since the conceptual activity of a human being is frequently interrupted, e.g. by sound sleep, without the human being ceasing to be the same person, why should the fact that an infant has not yet engaged in thinking disqualify him as a person? The onset of thinking is not the beginning of a new life wholly distinct from the life of the infant. Rather it is a normal and integral part of the maturational process which begins at fertilization.

The considerations which have been advanced against the humanity and right to life of the unborn apply equally to the newborn. Thus, the infant is much smaller than the adult, fully actualized human being. The organic development of the infant is also incomplete, and the infant is totally dependent on adults. On the other hand, what can be said in favour of the unborn child can also be said in favour of the infant, namely, that he has a human life of his own and is, therefore, a living individual of a rational nature, i.e. a person.

The fact that some people do not recognize the right to life of the infant also has this implication with regard to pluralism: If anti-abortion laws are unacceptable because they "violate" the conscience of some adults, then anti-infanticide laws are unacceptable for the same reason. On the other hand, if anti-infanticide laws are a requirement of justice, so also are anti-abortion laws.

5. ARE ANTI-ABORTION LAWS ENFORCEABLE?

There remains a popular argument from pluralism against anti-abortion laws which can be put as follows: In a society as divided over abortion law as ours, an anti-abortion law is unenforceable; ideally, perhaps, the unborn child ought to be protected; however, it is impossible in a pluralistic society to give effective legal protection to the unborn.

Contrary to this argument, anti-abortion laws do succeed in preventing abortions. No one knows how many illegal abortions are carried out in Canada or in any other country. At best we have educated guesses.[17] However there is no reason to think that withdrawal of legal protection from the unborn would encourage women to refrain from abortion who would have obtained illegal abortions under a restrictive law. On the other hand, the loosening of the law against abortion in Canada in 1969 has lent to abortion a respectability it did not previously enjoy in this country. Further, abortion is viewed increasingly by medical and social agencies as an attractive, quick and easy way of avoiding social problems. For example, since 1969 some Children's Aid Societies have been much less hesitant to arrange abortions for girls who become pregnant while under their care. Again, some doctors now routinely suggest abortion as a possible course of action when confirming to a patient that she is pregnant, especially if she is judged by the doctor to be someone who would be better off not having a baby. Dr. Carol Ann Cowell, a Toronto gynaecologist who regularly aborts teenagers, has made it clear that in her view, any unmarried teenager who is pregnant should be counselled to have an abortion.[18]

Thus, whatever may be the case with illegal abortions, it is clear that the 1969 loosening of the law against abortion has cost the lives of many unborn children who would not have been killed under more protective legislation. It would be naive not to expect further withdrawal of legal protection to cost the lives of a number who would not be killed under the continuation of even the present, modest legal protection. If all legal restrictions were removed, an increasing number of doctors, counsellors, and social agencies would be found encouraging abortions.

Now a policeman who, by his presence on the beat, prevents people from attempting to break the law, just as truly enforces the law as one who arrests a lawbreaker after the crime has been committed. In one sense, then, anti-abortion laws are clearly enforceable in a pluralistic society. They help prevent the killing of unborn children, even though their success, like that of many other laws, is less than one would desire. On the other hand, to abandon the task of defending the innocent from being killed by others would undermine respect not only for the legislators but for the entire system of legislation.

It is difficult to arrest and convict those who break anti-abortion laws. But the record of even this second kind of enforcement is not entirely discouraging. For five years prior to 1969, convictions in Canada for abortion or attempted abortion were: in 1963, 33; in 1964, 32; in 1965, 43; in 1966, 40; and in 1967, 54.[19]

It is worth emphasizing, however, that the most important type of enforcement of a law is the prevention of its violation. A law which is ideally enforced in the first sense never needs to be enforced in the second sense, because it is never violated. Well-publicized amendments to the Criminal Code and the Bill of Rights specifying that the child conceived but not yet born is a person with legal rights, together with the relocation of abortion law under the homicide section of the Code, might improve the enforcement of the law against abortion.[20]

On the other hand, any decrease of legal protection is likely to increase the toll of unborn children's lives. We must not allow this fact to become obscured by the intricacies of the abortion debate. Otherwise we may do no more than hide injustice by raising a learned dust.

Footnotes

[1] I shall use "abortion" throughout as an abbreviation for "induced abortion".

[2] "Unborn child" may strike some as a question-begging term. I have chosen it over the most likely alternative, "foetus", because "foetus" refers only to a roughly demarcated stage of life before birth, in the case of human life, from about eight weeks of gestation to birth. Also the Canadian Criminal Code speaks of the "child before its birth", but does not use "foetus ". The danger of question begging is slight once we have been alerted to it.

[3] Quoted by Professor Slayton on p. 173 of this volume.

[4] Leslie B. Arey, *Developmental Anatomy,* 7th edition, Philadelphia, W.B. Saunders Co., 1965, p. 100.

[5] Boethius, *Contra Eutychen et Nestorium,* III, Loeb Classical Library, p. 84.

[6] R. M. Yerkes, *Chimpanzees: A Laboratory Colony,* New Haven, Yale University Press, 1943; W.N. Kellogg and L.A. Kellogg, *The Ape and the Child,* New York, Wittlesly House, 1933.

[7] For example, Roy Lucas, executive director of the California Population Law Center, San Francisco, argued on the television show "Firing Line": "When you get up to, what is it, four weeks, the foetus is scarcely recognizable—5 mm. long, one-fifth of an inch. It has a tail. Would you call it a human being?" Transcript of the Firing Line Program taped at KCET in Los Angeles on July 25, 1972 and originally telecast on CBS on November 5, 1972. Columbia, S.C., Southern Educational Communication Association, 1972, p. 10.

[8] Joseph F. Donceel, "A Liberal Catholic's View", in Robert E. Hall (ed.) *Abortion in a Changing World,* Vol. 1, New York, Columbia University Press, 1970, pp. 39-45. See also Donceel's "Immediate Animation and Delayed Hominization", *Theological Studies,* 31(1970), 76-105.

[9] Donceel, *op. cit.* p. 43.

[10] Cloning refers to the asexual production of progeny in which the cell of a developed organism is caused to develop into an "identical twin" of the donor organism.

[11] *Abortion, A Study,* published jointly by the Board of Evangelism and Social Services and the Board of Women of the Division of Congregational Life and Work of the United Church of Canada, joint committee appointed in October, 1970, no publication date given, pp. 19-20.

[12] p. 51 of this volume.

[13] Michael Tooley, "A Defense of Abortion and Infanticide", in Joel Feinberg (ed.) *The Problem of Abortion,* Belmont, California, Wadsworth Publishing Co., p. 72.

[14] S.I. Benn, "Abortion, Infanticide and Respect for Persons", in Feinberg, *op. cit.* p. 99.

[15] Tooley, *op. cit.* p. 52; Benn, *op. cit.* pp. 94-95.

[16] Tooley, *op. cit.* p. 91.

[17] It should be noted that the evidence, on balance, does not support the idea that removal of legal protection from the unborn would decrease, or strengthening of legal protection for the unborn would increase, the number of "back alley" abortions in Canada. See, e.g., Fred E. Mecklenburg, "The Indications for Induced Abortion", in *Abortion and Social Justice,* edited by T.W. Hilgers and D.J. Horan, New York, Sheed & Ward, 1972, especially pp. 50-51.

[18] *The Medical Post,* Oct. 30, 1973, p. 19.
[19] Dominion Bureau of Statistics Daily, May 8, 1970, p. 6.
[20] An example is provided by the Quebec Civil Code, which, since January, 1972, has contained the following articles:

(18) Every human being possesses juridical personality. Whether citizen or alien he has the full enjoyment of civil rights, except as otherwise expressly provided by law.

(338) The persons to whom curators are given are:
(1) emancipated minors, (2) interdicted persons, (3) children conceived but not yet born.

Abortion and the Unwanted Child

by Ian Gentles

Ian Gentles is Associate Professor of History and Dean of Students, Glendon College, York University.

1. THE EXTENSION OF PROTECTION FOR THE IMMATURE

In ancient times abortion was practised widely and met with little disapproval. With infanticide, it constituted a primary act of self-defence of parents against the effects of famine, disease and other calamities of overpopulation. The killing of one's offspring was an elemental response to the pain and strain of life in an era when mankind, still dominated by nature, teetered at every moment on the brink of hunger and death. The circumstances that drove people to abortion and infanticide frequently drove them to kill the ill, the aged and the handicapped as well. Nevertheless, from about the fourth century A.D. there was a gradual shift in the prevailing attitude towards the weak and dependent members of society. Partly for economic, partly for religious and philosophical reasons, western civilization arrived at the view that the weak and dependent deserved special care and protection. Children obviously benefited from this ideological shift, and measures such as abortion, infanticide and abandonment became unacceptable. Not only theologians but the secular philosophers of the Enlightment too, urged respect for all human life—even that of the foetus in the womb. [1] In the twentieth century this consensus has been expressed in various United Nations declarations. The preamble to the Declaration of the Rights of the Child, for example, states "... the child, by reason of his physical and mental immaturity, needs special safeguards and care, including appropriate legal protection, before as well as after birth..."[2]

Paradoxically, it was the Industrial Revolution that first provided the conditions under which this philosophy of respect for life could flourish. In the short run the Industrial Revolution led to appalling living conditions and a probable drop in the standard of living of the masses, as well as a sharp increase in the repression, exploitation and alienation that they were compelled to endure. But it also created an insatiable demand for human labour. Children became an economic asset once they could be sent to work in the new mines, mills and factories. By multiplying percapita wealth many times the Industrial Revolution also furnished the means to implement the welfare state, with its assumption that all people—not just the intelligent and the strong—have the right to live their lives in dignity and comfort.

2. THE UNWANTED CHILD ARGUMENT FOR ABORTION: DEFORMED CHILDREN

Only during the past decade or so has the idea that unborn children merit special protection been called seriously into question. The argument of privatism is the one most frequently used to justify the removal of society's protection from the unborn child. Every person, we are told, has an absolute moral right to do whatever he or she wishes with his or her own body. The second most frequently used argument is that no child should be brought into the world unless he is wanted by his parents. It is to the second argument that this paper is addressed. It runs as follows: Every child should be a wanted child. A child is better off not to be brought into the world than to face neglect, hostility and abuse from parents who never wanted him in the first place. At the very least, abortion on demand will reduce the terrible toll of injury and death resulting from the ever-increasing rate of child abuse. Finally, a woman who knows that her baby has a high chance of being deformed should surely not be forced to bear it.

Let us deal with the last point first. Many people believe that it is the height of cruelty to expect a woman to go through with a pregnancy if she knows that her child will be born with congenital defects. Now that amniocentesis can be used to determine foetal deformity, how can a reasonable person oppose the use of abortion to avoid the misery that ensues when a deformed baby is brought into the world? What is rarely acknowledged is that amniocentesis is not 100 per cent effective. Normal children have been aborted on the basis of test results, and normal babies have been born to parents who ignored the advice to have an abortion when amniocentesis had revealed the child to be deformed. [3] It is worth keeping in mind that it is not the deformed themselves, or even their relatives, who advocate abortion to prevent more deformed children from being brought into the world. Indeed, the impression that only those born perfect can find happiness is an erroneous one, for most deformed people, despite their handicaps, are quite happy to be alive. According to a report presented by Dr. Paul Cameron and Dr. D. Van Hoeck to the American Psychological Association, handicapped, crippled and malformed people enjoy life as much as normal people. Although the malformed judged their lives more difficult, there was no difference between them and normal people in their degree of life satisfaction, outlook on what lies immediately ahead or vulnerability to frustrations. Unexpectedly, it was also found that a higher proportion of normal people had contemplated suicide.[4]

The real problem lies not with the deformed but with the rest of us. We find it distasteful to listen to those who cannot talk properly, or to look at spastics or limbless people. They offend us and we wish they did not exist. The demand for abortion on genetic grounds stems largely from a desire on the part of the normal to avoid emotional discomfort.

3. A SWEDISH STUDY OF UNWANTEDNESS

The proponents of abortion as the solution to the problem of unwanted children often cite a Swedish study which purports to show that children whose mothers did not want to bear them, suffer definite handicaps in life.[5] It is said that children whose mothers applied for and were denied abortions have a greater tendency to anti-social and criminal behaviour, drunken misconduct, dependence on public assistance, educational subnormality, early marriage and exemption from military service. The obvious conclusion, according to many commentators on the study, is that women who do not want to bear their babies should be encouraged to abort them. Free abortion alone will prevent the repetition of the tragedies that occur when children are born to parents who have rejected them in advance.

A critical examination of the evidence does not support the conclusions that are usually drawn from it. In the first place, the children who were subject of the study were born between 1939 and 1942. Over the subsequent thirty to thirty-five years there has been a vast improvement in the child welfare legislation of most western countries. Thirty-five years ago a baby rejected by his parents usually ended up in an orphanage or foster home; now he is adopted without any difficulty. Today there is much more generous financial assistance for mothers who need it. The number of daycare centres increases every year, and there is also a wide range of social services available. Moreover, society's attitude to illegitimacy is much different today from what it was thirty-five years ago. No longer is it a hideous disgrace to bear or raise an illegitimate child.[6] These trends hold for Canada as much as they do for Sweden. Indeed, the province of Ontario rightly boasts a body of child welfare legislation that is among the most advanced in the world.

Even if these changes in social conditions had not occurred over the past thirty-five years, there are several other reasons why the conclusions drawn by abortion advocates from the Swedish study do not stand up. The authors did not discover any statistically significant differences between the unwanted children and the control children in regard to criminal behaviour, drunken misconduct, educational subnormality, attendance at university, the fitness of the boys for military service, and marriage before the age of twenty-one. The areas in which significant differences were found included psychiatric consultation and hospitalization, juvenile delinquency, and receipt of public assistance between the ages of 16 and 21. However, these statistically significant differences are at least partly attributable to differences in social status. Eleven (9.2 per cent) more of the "unwanted" children were in the lowest social group. It is quite possible that their 10 per cent greater frequency of juvenile delinquency and their 11.7 per cent greater frequency of reliance on public assistance were functions of their lower social status rather than their unwantedness. The most striking of the authors' findings is that almost half (48.3 per cent) of the 120 unwanted children did not suffer from any ascertainable disadvantages at all. In the control group of children who were wanted by their parents, the percentage was — 68.3 — a difference of 20 per cent. It is questionable to argue that the "unwanted" children should have been aborted on the basis of a 20 per cent difference, which may have had a good deal to do with their lower social status, and with the fact that they were born before most of today's progressive child welfare legislation was enacted.

The chimerical effects of pre-natal unwantedness upon a child after he is born are demonstrated in a recent study carried out in Czechoslavkia. The families of 201 children whose mothers were denied abortions were scrutinized several years later. It is important to note that the Czechoslovakian study was more scientifically rigorous than the Swedish one — the purpose of the study for example was carefully concealed from the women who participated in it. What emerged was that "average normal conditions for the development of the child... existed in the great majority of the families". The researchers also found that" ... the care of these unwanted children as far as feeding, general health and actual state of health[was] very good; they practically [did] not differ from the siblings and other average children''.[7]

To argue that a child would be better off never born at all than born unwanted is to claim the right to make judgments about who is to be allowed the gift of life. It is also to accept the argument of despair, to turn one's back on the simple truth that where there is life there is hope. The right to life and the hope that accompanies it is higher than the right to be wanted. The right to be wanted is in any case an elusive concept, and as we shall see, impossible of prediction.

4. PARENTAL ATTITUDES, PRE-NATAL AND POST-NATAL

A woman's rejection of her pregnancy is almost never a constantly held attitude. Every obstetrician knows numberless women who reacted to the news of their pregnancy with feelings of resentment, frustration and depression. It is normal for these feelings to dissipate after the third month of pregnancy, and to be replaced by strong, genuine, positive feelings of acceptance as the pregnancy advances and foetal movements appear.[8] The evidence of obstetricians is strengthened by a study carried out in Denmark among 180 women whose applications for abortion were refused. Very few resorted to illegal abortion, and about 80 per cent reported that they were satisfied after having given birth.[9]

On the other hand, there are many parents who carefully plan and look forward to having their baby only to find it a disappointment when it arrives. Disappointment can turn into resentment, and occasionally into murderous hatred. Child care workers report that many babies become unwanted after they have reached the age of one year, *i.e.*, after they become mobile, begin asserting their own personality and become more demanding. It is at this stage that many parents discover they do not have the emotional resources to cope with a demanding child. They have not had enough mothering when *they* were young to give them the strength to be loving now. In short, their parental imcompetence is revealed. This revelation can be a very dangerous one for the baby. Babies can also become unwanted because they turn out to be a nuisance, interrupt careers and education, lower their parent's standard of living, and in general, cramp their life style.[10]

One of the puzzling facts about unwantedness is that while knowledge of birth control has been more widely disseminated and abortion has become more easily available in recent years, the frequency of child abuse has increased at an accelerating rate. In the five years from 1968 to 1972 the number of reported cases of alleged physical ill-treatment of children almost doubled in Ontario—rising from 267 to 491.[11] The frequency of ill-treatment will not be reduced by a freer abortion policy, because most battered children were not unwanted by their parents.

The paradox that most battered children were wanted children is dramatically illustrated by information that has recently come to light about the battered child and his parents. After studying 764 cases of child battering, Dr. E.F. Lenoski of the University of South California reports that 90 per cent of the children's parents planned and actively wanted the children they later abused. The parents' statements are supported by further objective measurement of their feelings.

Child naming.

In the control group of non-battering parents the child was named after his mother or father four percent of the time. Twenty-four per cent of the battered children were named after their mother or father.

Maternity clothes.

The mothers who battered their children began wearing maternity dress an average of 57 days earlier than the mothers in the control group.[12] The inference is plain: one cannot predict that a child who is unwanted before birth is in greater danger of being abused than a wanted child. If anything, it is the wanted child who stands a greater chance of being mistreated.

In summary, to use medical jargon, "post-partum parental attitudes cannot be predicted in the pre-partum interval".[13] Abortion to prevent unwantedness makes no sense. Logically far more cogent would be an argument for infanticide on demand to benefit those children who find themselves unwanted after they are born. Are proponents of abortion now ready to accept the inhumane and retrogressive "logic" of infanticide?

5. OVERPOPULATION AND TECHNOLOGY

The final observation to be made about the notion of unwantedness is that in Canada today *there is no such thing as an unwanted newborn child*. For several years there have been many more qualified adoptive parents than there have been babies to adopt. This situation has not arisen merely because the supply of babies has dried up. In Ontario the number of adoptions rose steadily until 1970, and only in 1971 did they begin to decline.[14] Changing social attitudes in the past fifteen years have meant a sharp rise in the number of people desiring to adopt. Waiting lists of adoptive parents are so long that some Children's Aid Societies in Ontario are no longer accepting applications.

Although there are at present more than enough qualified, loving parents for every "unwanted" baby, the current hysteria over population growth has convinced many people that children are a burden and a nuisance to society. The institutions that shape opinion have decided that to be childless is to be public spirited, while to have more than one or two children is selfish. The chief symptom of this population hysteria is misanthropy, and its effect is to make more pregnancies unwanted and more women ready to seek abortions.

The hysteria is unnecessary, since in North America population growth began levelling off more than fifteen years ago. Canada's birth rate dropped from a high of 28.2 per thousand in 1957 to 15.7 per thousand by 1972. The same trend is apparent in the United States where in 1972 the birth rate fell below the 2.1 per family needed to replace the existing population.[15]

Table One[16]
Canada's Population 1951-1971

Year	Population	Percentage increase since 1951
1951	14,009,000	—
1961	18,238,000	30.2
1971	21,569,000	54.0

Table Two[17]
Canada's Energy Demands 1950—1980

Year	Trillions of BTUs	Percentage increase since 1950
1950	2,560	—
1960	3,750	46.5
1970	6,360	148.4
1980 (projected)	10,300	302.3

The key to the current ecological crisis is not population but technology. Technological growth, energy and resource comsumption, and pollution race ahead unchecked, while population rises at an orderly rate.

Between 1951 and 1971 our population grew by about one half, while in a similar period (1950 to 1970) our energy consumption rose two and a half times. From a global perspective it is the countries with the greatest populations that consume the least energy and contribute the least pollution. The third-world countries of Asia, Africa and Latin America consume between 8 and 28 times less energy per capita than do Canada and the United States.[18]

To call for population control instead of technology control is to love machines more than people. A better way of showing concern for the environment would be to curb the technological gorgon and to reduce our per-capita energy consumption. Reducing population without attacking technology will accomplish little towards preserving the environment. Repeated assertions that bearing children is anti-social will bring more women to reject their pregnancies and seek abortions.

6. ALTERNATIVES TO ABORTION

The notion that unwantedness before birth is a fate worse than death has been shown to be a mythical one. Can anything be done to reduce the pressure for abortion on the mistaken grounds that the child will be unwanted? Many things can be done. First of all, it should be the responsibility of those who counsel women considering abortion to let them know that there are in Canada more than enough capable, loving parents to look after every "unwanted" child who is born. Since it is often other people—men in particular—who convince women to have abortions, an effort should be made to alter social attitudes. At present, for example, it is considered a far worse disgrace for a married couple to give away their child for adoption than to have him aborted.[19] Instead of acquiescing in the taboo against married people giving away their children, counsellors and social workers should combat it vigorously.

As a matter of public policy there should also be greater stress on the importance of active involvement by fathers in the family unit. Since it is men who frequently reject their unborn children, more training in fatherhood and a deliberate encouragement of paternal behaviour could alleviate the problem. We also need to find new ways of fostering motherly behaviour. Recently it has been shown that whether the mother wanted her pregnancy is of far less significance than the relationship that is established between her and her child during the first three days after delivery. It is now known that lengthy contact between mother and child during the first three days greatly fosters the development of good interaction between them. Affectional bonding is evidently enhanced by nothing more than the exposure of the mother to her child for one hour in the first three hours after birth, and for five extra hours each afternoon of the three days following delivery. "The standardization of this early exposure as routine policy for hospitals may have profound mental health-fostering effects and make the concept of unwantedness of pregnancy more irrelevant than it has already been shown to be."[20]

These are only a few of the possible alternatives to abortion for unwanted children. Serious thinking and research by those who are interested will undoubtedly produce many other feasible alternatives. The view that we must have abortion on demand to take care of the unwanted is only another symptom of a violent, alienated, uncaring society. The certainty of many people that the unwanted child would be better off dead is a disturbing indication of what Eric Fromm characterizes as the necrophilic behaviour of our civilization. The love of death, the desire to turn the animate into the inanimate, the sadistic drive to control and turn to stone everything that is living and free, is a chief characteristic of the oppressor consciousness.[21] According to this consciousness the human being is nothing more than a commodity to be disposed of when it interferes with the convenience or happiness of another human being who has power over it. Free abortion implies a callousness to human life that cannot but spread to other areas and lead to demands for "infanticide on demand", and death for the senile, the infirm and other useless and unwanted members of society. The mounting toll of abortions is but another instance of what Marshall McLuhan calls "the mechanization of death".

Footnotes

[1] Alfred Kadushin, *Child Welfare Services,* Macmillan, New York, 1967, pp. 31 ff.
[2] *Yearbook of the United Nations, 1959,* New York, 1960, p. 198.
[3] Thomas W. Hilgers, *Induced Abortion: A Documented Report,* 2nd. ed., Owatonna, Minnesota, 1973, p. 22.
[4] *Globe and Mail,* 7 September 1971, p. 8.
[5] Hans Forssman and Inga Thuwe, "One Hundred and Twenty Children Born After Application for Therapeutic Abortion Refused", *Acta Psychiatrica Scandinavia,* vol. 42 (1966), pp. 71-88.
[6] The increasing social acceptability of illegitimacy is mirrored in the rising numbers of unwed mothers who keep their children. From 1968 to 1972 the number of unwed mothers receiving family benefits in Ontario rose from 3,891 to 9,543. (Information supplied by the Ontario Department of Community and Social Services, Family Benefits Division.)

⁷ Vratislav Schuller and Eva Stupková, "The Unwanted Child in the Family", *The International Mental Health Research Newsletter,* vol. xiv, no. 3 (Fall, 1972), pp. 7, 8.
⁸ N. Eastman and L. Hellman, *William's Obstetrics,* 13th ed., New York, 1966, pp. 345-6.
⁹ Henrik Hoffmeyer, "Medical Aspects of the Danish Legislation on Abortion", in *Abortion and the Law,* David T. Smith (ed.), Cleveland, 1967, p. 201.
¹⁰ I am indebted to Veronica Fagan of the Catholic Children's Aid Society, Toronto, for the information on which this paragraph is based, and for many other valuable suggestions concerning this paper.
¹¹ Ontario Ministry of Community and Social Services, Child Welfare Branch, Year-End Survey (1973), p.4.
¹² I am indebted to Dr. Lenoski for making available this information from his forthcoming article, "Translating Injury Data into Preventive and Health Care Services", in the *Journal of the American Public Health Association.*
¹³ Samuel A. Nigro, "A Scientific Critique of Abortion as a Medical Procedure", *Psychiatric Annals,* vol. 2, no. 9, (September, 1972), p. 30.
¹⁴ I owe this information to Veronica Fagan of the C.C.A.S., Toronto.
¹⁵ Statistics Canada, *Vital Statistics, 1970,* p. 41.
Statistics Canada, *Vital Statistics,* vol. 20, no. 12, December, 1972; *New York Times,* 18 December, 1972, p.l.
¹⁶ Statistics Canada, "Statistical Information on Printouts", 1972, Table A.
¹⁷ *Energy in Ontario: The Outlook and Policy Implications,* The Draft Report of the Advisory Committee on Energy, Toronto, 1973, vol. ii, p. 30.
¹⁸ *Ibid.,* vol. i, p. 3, figure 0.1.
¹⁹ In Québec, for example, it was illegal until 1969 for a married couple to surrender a child for adoption.
²⁰ Nigro, *loc. cit.,* p. 26.
²¹ For an interesting discussion of Fromm's idea, see Paolo Freire, *Pedagogy of the Oppressed,* New York, 1972, pp. 45-52.

A Feminist for Life

by Jessica Pegis

Jessica Pegis is an undergraduate student, St. Michael's College, University of Toronto.

An editorial in *Women: A Journal of Liberation* (Vol. III, 1) recognizes and repudiates the existence of certain power relationships in Western culture, specifically, the patriarchal system, sexism and racism. The editorial indicates that such power relationships cannot be tolerated in a feminist context and that women must take it upon themselves to shape a new society in which every human individual possesses safeguards against his or her potential victimizer. The editorial has a remarkable spirit and one with which I can fully identify. My identification ceases, however, as I observe that the author mentions birth control and abortion in the same breath and condones the latter as a thoroughly sensible and legitimate tool of human self-determination. Reservations obvious to me may not be so to others: with this in mind I shall set forth my objections as succinctly as possible.

Embodied in the very notion of "feminism" is an unqualified acceptance of all human individuals. A feminist who brutalizes herself by victimizing another is a living violation of the principle of non-contradiction! If we are to repudiate all human oppression, then certainly we must not stop short of that form of subjugation which is closest to home—and that is abortion. In this respect I oppose abortion law repeal and I oppose it even more fiercely when it is paraded as a credible symbol of woman's liberation.

Feminists have traditionally exhibited concern for various groups of oppressed people over and above an immediate concern for the status of women. Such an involvement has manifested itself in a number of ways:

the fostering of male rap groups through feminist energy, male liberation and new views on male sexuality including an overhaul of the blatantly sexist literature currently available to male as well as female children, comparisons which have arisen between the feminist and the civil rights movement with an emphasis on the special problems faced by black women and, finally, the partial integration, at least in certain spheres, of the feminist movement with socialism and the anti-war movement, Weatherwomen, for instance. Feminists have also attempted to exert influence at many social levels over and above, again, the mass media stereotyped indication that all feminists are "career women". A recent Ontario Conference on Women held at the University of Toronto offered the following sampling of workshops: Women in the Professions, Women's Studies, Academic Discrimination, Women in Athletics, Women in Politics. One has only to pick up a feminist magazine to understand that the women's movement has infiltrated at many levels: female penitentiaries, homes for the aged, mental institutions and religious orders. Similarly, the woman who has chosen to take on the traditional role of motherhood is now beginning to receive a proportionate share of attention. *Women: A Journal of Liberation* suggests that feminists are continually "rediscovering traditions which we once considered 'unliberated' such as crafts and child rearing" and, in this same vein, *Ms* pulls no punches with a remarkable May, 1973 feature story (for once, no extremes!): "The Real Pleasures of Being a Mother—The Pitfalls of Trying to be Supermom!"

It would appear, from the description above, that the women's movement is and has been viable for some time as a front devoted to halting more than one aspect of human oppression. What I have tried to do here is to outline the structure of the movement as I see it—a movement which has grown up with the power and vigour to bring into actuality a radically absolute view of all living individuals. In this respect, I feel that the abortion law repeal movement constitutes one of the most brutal and reactionary movements of our time—specifically because it has matured in the context of feminism.

My two basic objections to a *feminist* abortion law repeal movement are:

(1) Abortion victimizes a living human individual who lacks the strength and the intellectual maturity to establish any form of resistance. Abortion exploits the weak. It is indicative of a chauvinist ethic and has no place in the women's movement.

(2) The abortion law repeal *movement*, as such, has interjected a note of mindlessness into feminist thought, ironically akin to the witless feminine mentality portrayed by the media and so fiercely denounced by feminists in general.

I shall now address myself to these two statements in some depth. My first objection is merely a specification of my basic antipathy to abortion: abortion takes a human life. A "potential" human life, someone will insist. But an embryonic human or a foetal human is not "potentially" human! He or she is *actually* human as all actual instances of individual humanity must be! He or she may be said to be a potential infant, adolescent or adult—but these labels refer only to stages of maturity and not to the species. "Human" can mean only "of the human species and conceived of human parents" for this is the broadest, most central sphere under which all human beings fall. The cliché, "A foetus is no more a human being than an acorn is an oak tree" has the speaker drawing a comparison in which no item has any sensible correlation with another precisely because the statement includes the term "foetus" as some sort of biological entity unto itself. Foetus? What does "foetus" mean? *Foetal human*? In that case, one ought to say so. (And the absurdity of this cliché becomes more pronounced.)

At this point in the discussion the subject of "personhood" invariably arises. The opposition takes great delight in bellowing about the ludicrous image of the "fertilized ovum as a person". The intimation is that all sensible souls ought to conjure up, for a moment, the image of fertilized ovums engaging in those tasks which we normally assign to human adults and immediately dismiss the situation as another example of anti-abortion eyewash: fertilized ovums fighting the subway rush, fertilized ovums reading the *Times*, playing golf, mixing drinks, fertilized ovums running for office and staging boycotts. "Personhood", it seems, has come to be known as some sort of exclusive adult commodity. "Personhood" is always referred to in such terms as the "woman's immediate situation" or as "her life as it is at the moment, full of commitments to other people, full of adult responsibilities, full of adult (and therefore important) dreams and expectations". The problem here, of course, is that such a notion of "personhood" can be applied only to particular people and that the number of non-persons who could be legitimately sacrificed would consequently include not only foetal humans but also human infants, the retarded, the senile, and the mentally ill. Do we mean this? Most of all, do we want it? Do we want to establish the prerequisite, "personhood", as the passport to freedom, as the key to liberation and independence? Do we really want to say that certain living human individuals count more than others because they happen to be more mature or brighter or more desirable to society? And as feminists, do we actually want to turn ourselves into obscene parodies of those persons who talk about feminine inferiority by mimicking their self-righteous claims with equally absurd annunciations: "The foetus is part of my body" or "At ten weeks the conceptus is a small blood mass, very jellylike, absolutely no arms or legs..." (scientifically inaccurate, fallacious and pitifully unfounded).

Certainly, the safest and most objective thing to do is to assign an absolute value to all. Restricted notions of "personhood" serve only to enhance the opportunities of certain oppressors to reap benefits at the expense of living human victims. Qualified notions of "personhood" severely limit any view of the human family which takes into account a diversity of human characteristics—diverse ages, diverse patterns of development, diverse looks, whims, quirks, intellectual capacities. Finally, less than absolute notions of "personhood" forbid us to examine these diverse human traits without judging their relative merits; they forbid us to recognize an absolute value of life, forbid us to understand that each human individual has the right to grow without the destructive interference of science or society. And this is why I believe that a movement devoted to eliminating sexism and class structure should not hinder the formation of legislation that would give pre-natal humans the legal protection that every human individual deserves. I suggest that feminists discard "personhood" as a prerequisite for legal rights and, in its place, adopt a radically broad and unbiased approach towards each member of the human species—recognizing as equal everyone at every stage of development and in any condition. In this, I feel that we could honestly say that we are working to abolish power relationships other than those directly affecting our immediate situations.

Now we may proceed to a second objection—my objection to the feminist abortion law repeal *movement*, as I have come to see it. My primary reservation with respect to the movement, as I stated before, is that it has introduced a wave of irrational "thinking" into the feminist front and has fostered a sense of community among its members that is blind, empty-headed, and arrogant. The women of the abortion law repeal movement deliver the standard lines concerning control of "their" bodies; they talk incessantly about acorns and oak trees and "quickening" (of all things!) in order to avoid the facts of prenatal life; they have committed to memory each and every insult that can be dredged up against those who oppose abortion and have been known to spit them back without discretion—(A feminist friend once remarked: "Someone was shouting at me and complaining that I and the rest of those *males* were oppressing women. I think she'd stopped looking at me by that time".)

Most unfortunate, though, is the fact that their sisterhood is no longer powerful in an honest sense. They exude a togetherness which has served only to draw them closer in defence; there is no room for questioning or for critical evaluation. At a recent Canadian national abortion law repeal conference, a representative of WONAAC made a little speech during the final plenary session of the conference. She talked about the abortion "victory" in the United States, referring, of course, to the recent Supreme Court decision to remove virtually all legal protection from foetal humans, and mentioned that the opposition had some sort of amendment up its sleeve—for this, she explained, was the only pitiful tactic left to the devices of all those terrible Catholics. So, in her coolest voice, she proceeded to pick apart what she considered to be the obvious flaw in the amendment: it would give a foetus the same status that you and I have, she told her audience. Now I'm sure you can appreciate, she continued, the absurd implications of this amendment... all the voting districts would have to be recounted in order to include pregnant women.

Everyone laughed; it was acceptably "funny". No woman showed any sign of understanding the fallacious reasoning behind such a bizarre statement. That voting lists include only those individuals who have a vote did not seem to occur to anyone. That foetal humans need only the legal recognition now given to infants was not mentioned. Mob psychology had taken over and any evidence of individual command was sorely lacking. It was this lack of individualism, this willingness to be led that impressed me as the sour note of the conference.

Do we want to be led? Do we actually want to be conned into believing that a foetus is merely "pregnancy tissue"? Do we really want to look back on ourselves twenty years from now and see ourselves laughing about Aquinas' Aristotelian theory on the beginning of life—forty days for males, eighty for females!—knowing full well that such humorous bantering was staged only to get us over the crucial question that will never go away: when does the human individual come into existence?

I certainly hope not. Feminists will recognize that some pregnancies are wanted and others are not, but I hope they always keep in mind, particularly in the latter case, that each pregnancy involves the welfare of another human individual. I also hope that a woman might never feel guilty about letting that individual be born—in marriage or outside of it—and subsequently be adopted out, because doing so means real self-determination both for herself and for her offspring.

And is this not what feminist ideology is all about? Human self-determination and independence for all? In that case, the right to existence must be of primary importance because without it such notions as human self-determination are absurd. Therefore, since all individuals are equal, I propose that feminists affirm the value of any human life over and above all other considerations.

Seeds, A Discussion of Euthanasia and Abortion

by **Denyse Handler**

Denyse Handler is editor of the newspaper, *The Uncertified Human.*

In the January 14/72 issue of *Life*, an article appeared outlining the dilemma of the mother of a one-year-old mongoloid child "still unwanted and still unnamed" who cost her parents much time, trouble and expense in treatments and care. Her mother is quoted as saying: "Why, when there are too many people in the world, keep alive an unwanted, malformed child... I still say if there was a place where I could take this child today and she would be put to sleep permanently I would do it." The story is a very sad one. It follows two articles on men who personally decided to discontinue agonizing treatments for terminal diseases and so die in peace. Yet strangely, the story of the mongoloid girl was also headed, "The Right to Die". Now really, the woman was campaigning for the child's death, not her own! She admitted in a subsequent letter her intention to get a bill passed permitting her to put the baby to sleep. Wouldn't "Right to Kill" be more appropriate?

The executive director of the fast-growing Euthanasia Educational Fund centred in New York State informed me in a personal letter that:

> Your letter is very perceptive about the other questions which arise and many of our members as individuals do believe in making a means of dying available, in providing for those who cannot speak for themselves and the humane withdrawal of support from defective babies. However, all of these are illegal and as an organization we do not advocate any of them.

If "providing for those who cannot speak for themselves" were legal,

I wonder what provisions they would advocate?

A Gallup Poll published in the *Toronto Star* for September 21, 1972, indicates that the majority of people in Canada seem to favour mercy-killing at the patient's request. Yet on the opposite page, a feature article by the United Church's former moderator concludes that the only reasons we do not similarly end the lives of those who have *not* requested it, but whose existences have become "meaningless", is "selfish indifference". It seems that the idea of killing at the patient's request and killing without it when we feel justified are, for the most part, difficult to separate. People are becoming particularly vocal on the question of deformed or defective children, who are generally considered, as such, to be unwanted. Dr. Colin Ferguson, president-elect of the Canadian Paediatrics Society, addressing the annual meeting, called for life-and-death guidelines for mongoloid children (*Toronto Star*, July 19, 1972). He said, "It is a supreme penalty to put on some families to save the life of a mongolian idiot." He noted that a young mother could have other normal children if the defective baby were phased out, and presumably the total happiness would be greater. "It would be easier for all concerned if socially acceptable guidelines were available," he concluded. Dr. Ferguson mentioned that another type of child also merited serious consideration, those afflicted with myelomeningoceles, which results in leg paralysis and lack of bowel control. He cited a Dr. David Morley of Britain who claims that such children cost the state one million dollars per year. Interestingly, on August 8, 1972, a surgeon at London's Hospital for Sick Children told the London *Sun* that these children should be left to die. He believes that a more selective approach is needed with respect to the survival of the handicapped. Of course, selectivity can pose problems, too. A controversy arose recently among anaestheticians, reported in *Obstetrical and Gynecological News*, January 1, 1971, as to whether an anaesthetician should attempt to revive an infant he had accidentally anaesthetized during the birth process, insofar as that infant might be mentally retarded. One doctor objected to allowing the infant to die on the grounds that, without prior knowledge of the actual IQ potential of the infant, one could not gauge *how much* below normal it would be, if at all. If he loses 60 points IQ from 150, that leaves him 90, or slightly subnormal. If he loses it from 90, he becomes an idiot. But prior to two years of age, no one can really know.

There is a good deal of confusion quite often about the meaning of the term "euthanasia". To some, it means allowing a person to die who wants to, and to others it means putting him to sleep. It has been used to mean withdrawal of support without the patient's consent or putting the patient to sleep without his consent.

Chaplain Reeves at Columbia University remarks that the dilemma in his view is basically this: There are two supreme challenges facing us all: to find an honourable equivalent to Spartan exposure on the rocks at the beginning of life, and an honorable equivalent to the Eskimo hole in the ice at the end of life (*National Observer*, March 4, 1972). One wonders in passing just what it is that the Reverend Reeves finds to be less than "honourable" about the Eskimo way. Insofar as the end result is the same, is it the primitive methods he objects to? Are antiseptic hypodermics more "honourable" than holes in the ice?

From my own point of view as a student of popular movements, all this bears a profound resemblance to the beginnings of many a successful abortion campaign, a fact which may disturb those who fear that this sort of thing may get out of hand. Indeed it may. Let me elaborate.

In the article in *Life*, the emotionally wrenching plea for a very hard case is reminiscent of the earlier pleas for abortion. "The mother whose child will almost certainly be born deformed" drew a great deal of sympathy for "the right to abort". The mother whose child *is born* deformed is beginning to draw sympathy for, well, infanticide. No one seems interested in considering the child, born or unborn, as other than a pawn in a "social problem" to be eliminated in favour of bigger pieces on the board.

The people who put forward ideas for abortion or euthanasia most often speak in high moral tones. Too high, in fact, because they invariably forget that the institutions that they propose are highly susceptible of abuse. Case in point? In Florida, a euthanasia bill has been introduced on the heels of an abortion bill. It did not pass the first year, but Rep. Sackett or his successors will introduce it every year until it does. There are a large number of elderly people in Florida whom the bill is meant to serve. One of the provisions of the bill is not at all a bad idea: it provides that a person may draw up a legal document asking that his life not be prolonged by medical means beyond the point of "meaningful existence". This, one hopes, will happen less often anyway, as doctors learn to make wise decisions with regard to sophisticated life-saving equipment.

But this bill is not content with letting the rational and healthy person draw up his or her own death-with-dignity document. Instead, it provides that:

> In the event any person is unable to make such a decision because of mental or physical incapacity, a spouse or person or persons of first degree kinship shall be allowed to make such a decision, provided written consent is obtained from:

(1) The spouse or person of first degree kinship, or
(2) In the event of two (2) persons of the first degree kinship, both such persons, or
(3) In the event of three (3) or more persons of first degree kinship, the majority of those persons.

The bill also provides that if any person is disabled and there is no kinship as provided in Section 3, death with dignity shall be granted any person if in the opinion of three (3) physicians, the prolongation of life is meaningless and if such opinion is stated before and approved by a circuit judge.

A bill like this, which will undoubtedly pass in one form or another, raises hordes of objections, from my own point of view. What does it mean when one says that a man cannot "make such a decision because of mental or physical incapacity"? That is, if he is paralysed or mentally deficient and therefore cannot be got to make such a decision, what guarantee is there that he *wants* it made? What do phrases like "meaningful existence", "disabled", or "the prolongation of life" *mean*? There is no carefully defined meaning for any of them, any more than for the "mental and physical health" clause which brought easy abortion to Canada. The thing to remember here is that we have a predominately aging population, so that euthanasia concepts will become more, not less, of an issue. Prolongation of life can mean giving food, water and bed care, in which case these could be withheld from the needy old, on the grounds that their lives are meaningless. Who is to guarantee that in a crowded institution such things will not happen? Doesn't it depend on who the three physicians and the judge are? For that matter, since the decision about the meaninglessness of a man's life is largely philosophical, why use physicians and judges? Would not plumbers and English professors do just as well, in the final analysis? Another thing: would parents be able to make such decisions on behalf of their undesirable children? Probably. Infanticide is merely an extension of abortion. Those who were not poisoned in the womb can be poisoned later, if they have not proved their usefulness.

Any euthanasia or infanticide procedure will probably be governed by the Therapeutic Abortion Committee formula, whereby a group of medical people decide to end a life for non-medical reasons. There is a trend in such matters for the persons who are least troubled by that particular form of extermination to wind up sitting on the committee. The others soon leave. The committee, having no conscience, becomes a legal rubber-stamp for the procedures, at which point people want to abolish it because it never fulfilled its function anyway. To see how this would work with respect to infanticide, consider that there is a very well-known Nobel prizewinning scientist, Sir Francis Crick, of Britain, who believes that children should be phased out if they are unsatisfactory up to the age of two years old. I have talked to pediatricians who share his view. Perhaps most pediatricians would not dream of condoning such things, but they need not, after all, sit on the committee. Perhaps the committee would start in a small way, eliminating only hopeless defectives. But where could they go from there?

Population hysteria helps the idea along, undoubtedly. Last year the U.S. reported the lowest birth rate in its history and Canada is in much the same position. Concern for population growth *as such* is by now a little misguided. The real concern, given present birth rates, should be to reduce population densities and repair damage to regional economies caused by mass migration to the cities. However, if we ignore problems caused by density and if the standard of living we wish to reach continually escalates, along with the unbelievable amount of waste generated by the Throwaway Society, there will always be too many people, even if we cut the population in half.

No, we do not need a population crisis to start us on the road to a systematic elimination of the "unfit". We need only consider the amount of money, time, and trouble saved in hospitals and institutions, if we "cease to permit useless suffering". Money that might better be spent on healthy young persons who know how to enjoy it. Tempting? Let's hope not.

The basic evil, unfortunately, lies rather deep. It lies in the assumption that killing is "all right" if we are only killing the unwanted, the unconscious, the unseen, the unhappy or "those whose lives do not affect us too much". This is the ethic on which abortion became acceptable, and it isn't just abortion that fits it.

Probabilism and Possible Abortifacients[1]

by **John Gallagher, c.s.b.**

John Gallagher is Associate Professor of Moral Theology, Toronto School of Theology.

Several methods currently in use to prevent pregnancy do so in ways that are not yet understood with certainty. For example, at the present (1972) state of medical knowledge we do not know precisely how the intrauterine device (I.U.D.) prevents pregnancy. It may be the case that the I.U.D. allows the fertilization of the ovum and then causes the ovum to be expelled from the womb before it can develop. If the I.U.D. causes the expulsion after the fertilized ovum has become implanted in the womb it is abortifacient. If the I.U.D. causes expulsion of the fertilized ovum before it becomes implanted some may not wish to call the process abortion. It is, however, the moral equivalent of very early abortion, since the fertilized ovum not implanted in the womb is equivalent, for purposes of moral evaluation, to the fertilized ovum which is implanted in the womb. Recent studies suggest, however, that possibly the I.U.D. does not prevent pregnancy in either of these ways, but rather by preventing the fertilization of the ovum by the sperm cells. Should this be the case the I.U.D. would have the same general moral significance as have other methods of artificial contraception. To sum up, there is doubt about whether, or how often, the I.U.D. produces abortion or the moral equivalent of abortion.[2]

In the case of certain "morning after" birth control pills there may be a similar doubt as to whether the pregnancy is prevented by simple contraception or by abortion. This paper will refer directly to the I.U.D., with the understanding that the same considerations apply to any methods of birth control that involve a doubt as to whether or not an abortion is effected.

Many people judge that in certain cases artificial contraception is morally justified but that deliberate abortion is immoral. For these people the use of the I.U.D. presents a problem. May one use the I.U.D., given this doubt about whether it is abortifacient? This paper attempts an evaluation of the morality of the I.U.D. and of any other method which involves this doubt. This paper considers these methods in view of the doubt as to whether they are abortive, but does not consider their morality insofar as they may be contraceptive.

Some claim that the use of the I.U.D. is morally permissible, and they support this claim by appealing to the doubt that is involved. They point out that if the intention is not to abort, and there is a good chance that the effect will be not abortion but contraception, the I.U.D. may be used, presuming that some artificial means of contraception may be used in the particular case.

This paper will argue for a contrary conclusion. Because there is a good chance the I.U.D. may be abortifacient, it is not morally permissible. To show why this is so it is necessary to consider several different meanings of this appeal to the doubt involved in the case.

1. THE BALANCE OF PROBABILITIES

The appeal to the element of doubt may be a sort of common sense balancing of a greater evil which might result against a lesser evil that is more likely to result. Such an appeal makes sense in general.[3] Applied to the use of the I.U.D., the argument would run thus: The use of the I.U.D. may, with some likelihood, result in abortion or its moral equivalent; not using such a method in a particular case may almost certainly result in such evils as the nervous collapse of the mother, or the neglect of older children. On the one hand, abortion is the greater evil. On the other hand, the evil effect will follow from the non-use of the I.U.D. with greater certainty than abortion will follow from the use of the I.U.D. So, the argument runs, one may choose to use the I.U.D. at least in some cases—where the greater evil of abortion is balanced by the lesser likelihood of its occurring.

Such an argument cannot justify the use of the I.U.D. On the one side, so far as we know the chance that the I.U.D. causes abortion is very real—perhaps a better than fifty per cent chance. If it is the case that such a method does cause abortions then its continued use will cause multiple abortions. On the other side, we must distinguish avoidable from unavoidable evil results of the non-use of the I.U.D. Certain evil results may be avoided by alternative procedures. Nervous collapse in some cases might be avoided by use of medical health facilities. Another alternative would be another type of birth control. Even permanent sterilization would be, I think, preferable to the risk of abortion. In each case, then, one must balance the use of the I.U.D. not against any collection of possible evil effects of its non-use, but against the smallest possible total of bad effects of its non-use after all has been done to produce as little evil as possible. I find it hard to conceive of a situation where, in the balance, the serious risk of abortion by use of the I.U.D. would be justified by the unavoidable evil effect of its non-use.

One can, however, at least imagine a situation where one might rightly acquiesce in the use of the I.U.D. by another. Suppose that a woman refuses to take any steps to avoid pregnancy except to use the I.U.D. Her doctor judges that if she does not use the I.U.D. she will almost certainly become pregnant and have an abortion. For the patient there is a better alternative than either abortion or use of the I.U.D., so she does a morally wrong thing if she does either. The doctor, however, knowing that she will not choose a morally good alternative, might perhaps be justified in trying to get the woman to choose the I.U.D. as the lesser of two evil alternatives.

2. PROBABILISM

The appeal to the element of doubt in the use of a possibly abortive method of preventing pregnancy may have a second meaning. It may appeal to the system of moral theology called "probabilism", a system widely used in Roman Catholic manuals of moral theology in recent centuries.[4] Probabilism came into being as a method to resolve doubts of conscience. It sought to provide guidance for those cases in which one cannot know with any assurance whether a particular course of action is morally good or evil.

Probabilism was one of several competing systems. We may compare these systems by using an illustration. Suppose that a person must choose between action A and action B. Action A is certainly morally good. There is real doubt about whether action B is morally good or morally evil. The system called "tutiorism" taught that in such a case one should choose the safer course, action A. This presupposes that there is a really significant possibility that action B is morally evil, and not just a slight or badly grounded suspicion. "Probabiliorism" taught that one may follow a course of action as long as it is more likely to be morally good than to be evil. The probabiliorist would say that the person could choose action B as long as it is more probable that action B is morally good than that it is morally evil. "Equi-probabilism" taught that one could follow a course of action as long as it was as likely to be morally good as to be morally evil. "Probabilism" allowed one to follow a course of action as long as there was what we might call a "solid probability" that it was morally good, even if there was a greater probability that it was morally evil. Solid probability could be considered from two points of view. From the point of view of the individual conscience, an opinion was solidly probable when the individual really had solid doubts about what was true, not being convinced either pro or con on a particular matter. From the point of view of the "state of the question" an opinion was considered solidly probable when a number of reputable authors, moral theologians in good standing in the Church, favoured an opinion. The opinion remained solidly probable even if a larger number of reputable authors opposed it. "Laxism", condemned by the Church, taught that one could follow a course of action as long as even one reputable author would say that it was good. The laxist would allow you to do action B rather than action A as long as one reputable author would approve such a choice.

In all of this the word "probable" does not mean "more likely than not", as it may mean in common conversation. Nor does "probable" here have a minimalist meaning, as though one may perform an action unless it has been proved conclusively to be bad.

Within this whole probabilist framework we must distinguish two "locations" of the doubt. First, the doubt may exist in the mind of the person who must choose whether or not to act, and this doubt may persist even after that person has tried all reasonable means to discover the truth. In section 3 below we will consider this type of doubt. Second, the doubt may be part of the "state of the question", some experts saying one thing and some saying the other. Section 4 below will consider this second type of doubt.

3. DOUBT IN THE MIND OF THE PERSON CHOOSING

It is conceivable that the probabilist argument might be applied in the following way, although probabilist theologians formulated their theory so that such an application is ruled out. A person, after using all reasonable means to discover the truth, still does not know whether a particular method, the I.U.D., causes abortion or not; one judges that there is a solid probability that the I.U.D. does not cause abortion, and is therefore not immoral. (Note that this could be called a "solid probability" even if the opposite were judged more likely to occur.) Probabilism allows you to act as long as there is solid probability that the course of action is not immoral. Therefore probabilism would allow you to use the I.U.D.

Traditional probabilists have excluded such a use of probabilism, for they demand that one choose the safer course where there is real danger of causing considerable harm to someone. Suppose that a hunter sees something stirring in the bushes. He thinks that it is probably a deer, though it may well be his neighbour. If he takes time to investigate the deer will escape. May the hunter shoot first and investigate later, on the grounds that there is a solid probability that he will not kill his neighbour? No reputable probabilist would allow this.

Probabilists make various exceptions to prevent the application of the probabilist principle from risking considerable harm to anyone. In 1697 Pope Innocent XI declared that the probabilist principle should not be applied to sacraments, to justice or to faith.[5] The reason is obvious. One should not risk making baptism invalid by using doubtfully valid form or matter. One should not risk harm to a neighbour's goods on the grounds that there is a good chance that there will be no harm. Philippe Delhaye holds that one must follow the surer (safer) course in dealing with others as well as in doubts of fact.[6] This latter term may require explanation. A "doubt of law" is a doubt about whether a certain class of action is immoral. For example, there might be a doubt of law about whether a borrower should pay compensation to the owner for damage done to property because of the borrower's non-deliberate negligence. A "doubt of fact" would occur, for example, if one did not know whether food one was serving were poisoned. Clearly the application of the probabilist principle to doubts of fact could lead to great harm.

Saint Alphonsus de Liguori, probably the foremost authority among Roman Catholic authors of textbooks of moral theology, is usually classed as an equi-probabilist. However, he clearly states that in cases of probability of fact where there is danger of harm to another or to oneself, one may not so act as to risk that harm. One must also follow the safer course in such matters as the requirements for salvation, (e.g., the validity of sacraments), and in a doctor's treatment of a patient.[7] Aertnys and Damen, later followers of St. Alphonsus, state clearly that whenever there is danger of harm to another which one should avoid one must follow the safer course.[8]

Traditional probabilists would not allow the application of the probabilist principle where it would risk grave harm to someone. Therefore they would not allow its application to justify use of the I.U.D.

4. DIFFERENCE OF OPINION AMONG EXPERTS

In section 3 we have considered the question insofar as there is doubt in the mind of the person choosing a method of preventing pregnancy. The doubt may, however, exist as part of the "state of the question"; this is the type of doubt when experts disagree. Appealing to this type of doubt, a probabilist may attempt to evade the consequences of the argument in this paper thus far. He may point out that the experts, including the Roman Catholic moral theologians, do not agree with the conclusions of this paper so far. In case of such a difference of opinion, the probabilists claim, you may act according to the opinion more lenient to you, even when that opinion conflicts with your own understanding, provided that this more lenient opinion is held by some good and reputable authors.

This argument may seem at first glance to be circular, and therefore invalid. That is, it seems to argue thus: probabilism teaches that one need not follow an opinion if experts disagree about it; the arguments here against probabilism are subject to disagreement among experts. Therefore I need not accept the conclusion from these arguments against probabilism. Such an argument apparently invokes a principle of probabilism in order to reject an argument against probabilism. It seems to presuppose the truth of a position in order to reject an attack on the truth of the position.

What saves the argument from being circular in this way is that it introduces a new element not considered in the previous exposition of probabilism. This new element is the appeal to authority. We may then restate the objection in three stages, to show better what is implied in it.

First, this probabilist objection adopts the position of being guided in moral matters by authority rather than by one's own understanding. Clearly this cannot be a pure position as though it implied that a person were guided only and completely by authority and not at all by one's own understanding; but it is a position which holds that in certain cases one will follow authority even when it disagrees with one's own understanding. (Otherwise, how could you justify following an opinion other than that which seems indicated by your own understanding?) The decision to be guided by authority in these cases may be very reasonable. The individual may judge that his own understanding about a particular point is inadequate, and that therefore he is more likely to be right if he is guided by authority than if he is guided by his own understanding.

The second stage in the probabilist objection can most easily be explained within the terms of the Roman Catholic moral tradition, though it could be operative in the case of anyone who reasons in the context of a more or less authoritative tradition in moral matters. For Roman Catholics in the probabilist tradition the second stage supposes that the authorities to be followed are the teachers of morality within the Roman Catholic Church. For several centuries now the moral theologians of the Roman Catholic Church, in union with pope and hierarchy, have generally accepted the probabilist position that in case of disagreement among experts one may follow the more lenient view, even if it goes against the consequences of one's own understanding, providing that this more lenient view is supported by good and reputable authors. Notice, at this point this particular probabilist opinion is established not by presupposing the truth of probabilism but by appeal to a general consensus of experts.[9]

The third stage in the probabilist objection supposes (continuing with its application only within the Roman Catholic tradition), that in fact some good and reputable Roman Catholic moral theologians maintain that one may use methods of preventing pregnancy even if there is a good chance that such methods cause abortion.[10]

If these three stages are all accepted as valid one might thus appeal to authority to overthrow the arguments of sections 1, 2 and 3 of this paper. But we must now ask our probabilist to be consistent. In accepting these three stages he has given a large role to authority, even choosing to be guided by it on points where it conflicts with his own understanding. Now the same tradition which emphasised authorities in probabilism was also quite generally agreed that the supreme among human authorities was the pope. To choose an authority to follow a more lenient opinion, as above, and then to choose not to follow the pope seems somewhat inconsistent.

Now in the matter of the I.U.D. there is a papal teaching that it is morally wrong insofar as it is an artificial contraceptive, quite apart from its possible abortive effect. Such teaching against artificial contraception has not only papal authority but the authority of a consensus, more or less, among moral teachers in the Roman Catholic Church, a consensus which existed for more centuries than did any consensus about probabilism.

If one is generally quite docile to authoritative moral teachings within the Roman Catholic Church he may reject the arguments in this paper. Then we can enter further discussion about whether the authoritative tradition to which he appeals is really of a compelling nature. Meanwhile such a docile person will presumably reject use of the I.U.D. because of papal teaching on birth control. Should one reject papal teaching on birth control, yet appeal to authority to escape the conclusions of this article, surely one must defend oneself against the charge of picking and choosing among authoritative statements rather than being guided by authority. Having thus ceased to be guided by authority, should one not surrender the luxury of following a more lenient opinion simply because to do so is justified by certain authorities?

There is a second reason for rejecting the probabilist objection elaborated at the beginning of this section. In section 3 we showed that probabilists did not allow the use of the probabilist principle when it involved real risk of harm to anyone. In section 3 we applied this to show that the traditional probabilists would not have allowed the appeal to probabilism to justify the use of the I.U.D. when there was doubt in the mind of the chooser about the morality of the effects of the I.U.D. I think it is legitimate to suppose that traditional probabilists would have rejected the practice of following the more lenient opinion in a case of doubt on the level of the "state of the question" when such a practice risked real harm to someone.

In conclusion, I find no logically defensible argument to justify the use of the I.U.D. or any other method of birth prevention concerning which there is real doubt about whether it is or is not abortive.

Footnotes

[1] This discussion arises directly out of the Roman Catholic moral tradition. However, many of the issues here discussed may be of interest to those outside of this particular moral tradition.

[2] In some minds there is another important doubt here—namely, whether the newly fertilized ovum is human or has a right to life as human beings have a right to life. I will not go into the question whether there are real grounds for this doubt. In this paper I will presuppose that abortion is not morally permissible and that the newly fertilized ovum has a human right to life. However, the argument of this paper would be relevant to answer any claim that one may cause early abortions on the basis of doubt about whether the newly fertilized ovum or the foetus at any stage has a human right to life.

[3] This type of balancing or calculation presents obvious difficulties. Some cases of such calculation seem clear enough. Suppose that one could calculate that action A has a one in three chance of resulting in the death of one person. Action B has a one in three chance of resulting in the death of two persons. Other things being equal, action A seems morally preferable. Of course one cannot usually calculate probabilities with this mathematical precision, especially when one compares quite different goods and evils. For example, how compare a risk to life against the danger of grave financial loss? Difficult as such calculation may be, some sort of balancing of alternatives is required in many moral judgments.

[4] A good extensive discussion of this development in moral theology is given by Thomas Deman in the article "probabilism" in *Dictionnaire de théologie Catholique*.

[5] Cf. Ph. Delhaye, *La conscience morale du chrétien*, Tournai, Desclée, 1964, pp. 195-6.

[6] Cf. *op. cit.* pp. 203-4.

[7] Alphonsus de Liguori, *Theologia Moralis*, Lib. I, tract. I, caput III, no. 42, 43, 44.

[8] Aertnys-Damen, *Theologia Moralis*, Roma, Marietti, 1947, t.I, Lib. I, tract. III, caput IV, art. II.

[9] One might choose to challenge this second stage regarding its validity simply as an appeal to authority. One might question whether there has been a consensus of

Roman Catholic moral theologians of the past several centuries that one may follow the more lenient opinion even if it conflicts with one's own understanding, provided that some good and reputable authors favour that more lenient opinion. Especially one might question whether there is still a consensus among Roman Catholic moral theologians on this point. Furthermore, supposing that such a consensus has existed for the past several centuries, what is its compelling force in view of the earlier and long-standing tutiorist tradition? Whatever be the answer to these questions, we will not pursue them here, but we will suppose for the sake of argument that there was a consensus on this subject over several centuries and that this constitutes a teaching from authority which Roman Catholics should take seriously and which they might be reasonably persuaded to follow because of its authoritative character.

[10]Again, one might challenge this third stage on whether it is factually correct. We will not here pursue this challenge but let the probabilist position stand in as strong a position as possible for the sake of our argument.

Section Four; Abortion and the Law

Law and the Sins of the Mothers

by Edward A. Synan

Edward A. Synan is Professor of Mediaeval Philosophy, Pontifical Institute of Mediaeval Studies, Toronto.

My intent in this paper is not to argue against abortion and still less to engage in anti-abortion rhetoric. It is to bring a fact of legal history before responsible readers. That our two traditions of civil legislation, Common Law and Roman Civil Law, both defended the foetus by attaching penalties to direct abortion is, of course, well known.[1] These two traditions intervened in another fashion, less often noticed, and two dramatic trials will serve to illustrate that intervention.

1. ENGLISH COMMON LAW

The 1692 trials for witchcraft at Salem, Massachusetts, were not mounted in order to provide the future with edifying reflections and few historians have found any in their appalling record.[2] Still, if the trials constitute a stone of stumbling for admirers of the Common Law under which they took place, one of those trials in one of its details goes a certain distance toward vindicating the proud claim by some apologists that Common Law is a legal structure developed to defend human life and, above all, to defend the lives of the more vulnerable members of society.

Elizabeth Proctor was one of the defendants in the exceptional trial. With her husband, and four other accused, Goodwife Proctor was found guilty of witchcraft on August 5th at the third session of a Special Court of Oyer and Terminer.[3] All six were promptly sentenced to death; two weeks later, on August 19th, all but Elizabeth Proctor were hanged. In this spectacular miscarriage of justice the edifying detail is that Goodwife Proctor was able to take refuge in a custom honoured by Common Law: pregnant, she had "pleaded her belly".[4] Her execution, accordingly, was stayed until such time as her child should have been born "on the ground", as an excellent historian of these grim events has not hesitated to put it, "that the child she was carrying was an innocent person".[5]

Although it is irrelevant to the legal and moral issues at stake, the reader will pardon if not welcome a brief note on the outcome of her appeal. By the time her child had been born, January of 1693, much had changed at Salem. Second thoughts had begun to torment influential people. The royal Governor of Massachusetts had returned from an expedition provoked by a threat from Canada—in those topsy-turvy days the thrust of empire ran from north to south—and found his wife "cried out upon" as a witch. The Puritan clergy were counselling restraint with a discretion we may deplore as excessive but, in the face of popular excitement, they did so with a firmness that compels our admiration.[6] In consequence, on October 29th the Governor allowed the Commission upon which the Court of Oyer and Terminer rested to lapse; the trials were over. A widow now, thanks to an "error... which cannot be retrieved",[7] Goodwife Proctor lived and so did her child—thanks to the persuasion of Common Law jurisprudence that what a woman has conceived is not a person who is guilty of any capital offense.

2. ROMAN LAW

Now it is on just such considerations as the escape of Goody Proctor and her child that the Common Law tradition, which has never lacked bards to hymn its virtues, is contrasted with Roman Law to the disadvantage of the latter. Sometimes the fact that Roman Law was a pagan construct, tardily and inadequately Christianized, is taken to mitigate its deficiencies.[8] As a distinguished former Chief Justice of China, John C.H. Wu, has written: "while the Roman Law was a deathbed convert to Christianity, the common law was a cradle Christian".[9] Professor Wu's image owes more than a little to the fact that he has undergone a conversion himself, but immediately before this sentence, he was able to cite his friend and correspondent, Oliver Wendell Holmes, an Associate Justice of the Supreme Court of the United States, on the technical superiority of "our law"—the Common Law—over Roman Law. Justice Holmes, we hardly need to insist, was not strongly moved by specifically Christian concerns.

Whatever the propriety with which a general superiority of Common

Law over Roman Law is asserted, the inviolability of a condemned woman's conception cannot be one of the grounds on which it is argued. For Roman Law, despite its severity at so many points, had included precisely the same temporary immunity for pregnant women, as two texts from the *Digest* of Justinian bear witness:

> (Ulpian) in the twenty-seventh *Book to Sabinum*: The Emperor Hadrian sent a rescript to Publicius Marcellus to the effect that a free woman who has been condemned to the extreme penalty bear her child, and it is the custom that she be preserved until she shall have given birth . . . [10]

The second text of the *Digest* evokes the horror of the Roman *quaestio*, "examination" under torture, for this brutality of the Roman legal procedure would have made the miscarriage of the foetus a foregone conclusion should the victim be a pregnant woman. If she could not be executed while a foetus remained within her, then consistency demanded that torture not put her conception in peril:

> (Ulpian) in the fourteenth *Book to Sabinum*: The penalty that must be undergone by a condemned pregnant woman is deferred until she has given birth. I know that this too is observed: For as long as she is pregnant, no *quaestio* that involves her is held. [11]

We may note the absence from this second text of Hadrian's specification that the woman concerned be a free woman. It is a point to which we shall return and it is in harmony with the Roman attitude that benign tendencies prevail over harsh ones. When Pope Boniface VIII introduced into the documentation of Canon Law the Rule: "It is right that hateful items be restricted and favourable ones extended",[12] he was canonizing a long-standing attitude of Roman jurisconsults.

As the Common Law protection of the unborn has been given a local habitation and a name in the mitigated tragedy that afflicted the Proctor family at Salem in 1692, so this parallel provision of Roman jurisprudence is enshrined in our memory of the Christian martyr Felicity who suffered with the matron Perpetua and others in the amphitheatre at Carthage, A.D. 203. Our totally reliable accounts[13] of their imprisonment, trial, and execution may reflect editing by the lawyer Tertullian (*ca.* A.D. 160 — *ca.* 220). In any event, the report of how Hadrian's rescript bore upon the execution of the slave woman Felicity is exact. We must remark that its application to a pregnant slave proves that Hadrian's restriction of his rescript to free women had indeed gone by the board in Ulpian's day, for Ulpian was to die in 228 and thus was a contemporary of Felicity, Perpetua, and their companions. The law he records is the law under which they suffered.

Perpetua was the twenty-two year old mother of a small boy at the time of arraignment, whereas Felicity was pregnant. Condemned to the beasts with other Christians, both men and women, who had refused to sacrifice to the gods of that time and place, Felicity feared that her pregnancy would delay her execution. The result would be that she would go later to her terrifying ordeal, without the support of her companions in the faith, and so would shed her blood among random criminals. Perhaps this very anxiety induced premature labour; she was delivered of her child before the day fixed for the execution when her pregnancy had run but eight months.[14] The people of Carthage who took pleasure, guaranteed them by law, in watching Perpetua and Felicity tossed on the horns of a maddened cow, by that same law were spared any conscientious scruples that might have been occasioned had the new-born daughter of Felicity died with—indeed within—her mother; the child, after all, had not spurned their gods.

3. THE CONTEXTS OF THE CASES

Roman Law is an inheritance from an Empire so wide-ranging that its populations thought of themselves as of all the men who mattered. In their own view, they constituted the "inhabited world", the *oikumenē*, ringed about by barbarians, to be sure, but barbarians were negligible (to give one reason from among many) because they lived outside the civilizing scope of Rome's law. Even as codified by Christian Emperors, first by Theodosius in A.D. 438 and 439, then by Justinian in 529 and 534, Roman Law consecrated slavery, imposed horrendous penalties, suppressed local and personal liberties, authorized recourse to torture. Under pagan emperors the gladiatorial games, with their murderous combats between man and man or between man and beast, were used to provide "entertainment" for the savage populace; so too, there was a debased interest to be garnered from that fearful capital, the execution of condemned criminals, for this was thought of as a kind of sacrifice to the gods of the City. One detail in the passion arranged for Perpetua and Felicity illustrates this also: for a moment, they were arrayed in ritual religious vestments to show that they and the other women in their company were dedicated to Ceres; the men were decked out as priests of Saturn. Perpetua protested that this indignity went beyond their sentence.

Condemned for their refusal to worship the gods, they ought not to be compelled to die in the livery of the gods. Anticipating Rousseau in her fashion, she claimed that this was the contract that the martyrs had made. Perpetua's plea was one that a legal mind can take in—"Injustice acknowledged justice", our account reads—and the victims died in common clothing.[15] From time immemorial, however, the Roman mentality had been open to the conviction that guaranteed life to the unborn child, even though the mother must die.[16] True enough, the motivation for excluding abortion in general (a husband must not be defrauded of his progeny)[17] is not likely to recommend itself to us and infanticide, in the same legal system, remained a discretionary right of the father. But in that desert of brutality, the unborn came to term within a legally sacrosanct oasis.

For most of the English-speaking world our legal tradition is that of English Common Law, not without influence from the Roman Codes. Here too the legal past is brutal. Torture may have been unknown to the Common Law, but until yesterday (as historians calibrate the past) torture was available as an "extraordinary" resource by royal prerogative, not only to compel the accused to confess or to name accomplices, but also as an ordinary resource at the disposal of local courts in order to persuade the accused to "put himself upon the country", the *patria*, that is, to accept trial by jury. For this celebrated blessing of jury trial found small enthusiasm among the Englishmen to whom it was first proposed and it still met resistance in the 17th century. Here too, Salem is instructive.

Giles Corey, one of those accused at Salem, refused to put himself at the mercy of jurymen provided by his *patria*. All available evidence must have persuaded him that they were a "hanging jury"; perhaps too he wished to avoid the confiscation of his property to the disadvantage of his heirs, a consequence of conviction by a jury, but not of death under torture designed to encourage him to accept trial at the hands of twelve good men and true. Giles Corey, insufficiently grateful for this blessing of Common Law, was submitted to what that law knew as *la peine forte et dure*, a method for dealing with such emergencies, traditional in various forms since the 13th century: he was pressed to death.[18]

Apart from torture in these circumstances, Common Law knew other brutal provisions. The death penalty obtained for a long list of offences, at times by grotesque procedures. For certain crimes, death was by burning, for some, an interrupted hanging, preceded by drawing on a hurdle to the place of execution and followed by quartering and disembowelling while the victim still lived.[19] When reform came to pass it entered through the back door. Executioners mercifully strangled before burning, hangmen did not cut down their victims alive for the disembowelling and quartering; juries began to refuse convictions where lesser crimes carried the death penalty.[20] Despite all encomia on the Common Law, our tradition of criminal justice remains a budget of horrors. Yet, among them there survived an important exception: the unborn enjoyed the protection of that otherwise savage Law. The Bible had proclaimed that children need not fear divine retribution for their fathers' sins (Deut. 24:16); Common Law blocked their destruction for the sins of their mothers. That Law would burn or hang a witch, but not a pregnant witch.[21]

The development of jurisprudence has been a prolonged effort to conquer excessive severity while achieving the goals of law. Torture is never authorized among us, capital punishment has been abandoned, either permanently or for a time, in Canada, England, and the United States; *la peine forte et dure* is hardly remembered outside the guild of historians; our diabolists go their way, restrained by no special statutes. Destruction of intra-uterine life must count in our legal structure as an exception to our all but universal tendency to mildness, whereas the immunity of the foetus was an exceptional provision in the harsh Roman Law and in the hardly more humane Common Law of England and her daughters. As we weigh abortion legislation for 20th century societies we shall do well to ponder the anxieties of Saint Felicity as she waited for the beasts at Carthage in 203 and those of Goodwife Proctor between August and October, 1692, at Salem.

Footnotes

[1] For English Common Law against direct abortion: *Bracton De Legibus et Consuetudinibus Angliae*, ed. George E. Woodbine, translation with revisions and notes, Samuel E. Thorne, Cambridge, Mass., Seldon Society Belknap Press of Harvard University Press, 1968, vol. 2, p. 341. Si sit aliquis qui mulierem praegnantem percusserit vel ei venenum dederit, per quod fecerit abortivum, si puerperium iam formatum vel animatum fuerit, et maxime animatum, facit homicidium... The terms *formatum* and *animatum* reflect ancient and mediaeval biological views on the advent of successively more advanced "forms" or "life-principles" in the development of the foetus—views lately revived in pro-abortion circles. See also, *ibidem*, p. 408: ... Item si quis mulieris visceribus vim intulerit quo partum abegerit, tenetur... For Roman Law against direct abortion: *Corpus Iuris Civilis*, ed. Theodor Mommsen and Paul Krueger, Berlin, Weidmann, 1922, *Digesta* 47, 11, 4; vol. 1, p. 836: MARCIANUS *libro primo regularum*, Divus Severus et Antoninus rescripserunt eam, quae data opera abegit, a praeside in temporale exilium dandam; indignum enim videri potest impune cam maritum liberis fraudasse.

[2] An excellent bibliography on the Salem trials is available in: Marion Starkey, *The Devil in Massachusetts*, New York, A.A. Knopf, 1949 and in a paperback edition of the same work: New York, Dolphin Books, 1961; the fundamental documentation is preserved in the Essex County Court House at Salem in three

typescript volumes under the title: *Salem Witchcraft 1692*, produced in 1938 from the manuscript records of the trials by the Works Progress Administration; Starkey and Chadwick Hansen, *Witchcraft at Salem*, New York, George Braziller, Inc., 1969 and a paperback edition of the same work, New York, Mentor Book, 1970, have seen the ending of the witchcraft excitement as a gradual triumph of good sense: Starkey, paperback edition, pp. 269-270; Hansen, paperback edition, pp. 259-278 and 284-286.

[3] On the nature of a Commission of Oyer and Terminer ("to hear and to decide") in English Common Law, see Sir William Holdsworth, *A History of English Law*, London, Methuen, 1903 ff., vol. 1, p. 274. Under the restored Stuart monarchy, Massachusetts had lost her charter (1684) and on the eve of the witchcraft at Salem, under the House of Orange, Increase Mather, with Sir William Phips, was in London where they successfully negotiated a new charter under which Phips became the royal Governor. A new Superior Court of Judicature was scheduled to sit in January, 1693; meanwhile, to meet the witchcraft emergency, Phips issued a Commission of Oyer and Terminer in order to provide a court to try the cases of those accused. For a discussion of these events see Hansen, *op. cit.* pp. 157-162.

[4] This phrase, and the legal practice it expresses has left its traces in English letters: John Gay, *The Beggar's Opera*, I, 2, 4: "Why, she may plead her belly at worst"; this satiric dramatist made room in this 1728 play for one character (Filch) whose duty it was to provide this immunity: *ibidem* III, 3, 5: "I have picked up a little money by helping the ladies to a pregnancy against their being called down to sentence"; the same immunity underlies lines that Shakespeare was not ashamed to ascribe to Joan of Arc: *Henry VI, Part I*, V, iv, 11. 26-31. For an instance of the way this guarantee appeared in written law see the *Statuta secunda Roberti primi* (of Scotland, A.D. 1306 ff.) in: *Traités sur les coutumes Anglo-Normandes qui ont été publiés en Angleterre, depuis le onzième, jusqu'au quatorzième Siècle*, par M. Howard, Paris and Dieppe, 1776, t. 2, p. 644: Cum mulier aliqua accusata de Crimine, dixerit se esse Praegnantem... tres Obstetrices... eam inspicient... Quae si concordaverint ipsae tres, vel duae earum, quod sit Praegnans... committetur illa Mulier accusata, honestae et securae custodiae, usque ad tempus, quo paritura credatur... Et cum partum aediderit (SIC); vel tempus pariendi transierit; fiat de eadem Muliere justitia, secundum quod demeruit. Et sicut de Muliere minime impraegnata.

[5] Hansen, ed. *cit.*, p. 179.

[6] One of several exceptional values of Hansen's work is his insistence upon the effective reality of witchcraft in any society that believes in it, an insight essential to a balanced judgment on the role played by the clergy at Salem; see his chapters 9 and 10, especially pp. 183-188 on Cotton Mather and pp. 192-193, 266.

[7] The phrase is that of the Reverend John Hale, author of *A Modest Inquiry into the Nature of Witchcraft*, cited by Hansen, ed. *cit.*, p. 255.

[8] I have done so myself: E.A. Synan, *The Popes and the Jews in the Middle Ages*, New York, Macmillan, 1965, pp. 20-21.

[9] J.C.H. Wu, *Fountain of Justice*, New York, Sheed and Ward, 1955, p. 65; on page 64, Professor Wu had noted deficiencies in Common Law, but he remarked that "defects... are incidental to all human institutions..."

[10] The *Digesta* is a collection of texts of interest to jurisprudence and forms a part of the "body" of Roman civil law; it appeared under the authority of Justinian in A.D. 533; see above, note 1, for the edition here cited, vol. 1, p. 36: IDEM *libro vicesimo septimo ad Sabinum* Imperator Hadrianus Publicio Marcello rescripsit

liberam, quae praegnas (SIC) ultimo supplicio damnata est, liberum parere et solitum esse servari eam, dum partum ederet... (I, 5, 18).

[11] *Ibidem,* vol. 1, p. 864: IDEM *libro quarto decimo ad Sabinum* Praegnatis (SIC) mulieris consumendae damnatae poena differtur quoad pariat. Ego quidem et ne quaestio de se habeatur, scio observari, quamdiu praegnas (SIC) est. (XLVIII, 19, 3).

[12] Odia restringi, et favores convenit ampliari; Bonifacius VIII, *De regulis iuris,* regula xv, *Sexti decretalium,* liber v, titulus xii, in: *Corpus Iuris Canonici,* ed. A. Friedberg, Leipzig, Tauchnitz, 1881, vol. 2, col. 1122.

[13] The text cited here is the edition by C.I.M.I. van Beek, *Passio sanctarum Perpetuae et Felicitatis, Latine et Graece,* Bonn, Peter Hanstein, 1938 (Florilegium Patristicum, fasc. 43): the same editor has produced an earlier edition (1936) and two English translations may be noted, that of E.C.E. Owen, *Some Authentic Acts of the Early Martyrs,* Oxford, Clarendon, 1927 (for Saints Perpetua and Felicity and their companions in this edition, see pp. 74-92), and that of W.H. Shewring, *The Passion of SS. Perpetua and Felicity MM; A New Edition and Translation of the Latin Text together with the Sermons of S. Augustine upon these Saints,* London, Sheed and Ward, 1931; for the structure of this document, part of which stems from two of the martyrs, see the Shewring edition, pp. xviii-xxiii.

[14] Circa Felicitatem vero, et illi gratia Domini eiusmodi contigit: Cum octo iam mensium ventrem haberet (nam praegnans fuerat adprehensa), instante spectaculi die in magno erat luctu, ne propter ventrem differretur (quia non licet praegnantes poenae repraesentari) et ne inter alios postea sceleratos sanctum et innocentem sanguinem funderet; ed. *cit.,* p. 46, 11. 3-9.

[15] ... Et cum ducti essent in portam et cogerentur habitum induere, viri quidem sacerdotum Saturni, feminae vero sacratarum Cereri, generosa illa in finem usque constantia repugnavit. Dicebat enim: "Ideo ad hoc sponte pervenimus, ne libertas nostra obduceretur; ideo animam nostram addiximus, ne tale aliquid faceremus; hoc vobiscum pacti sumus." Agnovit iniustitia iustitiam: concessit tribunus, quomodo erant, simpliciter inducerentur; ed. *cit.,* p. 54, 11. 1-7; but this was not permitted without a flareup of the obscenity usual in the arena: itaque dispoliatae et reticulis indutae producebantur. Horruit populus alteram respiciens puellam delicatam, alteram a partu recentem stillantibus mammis. Ita revocatas et discinctis indutae... *ibidem,* p. 56, 11. 16-19.

[16] According to Plutarch, *Moralia,* liber de sera numinis vindicta 7, 552 D, a comparable immunity had been "a most ancient law of the Egyptians".

[17] See the text of *Digesta* 47, 11, 4, cited above, note 1.

[18] For the fate of Giles Corey, see Hansen, ed. *cit.* pp. 198-199; on the history of *la peine forte et dure* to compel a prisoner to "put himself upon the country", see Holdsworth, *op. cit.,* vol. 1, pp. 326-327 where this historian notes the technicality that the prisoner must so consent if confiscation of his property is to follow upon an adverse judgment, the fact that the first mention of pressing as the form this might take (A.D. 1406) after various other tortures had been tried during the 13th and 14th centuries, and finally the fact that this "senseless barbarity" remained on the books until 1772.

[19] Holdsworth, *op. cit.,* vol. 11, pp. 556-560.

[20] *Ibidem,* vol. 11, pp. 561-566.

[21] *Ibidem,* vol. 4, pp. 509-511.

Queries About "Abortion to Save the Mother's Life"

by P.J. Micallef

P.J. Micallef is Professor of Philosophy, Notre Dame University, Nelson, B.C.

In its exclusive sense, abortion to save the mother's life involves the extreme case when either the mother or the child can be saved but not the two, and a choice has to be made between the life of one or the death of both.

In the present stage of obstetrics and gynecology, abortion to save the mother's life is hardly more than a theoretical question. While formerly it might have practically been the rule, it is now the proverbial exception.[1] To a growing number of theologians and moralists, Catholic and Protestant alike, abortion to save the mother's life is also increasingly ceasing to be a moral issue. While ruling out abortion for mere convenience, they concede that abortion is justifiable in the event of a mortal conflict between the mother and the child or when some value commensurate with life is at stake. However, in the light of medical practice and legal interpretation, the moral acceptance of abortion to save the mother's life might place the moralist in a vulnerable position. In their interpretation of the phrase, "to save the mother's life", the medical and legal professions have taken into account—foetal values aside—not so much the indication seriously threatening the life of the mother as the existential totality of the woman herself in relation to her family, her total environment and the community in which she lives and brings forth her child. In other words, if the moralist is going to find some justification for abortion on grounds of physical danger, might he not as well seek and find some justification for abortion to safeguard personal, psychological, social, economic and humanitarian values? Like the medical and legal professions, might he not as well be required to acknowledge the presence of values which earlier generations might not have suspected could possibly be involved in abortion to save the mother's life?

1. THE MEDICAL VIEWPOINT AND THE LAW'S INTERPRETATION

"It is difficult for an honest, conscientious physician to define the phrase 'to preserve the life of the mother' ", writes Dr. Alan F. Guttmacher, a leading advocate of liberal abortion laws. "Does this phrase actually mean to prevent her death, so that a death certificate will not be issued for her, or are there other things involved?"[2]

In the interpretation of the life-risk, imminent death does not appear to be the exclusive criterion for judging the necessity of a therapeutic abortion. "The inability to delimit the time interval between the non-performance of an abortion and subsequent death", says Dr. André Hellegers, "has facilitated acceptability of the so-called *maternal health indications*".[3] These indications may not be, as Dr. Kenneth Ryan calls them, "life-threatening", but they can be "life-devastating". He puts it at some length as follows:

> Pregnancy poses many threats to the mother and the family unit which are outside the "traditional" realm of medical practice but well within this expanded concept... Although none of these may be life-threatening, they are life-devastating, so apparently life-devastating that throughout the world, even in countries with "liberal" abortion laws, women desperately seek, and usually obtain, abortion by any means possible (even at considerable risk to life). It is not the pregnancy that is necessarily so terrifying as the sequelae. The pregnant woman with heart disease may not die while hospitalized for six months for optimal care but she may not be able to care for the child normally or see it reach full maturity. Living with children in poverty that sustains a pattern of futility of life, living with a hopelessly deformed or retarded child or bearing an illegitimate one is a life situation that many pregnant women will not accept...
>
> In short, a physician cannot for practical purposes list a group of "disease states" or conditions as medical indications for abortion. There are no absolute medical indications... [4]

The upshot of Dr. Ryan's description of the risks that pregnancy poses is this: while it can be said that there is hardly a pregnancy today which necessitates abortion for strictly therapeutic reasons, to save or prolong the mother's life and preserve her health, it can also be said that there is hardly an unwanted pregnancy which in one way or another may not be said to psychologically upset a woman's total life situation. Thus, in terms of abortion decisions, a broader and less distinguishable set of circumstances comes into play. Attention is not directed towards the illness as such: it is rather directed towards the existential situation or the future development of the woman herself, her other children, her whole family—paradoxically, even towards the future well-being of her unborn child himself. A broadly understood concept of maternal life and health has thus gradually become the real issue today. Whatever the reasons for abortion—be they the socio-economic, humanitarian, eugenic or otherwise—these indications are medically intended to cover something beyond saving the mother's physical life and preserving her physical health in the strict and traditional sense of the terms. They are statements about the mother's condition or specific instances of how the mother's life or health may be impaired.

By the use of such a formula, "to save the life of the mother", it is the intention of the medical profession to cover those particularly hard cases with exceptional or peculiar circumstances about them by relating or attaching them to the mother's life or health. These particularly hard cases are what the medical and psychiatric professions consider to be preventive medicine: the psychological, social and environmental conditions necessary for health and one's general well-being—conditions which are practically impossible to express in brief medical terms.

To cite the instance of abortion performed when there is the possibility that the child might be born deformed: where the eugenic indication is not specifically covered by the law's provisions—and in Canada, to mention one, it is not[5]—the medical reason for terminating such a pregnancy lies in the mental and psychological stress that may be provoked on the mother. So if an abortion is sought for eugenic reasons, as in fact it is, it receives its medical (and legal) blessing if months of apprehension that her child might be a highly deformed baby is considered to cause the mother undue mental or psychological stress. The premise is not, if the pregnancy is defective, then it may be terminated; but rather, if a woman pregnant with a possible defective pregnancy cannot psychologically and emotionally bear the very thought of such a pregnancy, then the pregnancy may be terminated—further underlining the point that even foetal indications are reducible to the maternal indication of saving a woman's life or preserving her health.[6] As Ralph J. Gampell puts it: "If you use enough semantic tricks there isn't any abortion problem, because there is no case which is not capable of being analyzed as being a threat to the life of the pregnant woman."[7]

In law, the question whether or not any abortion request may be subsumed under the comprehensive indication to save the mother's life first arose in England, in 1938, when Dr. Aleck Bourne, an eminent gynecologist, was charged with performing an abortion on a fourteen-year-old girl who had been gang-raped by a number of horse-guardsmen.

Until its sweeping revisions in 1967, Britain's legal provisions concerning abortion — and Canada's law and that of some American States were, before reform, based on and inspired by them — were contained in the *Offences Against the Person Act* of 1861 and, somewhat obliquely, in the *Infant Life Preservation Act* of 1929.

The carefully-worded Act of 1861 contained the all-important term "unlawfully".[8] Its real significance was not specified in and by the Act and both the medical and legal professions understood it to imply that some abortions might indeed be lawful after all. However, which instances could be considered lawful were by no means specified. In view of this lack of definition, what before very long became the accepted medical practice was to destroy the child *in utero*, shortly before birth or even at the very onset of labour, by embryotomy, when the procedure was considered necessary to save the mother's life. This form of child destruction was not strictly abortion because at this stage the foetus is quite viable and it had gone beyond the stage to which the term "abortion" applies. Nor was it infanticide/homicide because these terms were, as they still are, applicable to the human being and the unborn child is not, in law, a human being.

Since such a medical practice was covered by no Act, Bill or Statute, a step forward towards filling this legal gap was taken in 1929 when the English Statute created a special offence of child destruction, known as the *Infant Life Preservation Act* (1929). Originally proposed in England by various bills, dated as far back as 1867 and 1874 and by the Royal Commission's *Report of the Criminal Code* (1879), for some unexplained reason it was never enacted into law until 1929. Canada, however, filled that legal gap between viability and birth immediately this Report became available to the Parliament of Canada, which in 1892 it adopted with some changes and modifications as its Criminal Code. The *Infant Life Preservation Act*, which corresponds to Canada's Section 209 of the Criminal Code, was primarily designed to prevent children being destroyed at birth, once they had been spared abortion. However, the Act provided a very important limitation: "No person shall be found guilty of an offence under this section unless it is proved that the act which caused the death of the child was not done in good faith for the purpose only of preserving the life of the mother."

Strictly speaking, the 1861 and 1929 Acts were unrelated because they covered two distinct periods in foetal development. But so-called "therapeutic abortions" were performed nonetheless, no doubt in fear and trembling, on the strength of the term "unlawfully" of 1861 and the "saving clause" of 1929.

Dr. Bourne was charged under the provisions of the 1861 Act and his line of defence, which was accepted by the Court, proceeded in part on the saving clause of the 1929 Act (where the exception is limited to the preservation of the mother's life), and read into "unlawfully" of the 1861 Act the same exception covered by the 1929 Act, even though the 1929 Act did not concern abortion as such. Furthermore, his defence interpreted the preservation-of-life clause in a more extended sense to include as well the safeguarding of the mother's health. No clear-cut distinction could be drawn between the purpose of saving the mother's physical life, he argued, and the preservation of a mother's mental health, which was the indication in the present case. It was Dr. Bourne's intention "to establish in the eyes of the law that mental health was just as important as physical health, and in certain cases perhaps even more so".[9] He argued that there are many vague and almost indefinable conditions which, as serious dangers to health though not to life, are much more important than many straight cases of heart or chest disease. The latter often suffer little or no real depreciation of health, and they carry the label of a named disease which is readily accepted by laymen; the former class, by reason of the lack of concise clinical definition, may not be readily convincing cases in any subsequent investigation. These patients form the real problem.

In his summing-up on the Bourne case, Mr. Justice MacNaghten told the jury: "If the doctor is of the opinion, on reasonable grounds and with adequate knowledge, that the probable consequence of the continuance of the pregnancy will be to make the woman a physical or mental wreck, the jury are quite entitled to take the view that the doctor who, in those circumstances, and in the honest belief, operates, is operating for the purpose of preserving the life of the woman." They were further instructed to take a prudent view of the significance of the preservation-of-life clause. In his words: "The law is not that the doctor has got to wait until the unfortunate woman is in peril of immediate death and then at the last moment snatch her from the jaws of death ... Nobody suggests that the operation only becomes legal when a patient is dead."[10]

Dr. Bourne's line of defence has since become the now-celebrated

"Bourne Principle", a major landmark in the history of abortion law reform. Theoretically, it is applicable to cases where the woman, in no danger of losing her life, might otherwise be left impaired, physically, mentally or otherwise. Such cases include those that doctors in good faith consider part and parcel of good up-to-date therapeutic medical care, particularly those involving a greater risk of injury to health, in the form of mental or nervous shock or acute distress than even Bourne's particular case might have actually presented. More specifically, the principle established beyond reasonable doubt that therapeutic abortion is not limited to cases where the operation is performed for the purpose only of preventing the mother from having her life cut short; nor is it limited to cases where the threat to the mother's life or health is a somatic or bodily illness; nor need this threat be proximate or imminent. On the contrary, whatever is threatening the mother's life or health, psychiatric, psychological or otherwise, could well be diagnosed to be remote; furthermore, no proof is required of what other or prior measures had been or could be taken to overcome the potential danger; finally, the principle established that it is sufficient to operate in the honest belief that continuation of the pregnancy would or would be likely to endanger a woman's life or health.

Briefly, in law, as in medicine, the phrase, "to save the mother's life", has appeared to be meaningful only if it is construed in a large context which is by no means limited to the case of saving the mother from certain death; and which includes cases where the continuance of the pregnancy would even remotely make the woman a physical or mental wreck. Finally, all proof to the contrary, that an abortion was not performed to preserve the life or health (physical or mental) of the mother or that the doctor did not in good faith believe the abortion was necessary, lay with the state. In the circumstances, this was quite a heavy burden of proof.[11]

2. THE MORALIST'S POSITION

A typical attempt to see morality in general and by application a number of actions, including abortion, in a large context has been made by the Most Reverend Francis Simons, Bishop of Indore, India. He proposes "a number of moral positions which seem to be radically opposed to traditional Catholic doctrines" but he offers them "as a more faithful rendering of even more basic Catholic doctrines which teach that God made everything on earth for the sake of man, that he imposed laws only for man's good, and that love is the fulfilment of the law".[12]

The root source of a modern Christian morality, he suggests, is not so much the Bible or natural law as the consensus of what constitutes "the good or welfare of man — in society and individually".[13] Though some moral law is virtually self-evident and thus constant through history (for example, respect for life and property), there has also been change and development in man's understanding of morality. For instance, such practices as slavery and polygamy — which previous generation accepted as moral — have long since been regarded as wrong. Thus with "the greater good of men" or "the welfare of mankind" as his criterion, Bishop Simons argues that certain violations of traditionally accepted moral principles would today be regarded as reasonable exceptions to the general rule rather than sinful inconsistencies.

Speaking of the commandment, "You shall not kill", in relation to self-defence (individual and collective), he suggests that "whichever explanation is construed to justify the killing in these circumstances, there is no denying that they are exceptions to the general rule, 'You shall not kill', and thus show that the rule is not absolute. The reason why it is not absolute is that the general rule is meant to safeguard the greater good of man and does not apply when it becomes an obstacle to it". Applying the general rule to abortion, he further argues that although no valid reasons can be advanced for permitting abortion only to avoid an "unwanted child" or to escape shame or inconvenience—in such cases we can only speak of murder—there is a near-consensus of mankind that the commandment does not apply when the killing of the unborn child is honestly deemed the only means of preventing the death of both mother and child. He goes on to say that when abortion is performed to avoid almost certain or very probable serious harm to the health of the mother, its licitness is at least arguable.[14]

Father Charles E. Curran, of the Catholic University of America, also believes that an argument can be made to justify the priority of maternal rights over foetal rights. Without specifying any conditions, if there are any, he suggests that abortion can be justified without violating the principle of the sanctity of life:

> In discussing the problem of abortion, I believe that a Christian theologian must take the conservative position of treating the fetus at least from blastocyst as human life. However, even in the past the teaching of Catholic theologians and the statements of the hierarchical magisterium on abortion seem too restricted. Conflict situations cannot be solved merely by the physical structure and causality of the act. The human values involved must be carefully considered and weighed. In

Catholic theology there is a precedent for equating other values with life itself. As a Christian, any taking of life, must be seen as a reluctant necessity. However, in the case of abortion there can arise circumstances in which the abortion is justified for preserving the life of the mother or for some other important value commensurate with life even though the action aims at abortion "as a means to an end".[15]

In their study on the morality of abortion, the Church Assembly Board of Social Responsibility of the Church of England adopted a similar approach. Asserting as a fundamental premise "the general inviolability of the foetus" and "its right to live and develop" and, consequently, that "because of its potential future, there is a *presumption* that we ought to do what we can to preserve the foetus", they state that there may be good reasons for setting this presumption aside. While they did not accept abortion on the possibility of grave deformity or where pregnancy is the result of rape or incest—these grounds, they stated, rarely stand alone—they did concede that abortion may be a morally permissible or advisable course of action if a particular pregnancy is affecting the mother adversely. Again, they did not specify the conditions or the circumstances which may so affect the mother—it is up to her to specify and particularize them, for in making this concession they placed the burden of proof "firmly on those who, in particular cases, would wish to extinguish that right on the ground that it was in conflict with another or others with a higher claim to recognition".[16]

Karl Barth himself does not accept abortion for eugenic reasons. However, he does accept abortion in the event of a mortal (and near mortal) conflict involving the mother's life (and possibly health)—an approach that in the end might oblige him to accept what he so categorically rejects in the first place.[17]

Like Barth, John T. Noonan, Jr., who does not otherwise consider abortion as morally justifiable, sees some justification for it on the basis of St. Thomas' considerations on self-defence. Speaking of homicide, St. Thomas makes a distinction between killing "sinners"[18], and killing "innocents"[19], declaring that it is lawful, sometimes mandatory, to kill the former but "in no way lawful" to kill the latter. Speaking of self-defence as such, however, and without making any distinctions at all between "sinners" and "innocents", he declares that under the conditions of the double effect principle it is lawful for *someone* to kill *someone*.[20] On the basis of this principle, Noonan argues that, for an argument to be made to justify abortion to save the mother's life, "much would depend on how absolutely Thomas meant his declaration . . . that 'in no way is it lawful to kill the innocent'. If the statement held literally, it would seem to preclude capital punishment for a repentant thief, who has become innocent, as most men become innocent, by repentance; yet Thomas justified capital punishment''.[21] In my opinion, the texts cited by Noonan appear to leave no doubt that, from the moral standpoint, St. Thomas meant his declaration to be taken categorically. As for inflicting punishment on a repentant thief, Noonan appears to overlook the fact that the repentant thief is not innocent absolutely.[22] At any rate, he goes on to say that "it cannot be said definitely how Thomas would have answered... in the case of therapeutic abortion to save the mother's life", but later on in his discussion Noonan concludes that "once the humanity of the foetus is perceived, abortion is never right except in self-defence".[23]

The moral acceptance of abortion to save the mother's life is endorsed in similar terms by other contemporary moralists but none offer any criteria as to how self-defence or danger to the mother's life may be interpreted and applied in concrete situations.[24] In abortion decisions, self-defence may be so construed as to cover just about any situation: once the principle of self-defence in abortion is established and accepted, one immediately becomes involved in the same sort of situation that the medical and legal professions had put themselves when they first acknowledged the necessity of abortion "in good faith for the purpose only of preserving the life of the mother". One immediately becomes involved in questions of interpretation.

The approach of some contemporary moralists with regard to the moral problem of abortion is to do for the woman, pregnant with an unwanted pregnancy, what the medical and legal professions have been doing from their respective standpoint: to see maternal life and health in relation to her total life situation, considering the degree of "mental death" which occurs in the mother, if the pregnancy is not terminated, against the "physical death" of the unborn child.

Is such a moral concession towards abortion advisable? If the mental death of the mother is not a proportionately grave reason for permitting the death of the child, might one then be a little less unyielding and in the name of maternal life-values accept to argue for, say, Noonan's self-defence exception or Karl Barth's mortal or near-mortal conflict?

Indeed, one might never know that life itself is involved unless the mother dies. So when an attempt is made to justify abortion in the event of a mortal conflict, in self-defence or to save the mother's life, does this mean that the mother must be snatched from her deathbed before the abortion becomes a morally admissible course of action? Or might not (and must not) such danger as might exist be interpreted "reasonably", "prudently", meaning that the mother need not be *in extremis* before the abortion may be performed?

Dr. Ryan's analysis of what medically constitutes a risk to the mother's life or health and the legal latitude provided by the Bourne Principle are a guide to what may be the result of accepting abortion to save the mother's life. From the original medical necessity that the law recognized to the basic approach of the new moralists, the transition is easily made. If, from the moral standpoint, one were then to accept only the exception to save the mother's life, before too long the moralist may, like the medical and legal professions, find himself forced also to interpret this exception "reasonably" or in a "prudent" sense. For that reason, it seems to me one may no more draw the line at that one point (and exclusively at that one point)—"in good faith for the purpose only of preserving the life of the mother" (which was the law's original necessity to justify abortion)—any more than one may draw it, as the law found it necessary to draw it, a little further on and so on—unless a way can be found to limit the original justification to the case in which continuation of the pregnancy would cause the mother's physical death. But, as I pointed out earlier, that case no longer seems to occur under modern medical conditions. The law's original necessity to save the mother's life led it to the Bourne Principle; in turn, the Bourne Principle led it to whatever, in Canada's own abortion language, "would or would be likely to endanger her life or health"—in effect, any difficult personal situation. To this effect, Glanville Williams points out that "once abortion is permitted to save the mother's life and preserve her health and working capacity, there can be no convincing reason for stopping short at this point and refusing to take account of wider social grounds".[25]

More to our point, recalling the views on abortion of Rabbi Moshitz Vie, a former rabbi of Antwerp, Belgium, Rabbi David M. Feldman, of New York, said that "if we are going to allow abortion on grounds of physical discomfort, we ought all the more so to allow it on grounds of social, spiritual, emotional embarassment...". But Rabbi Vie stops short because, in the words of Rabbi Feldman, "he didn't want to carry the legal reasoning to its social consequences".[26]

Footnotes

[1] The literature on the subject is abundant. See, among others, Alan F. Guttmacher, "The Shrinking Non-Psychiatric Indications for Therapeutic Abortion", in Harold Rosen, Ed., *Therapeutic Abortion*, New York, Julian Press, 1954, p. 13: "Two decades ago the accepted attitude of the physician was that, if a pregnant woman were ill, the thing to do would be to rid her of her pregnancy. Today, it is felt that, unless the pregnancy itself intensifies the illness, nothing is accomplished by abortion"; "Abortion—Yesterday, Today and Tomorrow", in Alan F. Guttmacher, Ed., *The Case for Legalized Abortion Now*, Berkeley, Diablo Press, 1967, p.9: "Today it is possible for almost any patient to be brought through pregnancy alive, unless she suffers from a fatal illness such as cancer or leukemia and if so, abortion would be unlikely to prolong, much less save life"; R.V. Colpitts, "Trends in Therapeutic Abortion", *American Journal of Obstetrics and Gynecology*, October 1954: "Whatever indications we may use, therapeutic abortion always constitutes a failure of medical science."

For statistical analyses of the virtual disappearance of the medical necessity to save the mother's life by abortion, see: Irving K. Perlmutter, "Analysis of Therapeutic Abortions: Bellevue Hospital, New York 1935-45", *American Journal of Obstetrics and Gynecology*, 1947, 53:1008-1018; J.G. Moore and J.H. Randall, "Trends in Therapeutic Abortion: A Review of 137 Cases", *Ibid.*, 1952, 63:28; K.P. Russell, "Changing Indications for Therapeutic Abortion", *Journal of the American Medical Association*, January 10, 1953, 151:108, summarizes the results of the Los Angeles County Hospital from 1931 to 1950. Cf. Charles J. MacFadden, *Medical Ethics*, Philadelphia, F.A. Davis, 1966, p. 151, for additional data supplied by Dr. Russell himself for the period 1951-60; "Therapeutic Abortions in California in 1950", *Western Journal of Surgery*, October 1952, 60:497; G.W. Thomas, "The Effect of Pregnancy on the Course of Tuberculosis", *Canadian Medical Association Journal*, 1959, 81:710, discusses pulmonary tuberculosis as an outmoded indication for therapeutic abortion; Robert E. Hall, "Therapeutic Abortion, Sterilization and Contraception" *American Journal of Obstetrics and Gynecology*, 1965, 91:518, shows that in a number of American hospitals in as many as 24,417 deliveries there were no abortions performed at all, while in others there was an average of one abortion in about 36 deliveries.

[2] Alan F. Guttmacher, "Therapeutic Abortion: One Physician's Viewpoint", *Quarterly Review of Surgery, Obstetrics and Gynecology*, October-December, 1959, 16:237; Dr. G.B. Maughan, Montreal, in *Minutes of Proceedings and Evidence of the Standing Committee on Justice and Legal Affairs*, Ottawa: Queen's Printer, 1969, March 20, 1969, p. 578.

[3] André E. Hellegers, "Law and the Common Good", *Commonweal*, June 30, 1967, 86:419. Emphasis is author's.

[4] Robert E. Cooke *et al.*, Eds., *The Terrible Choice: The Abortion Dilemma*, New York: Bantam Books, 1968, pp. 68-70.

[5] Cf. Criminal Code of Canada, Section 237 (4) (c) where it is clearly stated that termination of pregnancy may be performed if "the continuation of the pregnancy of such female person would or would be likely to endanger her life or health". However, Mr. John C. Munro, Minister of National Health and Welfare, stated in Parliament on May 15, 1972, that "a small but important group of pregnancies

are terminated for congenital anomalies in the foetus'', *House of Commons Debates*, May 15, 1972, 116:2247.

[6] Kenneth R. Niswander, "Medical Abortion Practices in the United States", in David T. Smith, Ed., *Abortion and the Law*, Cleveland: Western Reserve University Press, 1967, p.54 (also in *Western Reserve Law Review*, 1965, 17:403, 414).

[7] Ralph J. Gampell, in Robert E. Hall, Ed., *Abortion in a Changing World*, New York, Columbia University Press, 1971, Vol. II. p. 165.

[8] Cf. *Offences Against the Person Act*, Section 58; The Earl of Halsbury, Ed., *The Laws of England*, London: Butterworth & Co., 1955, Vol. 10: "It is a felony by statute (1) for any woman with child unlawfully to administer to herself any poison or other noxious thing or to use any instrument or other means whatsoever with intent to procure her own miscarriage; or (2) for any person unlawfully to administer to or cause to be taken by any woman, whether she is with child or not, any poison or noxious thing with intent to procure her miscarriage, or to use any instrument or other means with that intent."

[9] Aleck Bourne, "Rex v. Bourne", *Lancet*, July 30, 1938, II:280. For a full account of the Bourne Case, see "Comment: Artificial Abortion Following Rape", *Lancet*, July 9, 1938, II:99; Lilian Wyles, *A Woman at Scotland Yard*, London, Gollancz, 1952, p. 221 *et seq.*; for the socio-legal aspects, see: Aleck W. Bourne, "Social Aspects of Abortion", *British Medical Journal*, February 25, 1939, I:408; Glanville Williams, *The Sanctity of Life and the Criminal Law*, London, Faber & Faber, 1958, pp. 152-176; for a critical comment on the legal and medical case, see *The Tablet*, July 23, 1938, 172:103.

[10] *Rex v. Bourne, All England Reports*, 3, 615, 1938.

[11] The Bourne Principle was subsequently upheld in other cases. See in particular: *Rex v. Bergman & Ferguson* (1948) which appeared to reinforce Bourne by implying that the mother's life must be considered in relation to its quality as well as its duration; *People v. Ballard*, 167 Cal. App. 2d 803, 335, P.2d 204-206 (Dist. Ct. App., 1959), was based solely on the statutory law which then provided only the exception "when necessary to preserve the mother's life": "There is a presumption of necessity when an abortion is performed by a licensed physician, which presumption cannot be overturned merely by showing prior good health ... Surely the abortion statute ... does not mean that the peril of life be imminent. It ought to be enough that the dangerous condition be potentially present, even though its full development might be delayed to a greater or less extent." Closer to our time is *U.S. v. Vuitch* (1971): "We are unable to believe that Congress intended that a physician be required to prove his innocence. We therefore hold that, under 22 D.C. Code 201, the burden is on the prosecution to plead and prove that an abortion was not 'necessary for the preservation of the mother's life or health'."

[12] Francis Simons, "The Catholic Church and the New Morality", *Cross Currents*, 1966, 16:429,445.

[13] *Ibid.*, p. 435.

[14] *Ibid.*, pp. 437-439.

[15] Charles E. Curran, *A New Look at Christian Morality*, Indiana, Fides Publishers, 1968, pp. 242-243.

[16] *Abortion: An Ethical Discussion*, London: Church Information Office, 1965, pp. 31-32,66. Emphasis is authors'. For a criticism of the Church's concession, see Letitia Fairfield, "Abortion and the Law: An Anglican Committee's Views",

The Tablet, January 15, 1966, 220:68-69: "An ingenious idea, but it opens doors to every abuse ... ".
[17] Karl Barth, *Church Dogmatics*, Edinburgh, T. & T. Clark, 1961, III:4, pp. 415-427. See also Paul Ramsey, "Points in Deciding About Abortion", in John T. Noonan, Jr., Ed. *The Morality of Abortion*, Cambridge, Harvard University Press, 1970, pp. 91-94.
[18] II-II, q.64, a.2; Noonan, *op. cit.*, p.25 *et seq.*
[19] II-II, q.64, a.6; also *De Malo*, q.13, a.4 ad 11: "To kill the innocent imports a determination of evil, and this can never be well done."
[20] II-II, q.64, a.7.
[21] Noonan, *op. cit.*, p.25.
[22] I-II, q.105, a.2, ad 9.
[23] Noonan, *op. cit.*, pp.25-26, 58.
[24] Cf. Cornelius J. Van der Poel, "The Principle of Double Effect", in Charles E. Curran, Ed., *Absolutes in Moral Theology*, Washington, D.C.: Corpus Books, 1968, pp. 204-205; William H. Van der Marck, *Toward a Christian Ethic*, trans. D.J. Barrett, Westminster, Md: Newman Press, 1967, pp.56-57; Daniel Callahan, *Abortion: Law, Choice and Morality*, New York: Macmillan, 1970, Chaps. XI-XII; Germain Grisez, *Abortion: The Myths, the Realities and the Arguments*, Washington: Corpus Books, 1971, Chaps. VI-VII.
[25] Williams, *op. cit.*, p.215.
[26] Hall, *op. cit.*, pp.95-96.

Roe v. Wade: A Canadian Perspective

by Philip Slayton

Philip Slayton is Associate Professor of Law, McGill University.

The Supreme Court of the United States has now pronounced on the abortion question. On January 22, 1973, the Court handed down its decision in the already famous case of *Roe v. Wade*.[1]

In this case action was brought for declaratory and injunctive relief respecting Texas criminal abortion laws which the plaintiffs claimed were unconstitutional. The Texas Penal Code made it a crime to procure or attempt an abortion, with the exception of an abortion procured or attempted on medical advice for the purpose of saving the life of the mother. Jane Roe, a pregnant single woman, claimed among other things that the Texas statute abridged her right of personal privacy protected by the First, Fourth, Fifth, Ninth, and Fourteenth Amendments to the United States Constitution.[2]

1. THE MAJORITY JUDGMENT IN ROE V. WADE

The majority judgment in *Roe v. Wade* was delivered by Mr. Justice Blackmun. Blackmun noted that the Supreme Court of the United States in a series of decisions "has recognized that a right of personal privacy, or a guarantee of certain areas or zones of privacy, does exist under the Constitution".[3] He then determined that the right of personal privacy includes the abortion decision:

> This right of privacy, whether it be founded in the Fourteenth Amendment's concept of personal liberty and restrictions upon

state action, as we feel it is, or as the District Court determined, in the Ninth Amendment's reservation of rights to the people, is broad enough to encompass a woman's decision whether or not to terminate her pregnancy. The detriment that the State would impose upon the pregnant woman by denying this choice altogether is apparent. Specific and direct harm medically diagnosable even in early pregnancy may be involved. Maternity, or additional offspring, may force upon the woman a distressful life and future. Psychological harm may be imminent. Mental and physical health may be taxed by child care. There is also the distress, for all concerned, associated with the unwanted child, and there is the problem of bringing a child into a family already unable, psychologically and otherwise, to care for it. In other cases, as in this one, the additional difficulties and continuing stigma of unwed motherhood may be involved.[4]

However, the Court felt unable to hold that this privacy right was absolute; the right was qualified by State interest in "safeguarding health, in maintaining medical standards, and in protecting potential life".[5] The Court found that the "compelling point" with regard to State interest in the health of the mother was at the end of the first trimester; until the end of this period mortality in abortion is less than mortality in normal childbirth.[6] The "compelling point" with regard to State interest in potential life is at viability; this is so because from then on the foetus has the capability of meaningful life outside the mother's womb. Mr. Justice Blackmun concluded:

> Measured against these standards, Art. 1196 of the Texas Penal Code, in restricting legal abortions to those "procured or attempted by medical advice for the purpose of saving the life of the mother," sweeps too broadly. The statute makes no distinction between abortions performed early in pregnancy and those performed later, and it limits to a single reason, "saving" the mother's life, the legal justification for the procedure. The statute, therefore, cannot survive the constitutional attack made upon it here.[7]

The Supreme Court in this manner endorsed a three trimester approach to abortion. In the last trimester of pregnancy (roughly the period of "viability") the State's interest in protecting potential life allows it to prohibit abortion (except in those cases where abortion is necessary to protect the health of the mother). In the middle trimester, a period in which statistically the medical danger of an abortion is greater than that of childbirth, the State's interest in protecting the health of the mother allows it to regulate (but not prohibit) abortion "to the extent that the regulation reasonably relates to the preservation and protection of maternal health".[8] But in the first trimester, the State has no constitutional interest in prohibiting or regulating abortion, and any State legislation dealing with abortion is invalid.[9]

The *ratio decidendi* of *Roe v. Wade* (and *Doe v. Bolton*) is clearly one of United States' constitutional law. The Supreme Court simply decided that a right of privacy embracing the abortion decision exists in the United States Constitution, probably in the Fourteenth Amendment, but that this aspect of the right is qualified by State interest in safeguarding health and potential life.[10] What is of interest to Canada and other jurisdictions not subject to the uncertainties of the United States Constitution, are the general principles and attitudes, existing independently of constitutional interpretation, which can be deduced from the case. What is the nature of the so-called "right to privacy", and what is the significance of this right for the abortion debate? What is the validity of the "three-trimester approach" to abortion?

2. THE "RIGHT TO PRIVACY"

In *Roe* the Supreme Court offers no general explanation of the elusive idea of privacy. All that the majority does is associate the concept with detriment suffered by a pregnant woman who does not want her child and who is unable to obtain an abortion.[11] The United States Constitution itself nowhere mentions a right of privacy, but in a series of previous decisions[12] the Supreme Court had identified a constitutionally protected zone of privacy incorporating activities relating to marriage, procreation, contraception, family relationships, and child rearing and education. The substance of these decisions can, however, be grossly overrated; Shirley Hufstedler, a Circuit Judge of the United States Court of Appeals for the Ninth Circuit, observed when giving the twenty-eighth Benjamin N. Cardozo lecture that "the content of the right (to privacy) remains elusive, the constitutional sources from which it springs are vaguely charted, and the remedies for its vindication remain largely ephemeral".[13]

General definitions of the term "privacy" abound. Westin, for example, defines "privacy" as "the claim of individuals, groups, or institutions to determine for themselves when, how, and to what extent information about them is communicated to others".[14] Arthur R. Miller writes that "of late... lawyers and social scientists have been reaching the conclusion that the basic attribute of an effective right of privacy is the individual's ability to control the circulation of information relating to him..."[15] Hufstedler claims that "the personal interest to be protected by a right of privacy is the individual's interest in preserving his essential dignity as a human being. It is his interest in securing the autonomy of his personality".[16] The recent Canadian government report *Privacy and Computers* identifies three major categories of privacy claims — territorial privacy, privacy of the person, and privacy in the information context. The report says of privacy of the person that "this sense of privacy transcends the physical and is aimed essentially at protecting the dignity of the human person".[17] A background study associated with this report defined privacy in general as "the capacity to exercise control over what a person or group of persons perceive to be a right to physical space (environmental) or over relationships with others (human-relational)".[18]

The most noticeable characteristic of these and other definitions and analyses is their lack of real content. The concept of privacy is like a ventriloquist's dummy; it shouts back at you what you shout at it.[19] Abstract philosophical writings on the subject generally recognize that this is the case; consequently they tend to explore the *nature* of privacy, without ever identifying what is private and what is not. Benn, for example, writes as follows:

> "Private"... is both norm-dependent and norm-invoking. It is norm-dependent because *private affairs* and *private rooms* cannot be identified without some reference to norms.... It is norm-invoking in that one need say no more than "This is a private matter" to claim that anyone not invited to concern himself with it ought to stay out of it.[20]

Similarly, W.L. Weinstein observes that "'public' and 'private' are contrast-concepts jointly exhausting the full range of *social* phenomena and... they typically have a normative basis and function in moral and political discourse".[21] The norm-dependent nature of privacy was recognized by the Privacy and Computers Report when it commented, in discussing privacy of the person, that "this 'personal space' is not bounded by real walls and fences, but by legal norms and social values".[22] It is my view that legal norms do *not* help define privacy; if they did, we could not say reasonably of a law that "this law infringes our right to privacy", and yet this statement is clearly one we should be permitted to make. The law should properly be considered as an indication, more or less reliable according to circumstances, of prevailing social norms.

Do Canadian social norms define a right to privacy that allows a woman an unregulated abortion choice? Section 251 of the Criminal Code of Canada provides that anyone who attempts to carry out the intention to procure a miscarriage is liable to imprisonment for life, and that every pregnant woman who uses any means or permits any means to be used for the purpose of procuring a miscarriage is liable to imprisonment for two years. (The section excepts from these provisions therapeutic abortions, provided various conditions for such abortions are fulfilled.) Can it perhaps be argued that in the case of abortion the law gives no indication of corresponding social norms? Is this one instance when the legislators have utterly failed to understand and respond to the standards of the Canadian people? There *is* a strong lobby in favour of relaxing or eliminating Canadian abortion laws. But equally there is strong sentiment for their retention and strict enforcement. There is probably as yet no consensus and perhaps not even a majority opinion on this question. Do we, then, face a situation in which there are no relevant societal norms? In such a situation should the law simply remain silent?

Section 251 of the Criminal Code should be taken to indicate, at the very least, that at the time of its enactment Canadian society was opposed to abortion in almost every case. My view is that while this or any other provision remains on the statute books the presumption is that it still reflects correctly the norms of society. The burden of proof to demonstrate otherwise must rest on those who claim otherwise, and this burden can only be discharged by successfully advocating repeal of the relevant provisions. This approach is, of course, an absurdity if the only basis on which Parliament could repeal the abortion laws is a demonstrable majority opinion that they are wrong. Then pro-abortionists would face the dilemma that only repeal would demonstrate existence of the necessary norms, but repeal could only take place following such a demonstration. The dilemma is, however, a false one, for Parliament can act on a basis other than expressed mores (and yet paradoxically itself demonstrate social standards when acting). This short note offers no opportunity to explore in depth the true nature and basis of law-making in a democratic society; suffice it to say here that law-making comprises due measure of both authority and response to the community's wishes.

There is a final quasi-technical objection to the idea that a right to "physical" privacy permits unregulated abortion. Any such right could extend only over the body of the individual claiming it. The unborn child is not just a part of the mother's body, but a separate body, with the potential of leading a separate existence. The right to be physically let alone does not encompass a right to destroy such a being.

3. THE THREE-TRIMESTER APPROACH TO ABORTION

What of the three-trimester approach to abortion? Putting aside considerations of American constitutional law, does it make sense to argue that in the first trimester abortion should be unregulated, that in the second trimester it should be regulated but not prohibited (in order to protect the life and health of the mother), and that in the third trimester it should be prohibited in most instances (in order to protect "potential life")?

It should first be noted that the Court in *Roe v. Wade* held that even after viability endangerment of the mother's health is sufficient reason to permit an abortion. Ely has severely criticized this approach on obvious grounds:

> This holding—that even after viability the mother's life *or health* (which presumably is to be defined very broadly indeed, so as to include what many might regard as the mother's convenience . . .) must, as a matter of constitutional law, take precedence over what the Court seems prepared to grant at this point has become the fetus's *life* . . . seems to me at least as controversial as its holding respecting the period prior to viability. (Typically, of course, one is not privileged even statutorily, let alone constitutionally, to take another's life in order to save his own life, much less his health.)[23]

An abortion prohibition which permits abortion to protect the broadly-defined health of the mother is a prohibition without meaning.[24] The only rational exception is protection of the mother's life, and a complete prohibition, with no qualification, is entirely defensible.

Secondly, there are inherent absurdities in the Court's justification of the third trimester qualified prohibition, seen in the context of the Court's overall analysis. The explanation of the prohibition is not that there exists in the third trimester a human being which merits the law's protection; but rather that there exists a *potential* life. If we are to talk in terms of potential life, then we must discuss the whole gestation period, for potential life (at the very least) exists during all that time. If we consider that the law must protect potential as well as actual life (and the Supreme Court apparently takes this view) then the third trimester prohibition must be extended, as it was not in *Roe*, to the entire gestation period. An additional feature of this analysis is that the favourite abortion debate as to when a human being comes into existence becomes irrelevant.

A further absurdity is the apparent view of the Supreme Court that *potential* life comes into existence at the moment of viability. If viability is to have any significance, it must be that it marks the beginning of *actual* life (if actual life does not exist throughout the entire gestation period, as many would argue). This feature of the Supreme Court's stance can only be supported by the view that only the born child has actual life; almost nobody in the history of the abortion debate has embraced such a crude viewpoint.

Finally the three trimester approach is remarkable for completely bypassing the fundamental philosophical and moral questions which must underly any significant debate of the abortion issue. What is a human being? What posture should the law adopt towards human life and potential human life? Mr. Justice Blackmun in *Roe v. Wade* casually passed over these critical issues, saying only that "we need not resolve the difficult question of when life begins. When those trained in the respective disciplines of medicine, philosophy, and theology are unable to arrive at any consensus, the judiciary, at this point in the development of man's knowledge, is not in a position to speculate as to the answer."[25] This passage indicates a profoundly unsatisfactory attitude. Even if the "difficult question" cannot at present be resolved, its full implications must be faced. First of all, it is scientifically tenable to argue that the unborn child is alive. Robert Byrn, one of the many who have collected the medical evidence, has observed: "The fetus at eight weeks has a pumping heart with fully deployed blood vessels and has all other internal organs. The face is completely formed, and the arms, legs, hands, feet, toes and fingers are partially formed. The fetus will react to tickling of the mouth or nose, and there is readable electrical activity coming from the brain."[26] Secondly, regardless of one's scientific stance, it is defensible to claim from a moral, religious or legal viewpoint that the zygote, embryo or foetus is "human". Many branches of the law, for example, treat the unborn child as a juridical person; a New York court in *In re Holthausen's Will* stated that "It has been the uniform and unvarying decision of all common law courts in respect of estate matters for at least the past two hundred years that a child en ventre sa mere is 'born' and 'alive' for all purposes for his benefit."[27]

Of course, the issue is not concluded by successfully arguing the "humanness" of the unborn child; it may well be that law-sanctioned destruction of human life is acceptable under certain conditions. What those conditions are (if they exist) is partly a profound legal problem which must not be obscured or ignored. The Supreme Court's analysis in *Roe v. Wade* was not worthy of a final appellate court in a division of powers system.

To summarize: *Roe v. Wade* was decided for reasons of United States constitutional law, and therefore its *ratio decidendi* offers no assistance to Canadians seeking an answer to the abortion issue. The idea of a right to privacy encompassing the abortion decision, accepted by the Supreme Court, should be rejected in Canada, for privacy is a creation of social norms, and Canadian social norms as suggested by Canadian law explicitly reject unregulated abortion. The three trimester approach to abortion, as enunciated by the Supreme Court, contains inherent absurdities and illogicalities and accordingly should be repudiated. Finally, nowhere in *Roe v. Wade* are basic problems dealing with the legal attitude towards life itself discussed; the abortion debate in Canada is worthy of better than that.

Footnotes

[1] 93 S. Ct. 705 (1973). Judgment was given the same day in the related case of *Doe v. Bolton*, 93 S. Ct. 739 (1973). For some details of this case, see no. 9, at p. 6.

[2] Similar constitutional deprivations were alleged in interventions by Halford, a licensed physician, and John and Mary Doe, a childless couple with the wife not pregnant; the Supreme Court dismissed these interventions for lack of standing. The action was first heard by a three-judge district court. The district court found that the Does did not have standing, granted declaratory relief to Roe and Halford on the basis that the Texas criminal abortion statutes were void on their face because they were both unconstitutionally vague and constituted an overbroad infringement of the plaintiffs' Ninth Amendment rights, but held that abstention was warranted with respect to the request for injunctive relief. Roe and Doe appealed to the Supreme Court from that part of the district court judgment denying injunctive relief; the District Attorney purported to cross appeal from the court's grant of declaratory relief.

[3] P. 726. All page references are to *Roe v. Wade* unless otherwise indicated.

[4] P. 727. The Ninth Amendment states: "The enumeration in the Constitution, of certain rights, shall not be construed to deny or disparage others retained by the people." Section One of the Fourteenth Amendment states in part: "No State shall make or enforce any law which shall abridge the privileges or immunities of citizens of the United States; nor shall any State deprive any person of life, liberty, or property, without due process of law; nor deny to any person within its jurisdiction the equal protection of the laws."

[5] P. 727.

[6] Pp. 731-2.

[7] P. 732.

[8] P. 732.

[9] In *Doe v. Bolton* 93 S. Ct. 739 (1973), Mr. Justice Blackmun, relying heavily on the analysis he had already given in *Roe v. Wade*, concluded that those parts of the Georgia abortion statutes which required an abortion to be carried out in a hospital accredited by the Joint Commission on Accreditation of Hospitals (a non-governmental body), which required approval of a hospital abortion committee and confirmation by two independent physicians, and which only permitted

abortions to be carried out on Georgia residents, were violative of the Fourteenth Amendment. In *Roe v. Wade*, Mr. Justice Stewart delivered a separate and brief concurring judgment. Chief Justice Burger and Mr. Justice Douglas each delivered a separate concurring judgment encompassing both *Roe* and *Doe v. Bolton*. In *Roe v. Wade*, Mr. Justice Rehnquist handed down a brief dissenting judgment; he argued that the right to privacy may not include the abortion decision; and in any event the Bill of Rights only guarantees against deprivation of such a right without due process of law. Rehnquist observed that "the test traditionally applied in the area of social and economic legislation is whether or not a law such as that challenged has a rational relation to a valid state objective", and then concluded: " . . . the Court's sweeping invalidation of any restrictions on abortion during the first trimester is impossible to justify under that standard, and the conscious weighing of competing factors which the Court's opinion apparently substitutes for the established test is far more appropriate to a legislative judgment than to a judicial one" (p. 737). Mr. Justice White delivered one dissent for both cases, and Mr. Justice Rehnquist joined with him. Said White: "The Court apparently values the convenience of a pregnant mother more than the continued existence and development of the life or potential life which she carries" (p. 763). Finally, Mr. Justice Rehnquist delivered an additional individual one paragraph dissent in *Doe v. Bolton*.

[10] Professor John Hart Ely of Yale Law School, commenting on the American constitutional law significance of *Roe*, has called the judgment "a very bad decision. . . . It is bad because it is bad constitutional law, or rather because it is *not* constitutional law and gives almost no sense of an obligation to try to be." Referring to a woman's newly-proclaimed freedom to choose an abortion, Ely writes: "What is frightening about *Roe* is that this super-protected right is not inferable from the language of the Constitution, the framers' thinking respecting the specific problem in issue, any general value derivable from the provisions they included, or the nation's governmental structure." See John Hart Ely, "The Wages of Crying Wolf: A Comment on *Roe v. Wade*", 1973, 82 *Yale Law Journal* 920, at p. 947, and pp. 935-6.

[11] P. 727; quoted, *supra* p. 3.

[12] For a list of these decisions, see pp. 726-7. Perhaps the most famous is *Griswold v. Connecticut* 85 S. Ct. 1678 (1965).

[13] The Honourable Shirley M. Hufstedler, *The Directions and Misdirections of a Constitutional Right of Privacy*, the Twenty-Eighth Annual Benjamin N. Cardozo Lecture, (New York: Association of the Bar of the City of New York, 1971), p. 12.

[14] A. Westin, *Privacy and Freedom*, New York, Atheneum, 1967, p. 7.

[15] Arthur R. Miller, *The Assault on Privacy*, Ann Arbor, University of Michigan Press, 1971, p. 25.

[16] *Supra* note 13, at p. 15.

[17] *Privacy and Computers*, A Report of a Task Force established jointly by Department of Communications/Department of Justice, Ottawa, Information Canada, 1972, p. 2.

[18] D.N. Weisstub and C.C. Gotlieb, *The Nature of Privacy*, (A study by the Privacy and Computer Task Force), p. 41.

[19] Or, as Weisstub and Gotlieb put it, "Privacy is . . . a receptacle or a mirror of a host of social, political, psychological and economic value variables." *Ibid*, at p. 39.

[20] Stanley I. Benn, *Privacy, Freedom, and Respect for Persons*, in J. Roland Pennock and John W. Chapman (eds.), *Privacy*, (New York: Atherton Press 1971), 1, at p. 2.
[21] W.L. Weinstein, *The Private and the Free: A Conceptual Inquiry*, in Pennock and Chapman, *ibid.*, 27, at p. 33.
[22] *Supra* note 17.
[23] *Supra* note 10, at p. 921, n. 19.
[24] S. 251 (4) of the Criminal Code allows abortion in Canada when the therapeutic abortion committee of an accredited or approved hospital issues a certificate stating that continuation of pregnancy would endanger the life *or health* of the pregnant woman.
[25] P. 730.
[26] Robert M. Byrn, "Abortion-on-Demand: Whose Morality?", 1970, 46 *Notre Dame Lawyer* 1, at p. 8.
[27] 26 N.Y.S. 2d 140, at p. 143 (Sur. Ct. 1941). Quoted by David W. Louisell and John T. Noonan, Jr., "Constitutional Balance", in Noonan, ed., *The Morality of Abortion*, Cambridge, Harvard University Press, 1970, 220 at p. 222. This essay contains an excellent summary of American law regarding the unborn child.

A Psychiatrist's Experience with Legal Abortion in Canada

by Eloise Jones

Eloise Jones is a practising Psychiatrist in Saskatoon, Saskatchewan.

Before discussing my experiences as a psychiatrist dealing with requests for abortion, I would like to refer to three events which were influential in bringing legal abortion to the Canadian scene.

1. ORIGINS OF THE 1969 CHANGE IN CANADIAN ABORTION LAW

First Event: In 1957 in Great Britain the Wolfendon Report, which was concerned with homosexual offences and prostitution, was published. It had nothing whatever to do with abortion, but it did lay down principles which were to be applied to the other areas. In brief, it separated *sin and crime*. This finally evolved into, "the State has no business in the bedrooms of the nation".

This concept of moral law as distinguished from civil law, and the personal as distinguished from the public good, was applied by politicians and others to the question of abortion. However, very few people appeared to notice at the time of the new legislation, that unlike homosexuality, abortion is a matter of life and death, and that a *third* life is directly involved—in fact is the target marked for killing. A homosexual relationship between two consenting adults is a far cry from the deliberate killing of an innocent, vulnerable child in the process of development.

It's one thing to say that the public good is not affected by a husband and wife practising contraception, but it is quite another to say that the killing of a child in the womb is a private and personal matter.

Second Event: In 1962, in Belgium, a mother who took thalidomide prior to delivery gave birth to a child without arms. After a lapse of one week, she and her husband, her mother and sister and their physician agreed on a course of action, and the infant was killed by the administration of barbiturates. They were charged with murder and acquitted. The public as well as the jury sympathized with their position. No voice was raised on behalf of the child.

In February 1974, a local newspaper in Saskatoon published a story, (complete with photograph) of an adult man without arms, who had developed the use of his feet and legs to compensate for his handicap. The article emphasized his claim that life for him was very much worth while. There was certainly no hint that he himself would have wished his life to be terminated either before or after birth. If he read about that trial in Belgium, he must have had some qualms. Will society in the future, in the name of mercy, or the public good, ask for his death because he is deformed?

Third Event: During the special hearings in the standing committee of Health and Welfare (special abortion Committee) in 1967, when it was suggested that there could be legitimate exceptions to a prohibition against abortion, Mr. Stanley Knowles, who is a veteran parliamentarian, said, "If you have the right to qualify in one instance, have not the others the right to qualify for some other reason?" Now that was absolutely right. He himself voted with his party for abortion. But his remark remains completely valid. If you make one exception, you are going to have people coming along wanting other exceptions. And that is exactly what has happened. Those who favoured abortion hoped to establish the fact that the need for abortion was recognized *in principle* by all, and that the difference between proponents and opponents was merely a difference in degree.

2. A PSYCHIATRIST'S EXPERIENCE WITH WOMEN SEEKING ABORTION

I would like now to talk about my own experience in private practice. On psychiatric grounds, I recommended approximately 500 therapeutic abortions between 1970 and the summer of 1972, at which point I stopped—after I had made certain observations; after I had paused to reflect more on the subject and its far reaching effects; after I had come to certain conclusions.

Contraception and Abortion

First of all, only 20% of those who requested therapeutic abortion had made *any* effort to avoid conceiving. There appeared to be several reasons to account for this:

(1) Side effects or complications of the pill, or the coil
(2) Fear of malignancy (mostly on the part of married women)
(3) Inability to obtain contraceptives because of age (minors)
(4) Fear of going to a physician for this purpose (This reason is related to the next.)
(5) Among the largest group, i.e. single 17-20 yr. olds who represented almost 60% of the total, and also among single women in their 20's and 30's, a reluctance to use birth control pills since this would force them to face the fact that they were intending to indulge in a sex relationship outside of marriage (Pregnancy then became an unfortunate, sometimes a tragic 'accident'.)
(6) Among younger adolescents, e.g. 15-16-(17) yrs., a not infrequent revolt against authority, and, often unconsciously, a use of pregnancy as a weapon to embarrass and hurt their parents (A 17 year old pregnant girl recently admitted this to me as a conscious insight.)
(7) Further the great reluctance on the part of some women (and men now too in an age of vasectomies) to have any chemical or surgical interference in their reproductive functions and potentialities (Any change in their sexual self-image was felt to be psychologically threatening — regardless of age.)
(8) Various "excuses", e.g., "too much bother", or "my husband didn't want me to use contraceptives", or, oddly enough under the circumstances, "I don't believe in contraceptives!"

It became increasingly clear to me that simply to push an educational program advocating the use of contraceptives such as the pill would not appreciably effect the growing number of candidates for therapeutic abortion. There was just no point to it. More and more pregnant women were deciding they did not want their pregnancy to continue; an increasingly large number were using therapeutic abortion as a means of birth control.

"Blob of Tissue" — Escape from Reality

Almost all the women applying for therapeutic abortion repeated the words, "Oh, it's not a baby, there's nothing formed, it's only a blob of tissue", or "It's mostly placenta — nothing much to it", or "I certainly don't have any feeling for it". Those words imply ignorance, and constitute wishful thinking, the desire to escape reality.

A University student who had a therapeutic abortion two years ago saw preserved foetal specimens at various stages in one of her classes. This made her acutely aware of the fact that the two month old foetus is fully formed, and with real regret, she exclaimed to me, "If I'd only known it was like that I mightn't have been so self-centred when I asked for an abortion." A two and one-half month pregnant Grade 12 student told me after she decided not to have an abortion, "When I looked at pictures and discovered that it wasn't just a piece of tissue, that it was fully formed and that it only had to grow in size until birth, I told all my friends about it and now we think this should be taught in school." On this subject, those who are pushing for sex education, birth control and abortion information in the schools have remained silent about the need to give information on the development of the baby in utero. But shouldn't it be taught? This young woman told me that once the abortion was rejected and the decision taken to give birth to the child, her anxiety and depression lifted. "I know I've got problems, but I feel better about it all." Parents need to realize this and be prepared to provide the kind of support their pregnant daughters really need.

A Private Decision?

If the decision to have an abortion were indeed only a personal one, as pro-abortionists say, then the moral burden of that decision would be increased for the pregnant woman, not lessened. When they first came to see me, many pregnant women were too disturbed and depressed, and often too pressured, to consider objectively the whole moral question either relating to themselves, to their unborn children, or to society as a whole, *so long as there was any alternative to continuation of their pregnancy.* That is, so long as they knew that abortion was a possible way out, they remained anxious, upset, disturbed, and unable to properly consider consequences.

An abortion can compound the psychological problems of a woman. This statement is based first of all on the premise that having an abortion must create a situation of conflict, because social acceptance of abortion is brand new in the history of our Western world, and conflict and controversy regarding it rage in the society surrounding the pregnant woman. How can anyone believe that women are so flexible as to absorb a brand new view of life and death without conflict and confusion? If human beings were so flexible, we would all rebound from the problems of childhood and the later crises quite easily, and there wouldn't be any need for psychiatrists. But we are not that flexible. Certain studies would have us believe we are, but I believe these suffer from lack of depth. I have concluded that there are no valid psychiatric grounds for deliberately killing an unborn child.

Why then do a growing number of women resort to this action? How do you brainwash people to make them do that which they previously felt was wrong? As a German psychiatrist has pointed out, history can answer this question very easily. Dictators know the answer. You distort certain values and principles enough to convince the person involved that the act you want her to agree to is a duty, an obligation, something to be done for the sake of others. This kind of brainwashing lasts for a variable length of time.

— Tell a woman that the world is already over-populated, and it would be wrong to have a child.
— Tell a woman that the standard of living of either family or culture is threatened by sharing food and care etc. with more people.
— Tell her that she will be unable to realize her career, or herself, if she has this child.
— Tell her she must not bring an unplanned child into the world, that it is unfair to the child, — after all, if he can't enjoy his rights, it is her duty to kill him rather than allow him to be born.

Therefore the unplanned child, the so-called unwanted child, assumes the role of villain; he *seems* to attack the home, the family, our culture, and our sense of duty as parents. What a terrible travesty of virtue and duty! All these kinds of justification I have heard over and over. I'm sure you have too. Pro-abortionists have used them over and over again.

But was this not supposed to be a private and personal decision? On the contrary, the so-called "moral" arguments which are actually based on a totally materialistic view of life have been and are being used to pressure pregnant women to seek abortion.

Since 1969, it has become clear that abortions are not purely private actions. They *require* the assistance not only of doctors and nurses, but of the entire hospital staff. Both technical knowledge, and also the consciences of others are intimately involved. We know that nurses are upset at the prospect of being forced to assist in a process they abhor. Psychiatrists have been called in to counsel and help "condition" them to new techniques. Again pressure is placed on those unwilling to conform, and the nurse who has a conscience may well feel isolated and helpless. After all abortions are legal in Canada, and therefore, acceptable. Pressure is also put on the public to agree to this new procedure. Those who oppose abortion are often regarded as narrow, self-righteous, anti-progressive and reactionary—damning epithet! Get on the band wagon, and live in the 20th century! Therapeutic abortion a personal decision, a personal point of view? Not by any stretch of the imagination.

Environmental Pressures and Stresses

What were the common environmental pressures and stresses on the 500 pregnant women I examined, stresses that would cause them to seek an abortion? To cite a few: inadequate emotional support, bad social conditions, too much responsibility, social stigma. In the case of teenagers, especially in their early teens, parents would apply strong pressure for abortion, or in the case of older adolescents, there would be marked anxiety lest parents, friends, employers, etc. discover the pregnancy. There was the prospect of interrupted schooling, lost jobs, lost opportunities etc. Sometimes it was the boy friend or husband who applied strong pressure for abortion. For example, a 30 year old woman became extremely disturbed and depressed following her abortion, and wrote to me, "An abortion may be the least desirable solution to an unplanned pregnancy." She described the guilt and hatred the abortion had brought into her life. This woman had originally been strongly motivated towards abortion. She rejected her unborn child. Since she had a chronic physical illness her family doctor felt termination was justified. But following the abortion she said she had been confused prior to it, and was pressured by her husband who was concerned about world population. He had had a vasectomy just prior to her abortion, and she felt he had trapped her into this action saying, "I wouldn't have done my part if I didn't think you would do yours." In other words, "It's your duty!" No wonder she was confused.

After Effects

What were the after effects? Following the abortion she became depressed, developed symptoms such as stomach aches and nausea, growing hatred for her husband, and sexual frigidity. She was preoccupied with her loss, and cried every time she saw a baby.

An abortion has not helped the self-image of any woman I have talked with. I was listening to one recently who shortly after her abortion claimed that it had not affected her, that it was a perfectly justified action. However I discovered that she was very frightened lest her teen-age daughter discover what she had done, and since the abortion she had become increasingly tearful, hostile and unresponsive to her husband, who is now wondering if he made a mistake in agreeing to this procedure. In her and in others, I have been presented with psychosomatic problems, sexual frigidity, hatred for the boy friend or spouse, sometimes transferred to "all men", anxiety, all kinds of neurotic disturbances and some deep depressive reactions. The self-image of these women has taken a severe beating. In one recent study it was found that 60% of a group of married (neurotic) women who were aborted 2 years previously were ashamed to have a daughter know of the abortion, would not advise a daughter to abort, wished they had the child, had never felt previously that they would regret the abortion, (or) felt the abortion had affected their health in ways not formerly thought possible![1] The conclusion is that post-abortal neurosis and psychosomatic disorder are more common than is often realized, and may be masked in terms of the presenting symptoms. Often a woman is reluctant, and understandably so, to admit that she has had an abortion. She will go to her physician complaining of headaches, backache, inability to sleep, irritability, depression, perhaps stomach or intestinal symptoms, and so on—the whole gamut of physical and psychological complaints.

It may take some time for symptoms of emotional disturbance reactive to therapeutic abortion to show up. They may not surface for several years, or even until the time of the menopause, when women are more vulnerable to unresolved conflicts and guilt over past actions.

These after-effects of therapeutic abortion are more likely to be found in those who have pre-existing emotional problems. Therefore, those having abortions on psychiatric grounds are likely to be at greater risk. Since this includes approximately 97% of all those receiving legal abortions, it seems inevitable that we are going to be presented with psychiatric problems triggered by abortions for years to come. It looks as though short-term expediency will give rise to long-term suffering.

In those who manage for variable lengths of time to suppress and bury their guilt and disturbance the self-hatred continues to fester and it may well be projected onto other people. Hatred then becomes a way of life. In those who are more psychopathic in character, there may be found a growing indifference and even callousness toward the deformed, the debilitated, and the unwanted.

If technology and an increasing knowledge in many fields means greater safety, an easier life, better physical health, and the prevention of illness, what good will this be to us if more and more individuals become the vehicles of fear, hate and indifference, and more and more people are nursing what amounts to a pathological death wish? The cry, ''My body is my own to do with as I like,'' regardless of the silent claims of the developing child, regardless of others around me, this false claim to autonomy is not based on reality. It is rooted in death itself.

3. ABORTION AND THE FUTURE OF SOCIETY

I wonder whether we are entering a reign of terrorism. The target of terrorism is always the innocent, the weak, the helpless, such as the unborn child, the deformed infant and child, the debilitated, the elderly. In what direction are we moving when we speak of mercy in the form of deliberately killing off those chronically ill, and those in the terminal stages of disease? Is justice served by the calculated power which destroys the useless, the inconvenient, those weak individuals who are unable to plead their cause? If expedient killing is socially accepted, then our civilization is indeed not only ill, but dying; and reverence for life a thing of the past. Meanwhile the number of abortions rises rapidly, and abortion on demand is for all practical purposes with us. In the eyes of the law, the unborn child is denied the protection afforded every other human person, citizen or not. What about infanticide? What about euthanasia? Both are being practised more often than is usually recognized. What about elimination of all unwanted children and adults? How far have we travelled down the road to rejection of life itself?

Most people don't want to become involved with the question of abortion, because they feel that it is an ugly subject, and too controversial. Sometimes it touches on a personal experience, which they would rather leave buried. Often they aren't sure enough of their own values and principles to be able to confront these questions, or know where they stand. It's not popular now to have moral values, especially traditional ones. People are very quick to say, "In this pluralistic society you mustn't be moralistic!" I agree, you mustn't be moralistic when matters of small importance are being considered, but can morality be over emphasized when dealing with questions of life and death?

A local newspaper in Saskatoon has carried several advertisements dealing with shop-lifting which state, "Stealing is a Crime". Is that moralistic? Did anyone complain about that approach? I saw no letters to the editor protesting this action, letters saying, "But this is a pluralistic society. Everyone has a right to his own point of view, to satisfy his own conscience. Some steal, some don't. Don't be narrow."

It is nonsense to state that physicians should not inject their moral values into the treatment of people they are endeavoring to help. In any event their morality makes itself felt. And people are looking for direction. They need it. Certainly those who are in favour of abortion do not hesitate to let patients and others around them know their views, do not hesitate to attempt to persuade them to adopt and act on their values. Do not be naive about this. Are not pro-abortionists telling women that for various reasons, mainly materialistic, it is their duty to society to have an abortion?

Somehow things have gotten twisted. The anti-moralizers are calling moral those actions that we used to regard as evil, and they are condemning those values we used to regard as good, and beneficial to life. How have things become so distorted?

In the 60's and 70's our world has seemed to be increasingly concerned with practicality, with the art of the possible, with what is feasible, with what is efficient, with what is appropriate from the short term or immediate point of view. This is the age of pragmatism. And thus we lose our perspective, our sense of values. We are unable to grasp the significance of what we are doing. We see life fragmented, piece-meal, not in its totality, and therefore all our actions become disordered, insignificant. Everything becomes a prey to impulse. Finally all becomes futile, and we sink into an abyss of meaninglessness. It is not possible to live a rudderless, meaningless life and be in good mental and moral health.

What are the alternatives to the dilemma in which we find ourselves? I believe that as individuals we need to pause now, and examine the values by which we live. To what extent are we rooted in reality, in what is truly good and favourable to life? We need to decide where we stand on basic issues, such as life and death, and declare ourselves to each other and to our governments. Indeed the polarization process is already underway, and we will finally *have* to choose which we will serve, life or death.

I am against the deliberate killing of any individual, born or unborn. I believe the unborn child deserves the same protection, before the law, given to every other human person.

I believe there should be much greater concern and action to provide support and assistance of all kinds for the woman who has an unwanted pregnancy, whether she is single or married, and also to provide follow-up care for her after delivery, whether or not she is able to assume responsibility for her child.

Birthright deserves more support from all of us who have decided for life; it also needs more publicity so that pregnant women in distress will know where they can go for help.

Family physicians, obstetricians, psychiatrists, social workers, and sometimes lawyers, as well as other community "care" people have a definite role in helping the distressed pregnant women to come to terms with her problem.

I believe there should be better educational efforts both in and out of the school system to inform children and parents not only about sexual development, and adult anatomy, physiology and psychology in relation to sex, but also advice about responsible family planning which will not include the possibility of abortion, but which will include explicit information in regard to the intrauterine development of the child.

The whole abortion problem is part of the sexual ethics problem. We need to deglamorize sexual abuses and excesses, along with the whole ugly process of the killing of the unborn child who is irresponsibly and thoughtlessly conceived.

A world in which *Playboy, Hush, Flash,* and *Midnight* are produced and fed to sex-preoccupied and obsessed people is hardly evidence of a balanced and soundly based approach which would justify the decision to kill the unwanted child.

We have a responsibility toward the advancement of life in all its aspects, and only as we actively discharge this responsibility, only as we take up this challenge, do we even begin to have a basis for personal and societal growth and development.

(The contribution of Doctor Jones is the text of a talk she delivered at a Pro-Life Seminar in Saskatoon on 27 April 1974.)

Footnote

[1] L.K. Gluckman, "Some Unanticipated Complications of Therapeutic Abortion", *New Zealand Medical Journal* 74, August, 1971, pp. 71-78.

Index

Index • 189

Abramovich, D.R., 60, n. 16
Acta Psychiatrica Scandinavia, 126, n. 17; *Supplementum*, 74, n. 63
Advisory Committee on Energy, Toronto, 126, n. 17
Aertnys-Damen, 141, 144, n. 8
Aitken, Dr., 22
Alexander, S., 77
Allemang, Dr. W.H., 47, 48, n. 7
Alphonsus de Liguori, Saint, 141, 144, n. 7
American College of Obstetrics and Gynecology, 69;
  College Statement and Minority Report on Therapeutic Abortion, 74, n. 53;
  Amicus curiae Brief, 72, n. 19
American Journal of Cardiology, 72, n. 7
American Journal of Nursing, 74, n. 68
American Journal of Obstetrics and Gynecology, 73, n. 27, 74, n. 57, 164, n. 1
American Law Institute, 14
American Psychological Association, 119
Anderson v. Raleigh Fitkin-Paul Morgan Memorial Hospital, 73
Anglican Church of Canada, 30;
  Brief to Divorce Committee, 36
Aquinas, Saint Thomas, 131, 161, 166, nn. 18, 19, 20, 22
Arantius, 62
Archives des maladies du coeur, 73, n. 34
Arey, Leslie B., 60, n. 7, 73, n. 36, 115, n. 4
Aristotle, 131
Association for Research in Nervous and Mental Disease, *Proceedings*, 72, n. 14

Ballard, Dr., 73, n. 21
Ballard v. People, 165, n. 11
Basford, Ronald (L, Vancouver Centre), 33
Barrett, D.J., 166, n. 24
Barth, Karl, 161, 162, 165, n. 16
Bazos, Anthony C., 29

Bengtsson, L.D., 74, n. 60
Benn, Stanley I., 111, 112, 115, nn. 14 and 15, 170, 176, n. 20
Bergman and Ferguson, Rex v., 165, n. 11
Berman, Peter, 73, n. 30
Bernhard, Dr. P., 68
Birthright, 185
Boethius, 103, 108, 115, n. 5
Bolton, Doe v., 169, 174, nn. 1, 2, 9, 175, n. 9
Blackmun, Mr. Justice, 101, 167, 168, 171, 173, 174, n. 9
Boniface VIII, Pope, 148, 153, n. 12
Borins, Norman, Q.C., 16, 18
Bourne, Dr. Aleck (*B. Principle*), 157, 158, 159, 163, 165, n. 9
Bourne, Rex v., 165, nn. 10 and 11
Bowman, David, 30, 31
Bracton, Henry, 151, n. 1
Brand, Dr. Lewis (PC, Saskatoon), 22, 42, n. 76
Brief to the Bishops, 34
British Columbia Catholic Lawyers' Guild, 19, 20
British Medical Journal, 72, nn. 50 and 56, 165, n. 9
Broad, C.D., 77
Buddhist culture, 2
Burger, Chief Justice, 175, n. 9
Burke, Edmund, 104
Burton, John (NDP, Regina East), 46
Byrn, Robert M., 171, 173, 176, n. 26

California Population Law Center, 115, n. 7
Callahan, Daniel, 166, n. 24
Cameron, Dr. Paul, 119
Canadian Bar Association, 19, 21, 22, 23, 27, 28, 30, 32, 34, 41, n. 63, Section on Criminal Justice, 19 *Proceedings*, 40, nn. 17, 18, 21, 22, 24, 25, 27, 33; 41, nn. 62, 64, 65; 42, nn. 66, 68, 69, 70, 80
Canadian Bar Journal, 41, n. 56
Canadian Churchman, 25, 41, n. 43
Canadian Criminal Code, 44, 45, 99, 114, 115, n. 2, 164, n. 5, 171, 176, n. 24
Canadian Medical Association, 15,

19, 21, 22, 23, 27, 32, 34
Maternal Welfare Committee, 22
Canadian Medical Association Journal, 40, nn. 32, 33; 41, n. 38; 42, n. 66; 60, n. 14
Canadian Paediatrics Society, 133
Canadian Press, 21
Cannell, Douglas, 16
Cardin, Lucien, 33
Cardozo, Benjamin N., Lecture, 169, 175, n. 13
Catholic Children's Aid Society, Toronto, 126, nn. 10 and 14
Catholic Digest, 74, n. 61
Catholic Lawyer, 72, n. 2
Catholic, Roman; teaching, theologians, moralists, 2, 10, 36, 38, 59, 99, 131, 139, 140, 142, 143, 144, n. 1, 145, n. 9, 154, 159, 160, 161
Bishops of Canada, 34, 36
Catholic Women's League, 26
Central Ontario Women's Institute, 26
Cepelak, J., 74, n. 65
Ceres, Roman goddess, 149
Chapman, John W., 176, nn. 20 and 21
Chatelaine, 14, 15, 18, 39, nn. 1, 5, 9, 10
Church of England, 24
  Church Assembly Board of Social Responsibility, 24, 161, 165, n. 16
Colpitts, R.V., 164, n. 1
Commonweal, 164, n. 3
Connell, Dr. D.E., 16, 22
Constantineau, G., 39, n. 2
Cooke, Robert E., 164, n. 4
Corey, Giles, 150, 153, n. 18
Courtney, L.O., 74, n. 59
Cowell, Dr. Carol Ann, 113
Crick, Sir Francis, 136
Cross Currents, 165, nn. 12, 13, 14
Curran, Fr. Charles E., 1, 13, n. 1 160, 165, n. 15, 166, n. 24
Currie, G.A., 60, n. 2

Daly, Bernard, 43, nn. 89 and 93
Damen, 141, 144, n. 8
Damude, Earl, 39 n. 5
Dawe, Arthur, 20
Day & Liley, 72, n. 6

Delhaye, Philippe, 141, 144, n. 5
Deman, Thomas, 144, n. 4
Descartes (René), 112
Deutsch, Helene, 74, n. 67
de Valk, Alphonse, 13, n. 8, 48, n. 13
Diamond, Eugene, 62, 65, 72, n. 2, 73, n. 24
Dietrich v. Northhampton, 72, n. 3
Dillon, Valerie Vance, 73, nn. 22 and 31
Diplock, Donald, 29
Doe v. Bolton; see *Bolton, Doe v.*
Dominion Bureau of Statistics Daily, 115, n. 19
Donald, Dr. Ian, 68, 74, n. 49
Donceel, Joseph F., 104, 105, 115, n. 8
Douglas, Mr. Justice, 175, n. 9
Down's Syndrome, 52
Drefus (Alfred), 12
Droegemuller, Dr. W., 69, 74, n. 57
Duchenne Muscular Dystrophy, 52

Eastman, N., 126, n. 8
Ecclesiastes, 75, n. 77
Eichmann, 11
Einhorn, Richard N., 60, n. 5
Ekblad, Dr. Martin, 70, 74, n. 63
Ely, Professor John Hart, 172, 175, n. 10
Emerson, Bruce, 20
Euthanasia Educational Fund, 132
Exchaquet, J., 67, 73, n. 34

Fagan, Veronica, 126, nn. 10 and 14
Fairfield, Letitia, 39, 41, n. 40, 165, n. 16
Family Life, 74, nn. 61 and 62
Family Planning Federation of Canada, 48
Family Planning and Population, 48, n. 12
Feinberg, Dr. Abraham, 16, 17
Feinberg, Joel, 115, nn. 13 and 14
Feldman, Rabbi David M., 163
Felicity, Saint, 148, 149, 151, 153, nn. 13 and 14
Ferguson, Dr. Colin, 133
Filch, 152, n. 4
Finkbine, Mrs., 17, 40, n. 15

Finnigan, Joan, 39, n. 1
"Firing Line" television show, 115, n. 7
Flannagan, G.L., 60, n. 6, 72, n. 9, 73, nn. 15 and 35
Flash, 186
Floyd, Dr. W., 73, n. 27
Foulkes, Dr. Richard, 48
Forssman, Hans, 126, n. 5
Fracastoro, 73, n. 27
Freire, Paolo, 126, n. 21
Freud, Dr. Sigmund, 12
Fromm, Eric, 125, 126, n. 21
Froomkin, Saul, 30

Gallup Poll, 133
Gampell, Ralph J., 156, 165, n. 7
Gardiner, Dr., 74, n. 53
Gay, John, 152, n. 4
George, Gordon, 16, 17
Gesell, Arnold, 60, n. 8, 72, nn. 13 and 17, 73, n. 38
Gilbert, John (NDP, Broadview), 46
Gilmour, G.P., 16, 17
Globe and Mail (Toronto) 14, 15, 16, 18, 20, 21, 23, 25, 27, 28, 32, 34, 38, 39, 40 nn. 11, 12, 13, 15, 16, 19, 20, 23, 36, 41, nn. 47, 49, 50, 53, 54, 60, 42 nn. 69, 73, 74, 83, 43 nn. 84, 85, 87, 48, nn. 10, 11, 99, 126, n. 4
Gluckman, L.K., 186, n. 1
Goodall, Rev. Roy, 15, 39, nn. 5, 6, 7, 40, n. 14
Goodman, P., 73, n. 27
Gospel according to John, 60
Gotlieb, C.C., 175, nn. 18 and 19
Granfield, David, 72, n. 5
Gray, Dr. Kenneth G., 22
Grisez, Germain, 166, n. 24
Griswold v. Connecticut, 175, n. 12
Guttmacher, Dr. Alan F., 155, 164, nn. 1 and 2

Hadrian, Roman Emperor, 148, 152, n. 10
Hale, Rev. John, 152, n. 7
Halford, licensed physician, 174, n. 2
Halifax Herald, 42, n. 83
Hall, Robert E., 115, n. 7, 164, n. 1, 165, n. 7, 166, n. 26
Halsbury, Earl of, 165, n. 8
Hammurabi, Code of, 40, n. 14
Hansard, 48, nn. 1, 2, 3, 4, 5, 6
Hansen, Chadwick, 152, nn. 2, 5, 6, 153, n. 18
Harkens, Dr. L., 16, 17
Harley, Dr. Harry (L, Halton), 33
Harrington, P. V., 40, n. 14
Harris, Paul T., 42, n. 83
Heenan, John Cardinal, 24, 25
Hellegers, Dr. André, 60, n. 15, 67, 73, n. 40, 155, 164, n. 3
Hellman, L., 126, n. 8
Hemophilia A: see Duchenne muscular dystrophy
Hilgers, Thomas W., 74, n. 52, 115, n. 17, 126, n. 3
Hindu culture, 2
Hippocratic Oath, 10
Hiroshima, 8
Hitler, 11
Hodari, A., 73, n. 30
Hoffmeyer, Henrick, 126, n. 9
Holdsworth, Sir William, 152, n. 3, 153, nn. 19, 20, 21
Hollobon, Joan, 40, n. 15
Holmes, Oliver Wendell, 62, 147
Holthausen's Will, In re, 173
Hooker, Davenport, 60, nn. 9 and 10, 72, n. 9, 73, nn. 14 and 42
Horan, D.J., 115, n. 17
Hord, Rev. R.J., 25
Horger, E., 73, n. 27
House of Commons:
  Committee on Health and Welfare; Contraception bills to, 33, 35;
  Hearings on abortion, 24, 28, 31, 32, 42, nn. 76, 77, 79, 80, 81, 83
  Committee on Justice and Legal Affairs; divorce bills to, 33
House of Commons Debates, 164, n. 5
Huband, Rev. A.R., 26
Hufstedler, Judge Shirley M., 169, 170, 175, n. 13
Humanist, 42, n. 67
Hume (David), 104
Huntington's Chorea, 52
Huser, R.J., 40, n. 14
Hush, 186

Hutchinson, Dr. D., 73, n. 27
Hyman, Ralph, 40 nn. 19 and 20

Induced Abortion: A Documented Report, 74, n. 52
Infant Life Preservation Act, 157
Ingelman-Sundberg, Axel, 60
Innocent XI, Pope, 141
International Journal of Gynaecology and Obstetrics, 74, n. 71
International Mental Health Research Newsletter, 126, n. 7

Jerusalem Bible, 60, n. 18
Jews: see Judaism
Joan of Arc, 152, n. 4
Johnson, Life of, 102
Journal of the American Medical Association, 73, n. 20, 164, n. 1
Journal of the American Public Health Association, 126, n. 12
Journal of Clinical Endocrinology, 60, n. 17
Journal of Neurological Science, 60, n. 12
Journal of Obstetrics and Gynecology of the British Commonwealth, 60, n. 11, 72, n. 18
Journal of Pediatrics, 73, n. 27, 74, n. 30
Journal of the Washington Academy of Science, 72, n. 8
Judaism, teaching, theologians, moralists, 2, 10, 18, 74, n. 48, 99
Justinian, Roman Emperor, 148, 149, 152, n. 10

Kadushin, Alfred, 126, n. 1
Karasich, Rabbi, 74, n. 48
Kelaris, Dr., 71
Kellogg, W.N. and L.A., 115, n. 6
Klinger, A., 74, n. 71, 75, n. 76
Knowles, Stanley, 178
Kremer, Elmar J., 9, 13, n. 7
Kuck, M., 75, n. 73

Lakartidninger, 74, n. 60
Lancet, 73, n. 30, 74, nn. 54 and 55, 165, n. 9
Langdon, Judge Ken, 18

Laputa, 1
Lawrence, Mr., Minister of Health, Ontario, 47
Lekhter, A.M., 74, n. 58
Lemarie, Rev. Jean Guy, O.M.I., 42, n. 81
Lenoski, Dr. E. F., 122, 126, n. 12
Le Roux, R., 74, n. 68
Levy, Mike, 73, n. 21
Lewis, David (NDP, Scarborough West), 31
Lewis, Stephen, 31
Liberal Party, majority, 1967-1969, 45
Life, 132, 134
Liguori: see Saint Alphonsus
Liley, Dr. Albert W., 63, 64, 65, 72, nn. 6 and 11
Liley, Dr. H.M.I., 60, n. 13, 62, 64, 65, 67, 72, 73, nn. 23, 26, 41, 42
Linacre Quarterly, 40, n. 14
Locke, (John), 112
Loffmark, Mr., Minister of Health, British Columbia, 47
Lorna, T., 73, n. 30
Louisell, David W., 176, n. 27
Low, Dr. D.M., 22, 27
Lutheran Church, 36
Lucas, Roy, 115, n. 7

MacFadden, Charles J., 164, n. 1
MacInnis, Mrs. Grace (NDP, Vancouver-Kingsway), 46
MacLean's, 14, 39, n. 2
MacNaughten, Mr. Justice, 158
Mainichi survey, 70
Malinowski, 5
Marcel, M., 67, 73, nn. 34 and 37
Mather, Cotton, 152, n. 6
Mather, Increase, 152, n. 3
Matte, Jean Paul (L. Champlain), 34
Mattingly, Dr., 74, n. 53
Marx, Dr. Paul, 74, n. 66, 75, n. 75
Maughan, Dr. G.B., 164, n. 2
McCoy, Dr. E.C., 15
McGeer, Professor P.L., 16
McLuhan, Marshall, 125
McMaster University Hospital, 47
McMorran, A. Stewart, 19, 29
Mecklenburg, Fred E., 115, n. 17

Medical Journal of Australia, 60, n. 16
Medical Post, 115, n. 18
Medical Tribune Report, 72, n. 11
Mendel, Mendelian Laws, 50, 53
Mennonite Church, 36
Merchant of Venice, 61 ff.
Micallef, P.J., 13, nn. 1 and 6
Midak, E., 74, n. 64
Midnight, 186
Miller, Arthur R., 170, 175, n. 15
Minnesota Medicine, 74, n. 51
Mongolism: see Down's Syndrome
Monroe, 60, n. 14
Montagu, Ashley, 65, 73, nn. 28, 32, 33, 44, 45, 46, 95
Montreal Gazette, 42, n. 83
Moolgaoker, A.S., 74, n. 54
Moore, J.G., 164, n. 1
Morley, Dr. David, 133
Mortimer, Rt. Rev. Robert Cecil, 25
Ms, 128
Munro, Mr. John C., Minister of National Health and Welfare, 164, n. 5
Munsinger, Gerda, 42, n. 83
Murray, George L., 19

Nagasaki, 8
Nagoya survey, 70
Narcissus (mythical lover of his own image), 71
National Canadian Conference on Abortion, St. Michael's College, Toronto, 48, n. 7
National Council of Women of Canada, 18, 26, 32, 41, n. 53
National Observer, 134
National Symposium on Abortion, Chicago, 1970, 60, n. 15
New Democratic Party, 16, 46
New York State divorce law, 35
New York Times, 98, n. 3, 126, n. 15
New Zealand Medical Journal, 186, n. 1
Nigro, Samuel A., 126, nn. 13 and 20
Niswander, Kenneth R., 164, n. 6
Nixon, President Richard M., 1
Noguchi, Dr. Ayao, 47
Noonan, John T. Jr., 161, 162, 166, nn. 17, 18, 21, 23, 176 n. 27

Northhampton, Dietrich v., 72
Northwestern General Hospital (Toronto), 47
Notre Dame Lawyer, 176, n. 26

Obstetrical and Gynecological News, 133
Obstetrics and Gynecology, 73 nn. 27 and 30
O'Doherty, N., 73, n. 30
O'Driscoll, John, 34
Offences against the Person Act, 157, 165, n. 8
O'Lane, Dr. J.M., 68
Omnibus Bill, 44, 45
Ontario Conference on Women, 128
Ontario Department of Community and Social Services, 126, n. 6
Ontario Medical Association, 21, 22, 23, 40, n. 35
Sterilization and Therapeutic Abortion Committee, 21, 23
Ontario Medical Review, 23, 40, nn. 28, 29, 30, 31, 34, 41, n. 37
Ontario Ministry of Community and Social Services, 126, n. 11
Osservatore Romano, 73, n. 25
Ottawa Journal, 42, n. 83
Owen, E.C.E., 153, n. 13

Paiken, Sydney, 30
Papola, Dr. Gino, 65, 73, n. 25, 74 n. 48
Parmley, 73, n. 27
Patten, Bradley M., 60, 72, n. 12, 73, n. 41
Paul, Rev. Gerald W., 15, 39, n. 9
Pearson, Lester, 32, 39
Pegis, Jessica, 11
Pennock, J. Roland, 176, nn. 20 and 21
Perlmutter, Irving K., 164, n. 1
Perpetua, Saint, 148, 149, 150, 153, nn. 13 and 15
Petre-Quadens, O., 60, n. 12
Philosophy and Public Affairs, 13, nn. 1 and 2
Phips, Sir William, 152, n. 3
Pisani, Dr., 74, n. 53
Planned Parenthood (Edmonton), 26

Playboy, 186
Plutarch, 153, n. 16
Popenoe, Dr. Paul, 74, n. 61
Prairie Messenger, 41 nn. 42 and 54, 42, nn. 78, 79, 80, 81, 43, nn. 84, 87, 98, 91, 92, 95
Presbyterian Church, 36
Prittie, Robert (NDP, Burnaby-Richmond), 33, 34
Proctor, Elizabeth, 146, 147, 148, 151
Progressive Conservative Party, 16
Protestant Churches, teaching, theologians, moralists, 2, 10, 18, 99, 154
Psychiatric Annals, 126, n. 13
Publicius Marcellus, 148, 152 n. 10

Quarterly Review of Surgery, Obstetrics and Gynecology, 164, n. 2
Quebec Civil Code, 116, n. 20

Raleigh Fitkin-Paul Morgan Memorial Hospital v. Anderson, 73, n. 29
Ramsey, Paul, 166, n. 17
Randall, J.H., 164, n. 1
Reeves, Rev., Chaplain, Columbia University, 134
Rehnquist, Mr. Justice, 175, n. 9
Robert I, King of Scotland, 152, n. 4
Roe v. Wade, 4, 13 n. 4, 101, 167 ff.
Roebuck, Senator, 35
Rosen, Harold, 164, n. 1
Rosenfield, A.B., 69, 74, n. 51
Roman Law, 11, 147 ff.
Rousseau, J.-J., 150
Royal College of Obstetricians and Gynaecologists, 68
Royal Commission on Health Sciences, 18
Royal Society of Medicine; *Proceedings*, 74, n. 59
Rugh, Robert, 60, 63, 72, n. 10
Russell, Dr. K.P., 164, n. 1
Ryan, Dr. Kenneth, 155, 163

Sackett, Representative, 134
Sarchuk, Alex, 30
Saturn, Roman god, 149
Schaeffer, A.J., 73, n. 47
Schlesinger, Professor Benjamin, 16, 17

Schuller, Vratislav, 126, n. 7
Schollin, John, 19
Scotsman, 74, n. 49
Sedzmir, Dr. C.B., 66
Sevilla, Rafael, 73
Shakespeare, 72, n. 1, 73, n. 20, 152, n. 4
Shearin, Dr. Robert, 74, n. 52
Shephard, Thomas, 60, n. 17
Shettles, Landrum B., 60, 63, 72, n. 10
Shewring, W.H., 153, n. 13
Shylock, 61, 71
Sign, 72, n. 22
Silkin, Lord, 41, n. 64
Simmons, Francis, Bishop of Indore, 1, 13, n. 1, 159, 160, 165, n. 12
Sisters Today, 74, n. 66
Slayton, Professor Philip, 13, n. 4, 115, n. 3
Smith, David T., 165, n. 6
Soltan, Dr. Hubert C., 48, n. 9, 111
Sood, S.V., 69, 74, n. 56
Southern Educational Communication Association, 115, n. 7
Special Joint Committee of the Commons and the Senate on Divorce, 35, 36
Stackhouse, Professor R.F., 31
Stalin, 11
Stallworthy, Dr. J.A., 69, 74, n. 54
Stanbury, Robert (L, York-Scarborough), 22, 23
Starkey, Marion, 151, 152, n. 2
Star-Phoenix (Saskatoon), 40, n. 26, 41, n. 52
Statistics Canada, 126, nn. 15 and 16
Steen, Mrs. H.H., 32
Stern, Dr. Karl, 70, 74, nn. 67 and 69
Stewart, Mr. Justice, 175, n. 9
Still, J.W., 72, n. 8
Straus, Reuben, 67, 72, n. 7, 73, n. 39
Stuart (monarchy), 152, n. 3
Stupková, Eva, 126, n. 7
Sun (London), 133
Synan, E.A., 11, 152, n. 8
Szasz, Professor Thomas, 29, 42, n. 67
Szijarto, 73, n. 27

Tablet (London), 41, n. 40, 165, nn. 9

and 16
Talmund, 68
Taylor, Rattray, 17
Tay Sachs Disease, 52
Tertullian, 148
Texas Penal Code, 167, 168
Theodosius, Roman Emperor, 149
Theological Studies, 73, n. 40, 115, nn. 8 and 9
Thomas, G.W., 164, n. 1
Thompson, Judith Jarvis, 4, 5, 6
Tompkins, Dr. M.G., 22, 27, 28
Thuwe, Inga, 126, n. 5
Tooley, Michael, 111, 112, 115, nn. 13, 15, 16
Toronto General Hospital, 47
Toronto Star, 48, n. 8, 133
Triumph, 73, n. 21
Trudeau, Pierre Elliot, 37
Turner, John, 45, 46, 47

Ulpian, 148, 149
Uncertified Human, The, 132
United Church of Canada, 6, 15, 22, 25, 30, 36, 38, 108
  Joint Committee on Abortion, 9, 108, 109
  Board of Evangelism and Social Service, 25, 26, 115, n. 11
  Board of Women, Division of Congregational Life and Work, 115, n. 11
  Brief to the Divorce Committee, 36
  19th General Council (1960), 13, n. 8, 14, 26
  22nd General Council (1966), 26, 41, n. 48
  Former moderator of, 133
United Church Observer, 14, 15, 18, 36, 39, nn. 6, 7, 8, 40, n. 14
United Nations
  Declaration of Human Rights (1959), 2, 8, 10, 30
  Declaration of the Rights of the Child, 117
  Yearbook of, 126, n. 2
United States Supreme Court, 4, 8, 167 ff.
University of Toronto Medical Journal, 14

VandePut trial, 17, 40, n. 15
Van der Marck, William H., 166, n. 24
Van der Poel, Cornelius J., 166, n. 24
Van Hoeck, Dr. D., 119
Vezina, Rev. Louis P.,O.M.I., 34, 42, n. 81
Vie, Rabbi Moshitz, 163
Voice of Women, 34
Vuitch, U.S. v., 165, n. 11

Wade, *Roe v.*, 4, 101, 167 ff.
Wahn, Ian (L. Toronto-St. Paul's), 31 32, 33, 34, 42, n. 82
Walsh, J.J., 74, n. 54
Waring, Gerald, 22, 31
Weinstein, W.L., 170, 176, n. 21
Weisstub, D.N., 175, nn. 18 and 19
Wertheimer, Roger, 13, n. 1
Western Catholic Reporter, 32, 39, 41 nn. 41, 42, 45, 46, 51, 42 n. 75, 43, nn. 84, 90, 93, 48, n. 13
Western Journal of Surgery, 164, n. 1
Western Reserve Law Review, 165, n. 6
Westin, A., 169, 175, n. 14
Westminster Cathedral Chronicles, 41, n. 41
Wheeler, Professor Michael, 16
White, John, 30
White, Mr. Justice, 175, n. 9
Wilkinson, Rt. Rev. F.H., 16, 17
Williams, Glanville, 163, 165, n. 9, 166, n. 25
Willke, Dr. J.C., 67, 72, n. 16, 73, nn. 43 and 47
Willke, Mrs. J.C., 72, n. 16
Wilson, Dr. F., 66
Wilson, P., 73, n. 27
Winnipeg Free Press, 37, 42, n. 83, 42, n. 96
Wirsen, Cloes, 60
Wolfendon Report, 177
Women: A Journal of Liberation, 127, 128
Women's liberation, 9, 11
WONAAC, 131
Wood, Carl, 60, n. 11, 72, n. 18
World Health Organization, 70
  Technical Report Series, 74, n. 70

Statistics Report, 74, n. 72, 75, n. 74
Wu, John C.H., 147, 152, n. 9
Wyles, Lilian, 165, n. 9

Yagoda, 11
Yale Law Journal, 175, n. 10

Yerkes, R.M., 115, n. 6

Zabriskie, Dr. J.R., 68
Zdravookhr, 74, n. 58